A SHORT HISTORY OF FRENCH
LITERATURE

Sincerely yours,
Lothair H. Hudson

A SHORT HISTORY

OF

FRENCH LITERATURE

BY

WILLIAM HENRY HUDSON, *1841 – 1922*

WITH MEMOIR OF THE AUTHOR BY

A. A. JACK, M.A., LL.M.

KENNIKAT PRESS
Port Washington, N. Y./London

A SHORT HISTORY OF FRENCH LITERATURE

First published in 1919
Reissued in 1970 by Kennikat Press
Library of Congress Catalog Card No: 72-103227
SBN 8046-0864-4

Manufactured by Taylor Publishing Company   Dallas, Texas

WILLIAM HENRY HUDSON

A MEMOIR

Mr. Hudson's death on the 12th of August 1918, at Droitwich, came as a shock; but not altogether to those by whom he was best known as an unanticipated blow. In 1913 he had had a disabling attack of rheumatic fever, and he was well aware his heart was weak. Indeed, he once remarked to one who some eight years ago remonstrated with him for overtaxing his strength that he had good reason to suppose his span of life would be short, and that he had much that he wished to write.

This is the nemesis of the critical profession. Before one can criticise, one must have read and studied; and when at fifty "the ship is cheered," one may perhaps hear the evening bell. Not that Mr. Hudson's energy was in any degree abated. His last book on *Nineteenth Century Literature* was as ripe and easy as anything he had produced, a thing let fall from copiousness and a mind stored to the full.

Learning is a word that in this country has come to bear a very particular connotation. One must know more about some one subject, however minute or subdivided, than others do; or one must labour in the mine and bring to the surface what has not been properly accessible before. But leaving out of account this

v

limited meaning of Learning, there were few literary men in England more generally learned than Mr. Hudson : he knew more about everything than anybody else.

Starting life as secretary to Herbert Spencer, he had a sound philosophical basis, and wrote books on Spencer and Rousseau. In later years he told *The Story of the Renaissance*, or wrote of *The Man Napoleon*, just as when, in California, he had written *The Strange Adventures of John Smith*. In his list of books there are five with such titles as *Studies in Interpretation, The Meaning and Value of Poetry*, or *Idle Hours in a Library*. More directly in the line of his teaching is *An Outline History of English Literature*, with its accompanying volume of *Representative Selections*. One finds that he edited or wrote introductions to various works by Carlyle, Dryden, Goldsmith, Addison, Spenser, Bacon, Macaulay ; and in the admirable *Poetry and Life* series which he originated he was himself responsible for seven monographs. Besides these and many other writings he had to his credit a volume of original verse, *The Sphinx and other Poems*.

It would be idle to attempt here to assess the amount of good work, the product of an always living intelligence, enclosed in this little library (some forty publications that appeared mainly in some twenty years), but he himself had a fondness for his volume on Rousseau. Others would put forward claims for his Literary histories ; while there is one book—his *Introduction to the Study of Literature*—which is easily the best as it is also the most painstakingly simple introduction to the foundations of Literary appreciation. With this exception his specially original work was of a different character, the very modern and characteristically lucid introductions to those volumes of *The Elizabethan Shakespeare* which have been published in this country. Interest in these extended to Germany, and it may safely be said that nowhere are the problems of modern Shakespearian criticism handled more competently or with a firmer grasp of the essentially modern issues.

Mr. Hudson did not write on out-of-the-way subjects. His business always was with the best, and his walk consequently almost always on trodden ground. But no one was less of the type that smoothly accepts the reigning opinion. He knew exactly what he wanted to bring out. He had the greatest powers of arrangement, and his own and very definite notions about his various subjects. If one wished to show the difference between Compilation and Exposition, one would only have to point to any one of his little masterpieces in the latter art—to his Milton or his Gray.

It was emphatically the skill of an expositor, of a teacher, and it was this skill that served him in peculiar stead throughout his career as an Extension Lecturer. He had started, very happily, as a definite professor in California, and it was there, in Stanford University, that for nine years he laid the foundations of the wide-ranging knowledge essential for his subsequent and more arduous career. When he came to London in 1902, Mr. Churton Collins, already overtasked, was in the evening of his Extension days, and from the first Mr. Hudson, *facile princeps* among his literary successors, took up without effort the work he was laying down. Dissatisfied with the fragmentary nature of Extension work, he fell in delightedly with Dr. Roberts' scheme of Sessional courses, and, excepting only Professor Gollancz's courses at King's College, it was he, almost unaided, who did the work of the University of London Diploma in Literature. He had two courses for this work : one purely English, 75 lectures covering the outline from Chaucer to Tennyson,

and one General, 25 on Ancient, 25 on Mediæval, and
25 on Modern European Literature.

Of the first course a fellow-teacher of English may be
permitted to say that its circular and recurrent delivery
was in itself an arduous task. Sometimes it happened
that in one year he would be giving its first portion in one
Centre, its second in another, and its third in a third. In
any given week he might be lecturing, among his other
duties, upon Bacon, Addison, and Burns. Besides, it
always happened that the course on General European
Literature was running concurrently, and in the Bacon,
Addison, Burns week he would also be speaking, perhaps,
on Horace, Cervantes, and Molière. As he lectured without notes, or with the scantiest, from a singularly full
syllabus only, it meant that he had to have perpetually at
his fingers' ends most of the chief books of the chief authors
of Europe.

The powers needed to pursue such a life, and to pursue
it with unvarying and even success, are not to be estimated
easily. A much greater flexibility of spirit, a much
greater control of nerves is required than is demanded
from any College teacher. The perfect Extension lecturer
(and surely if there is ever to be one Mr. Hudson was
he) has no time to air crotchets or to run off on himself
rather than on his subject ; and yet how tempting are
these diversions. What is one to say of Keats in an hour ?
It has been said ; and the one thing that is interesting to
oneself is one's own history of personal contact. Never-
theless for the auditor who has never even properly heard
of the poet, and may not again properly hear, the one
thing needful is that the foundations should be well and
truly laid. It is difficult to do this constantly and on
common topics. To do it as Mr. Hudson did it, and to
preserve interest while doing it even in those who had

heard the main part of the story before ; to do this without ever descending to the popular or deviating from the seriousness of study, to promote always a liberal atmosphere while speaking without fence and so as always to be plainly understood, necessitates a forgetfulness of self and a care for one's auditors that is not only a literary but a social virtue. One does not find El Dorados by such conscientiousness, but one must not think, because the rewards in personal *réclame* are not immediate, that the real rewards are small. And, indeed, what social work, done unostentatiously among us, has been more fruitful ! I should imagine, without attempting a precise estimate, that in his sixteen years in London some ten thousand thinking people, and many of them often, must have heard his voice. These are small numbers, perhaps, when one remembers Robert Chambers or Charles Knight. But the spread of printed information is one thing, and that of personal education necessarily another. In his own sphere, dealing with a restricted public and working with his own method, he has a right to be classed with those great popularisers of knowledge.

This was the true work of his life, and he would wish it to figure in his epitaph. Among his numerous publications there are several that have already secured their hold in the educational world, and are likely to retain it. They will keep his memory green, as he wished, by the written and not the spoken word. His contributions to the understanding of Shakespeare will preserve his name in Scholarship ; but I am not attempting a presumptuous estimate, and it is true that his national service was as an Extension lecturer.

It is hard that he should have died just when the social greatness of the work he was doing was coming to be widely understood, and before the cessation of the

War, when there would have been leisure for due recognition. But I do not think of him as not content. He was a man singularly absorbed in the present labour and satisfied with it. He was not thinking of what the work would lead to, but of the work ; and if he was ever worried, it was not with what his students were thinking about him, but with his thoughts about his students. I think he had a consciousness that he had found work worth doing which no one else could do just as he. Not that I mean that it was a conscious consciousness, or that he flattered himself on that or on any account. It was as a good bowler will take the ball when he begins the over, or some mower will give a contented swing to his scythe. Personally of a natural and unassuming modesty, he would, on question, open his stores without parade, and I can still hear him telling me about Dante as we crossed Blackheath Common " when the clock was striking the hour." To many of us he was an elder brother in the craft that is " so long to lerne "—the craft of disinterested teaching ; and it seems to me, as I write this, of all things connected with his death perhaps the most remarkable that I, and I suppose others who were his companions, associated with it so little of the feeling of disaster. I suppose it was because we, and the whole Extension System with us, realised that, though his years were not many, few men had done a more useful life's-work or lived a gentler or more honest life.

A. A. JACK.

The following biographical details have been furnished by a near relative.

William Henry Hudson was born in Victoria Gardens, Kensington, on May 2, 1862. His father, Thomas Hudson, a man of marked individuality, was, in his day, a prominent advocate of temperance and political reform and an effective platform speaker. His mother, a thoughtful and saintly woman, was a native of Bristol. Though a very intelligent boy and a good average student, he did not labour at his work or look upon the passing of examinations as the end of study. Literature claimed him from very early days : he wrote little stories for the entertainment of his immediate circle, and one of these, a fairy tale in thirty chapters, is still in possession of the family. In London he attended the old "Brixton Lodge" school : the school-house is still standing, though hidden away behind newer buildings. Here the boy's personality and high spirits soon made him a leader and he became very popular among his fellows. He was an excellent cricketer, strong on the "leg" side and a good bowler. Some time after leaving Brixton Lodge young Hudson accompanied the family to Bristol, where he entered a solicitor's office. But his heart was not in the law, and he declined the offer of his articles made by his employer. His devotion to literature increased, and he read voluminously, assiduously visiting the "Arcades," well known to Bristolians as the special market for second-hand books. In this period, culminating when he was about twenty years of age, he wrote a good deal of poetry for the Bristol papers, and took an active part in temperance and political work. Joining the Bristol Parliamentary Debating Society, he became the leader of an advanced Radical wing, and soon gained a public reputation as a speaker. He also acquired great proficiency as a linguist, and could read most of the masterpieces of European literature in their original language.

He came to London in the autumn of 1882, and in the following year sailed for New York, where he spent a year in a secretarial capacity. Then returning to London he became in due course private secretary to Mr. Herbert Spencer, and subsequently to Lord (then Sir Frederick) Leighton.

In 1893 he again went to America, and settled down for some years as a professor in Stanford University, California. A later appointment in the University of Chicago was held during a third visit to the United States.

During recent years several serious illnesses interfered with Mr. Hudson's lecturing and general literary work in London, greatly impairing his health and leading to the fatal attack of the summer of 1918. Towards the close of July he expressed a desire to visit Droitwich to take the baths, from which, some years previously, he had derived saving benefit. Unfortunately, though he reached his destination, he was not able to undergo the special treatment, but gradually grew weaker, and passed away on August 12. He was buried in the St. Andrew's Cemetery outside the town.

AUTHOR'S PREFACE

IN two fundamental respects this *Short History of French Literature* follows the plan of my *Outline History of English Literature*, explained in the preface to that volume: it attempts to record, not merely the achievements of individual writers, but also the general movement of literature as a whole; and in doing this, it seeks to exhibit the vital connection of the literature of each period with the changing movements of national life. I have not, however, endeavoured to make the book quite as comprehensive as the *Outline History*, and have, indeed, especially in the earlier chapters, ignored many minor writers in order to focus attention upon the few really important men. This is because the book is designed for the English student of French literature, whose first concern is with these important men. For the same reason, in the arrangement of my material I have given what is relatively a large amount of space to modern literature as a division of the subject which is naturally of particular interest to English readers.

It is hardly necessary to say that I have freely used not only the standard French histories of French literature, but also innumerable monographs on special authors, epochs, and movements. It would be difficult to indicate in detail my indebtedness to such works, and I must therefore be satisfied with a general acknowledgment of it here. At the same time I think it only fair to myself to state that this is in no sense a mere compilation. I have been a lover of French literature from my boyhood, and a systematic student of it for a longer period than I quite care to remember, and thus this *Short History*, modest as it is in aim and compass, has really behind it a good many years of independent work.

W. H. HUDSON.

PUBLISHERS' NOTE

THE proofs of this little book were finally corrected by Mr. Hudson in 1917, but its appearance was delayed, with the approval of the Author, on account of difficulties occasioned by the outbreak of war. In presenting the present memorial edition the publishers would express their indebtedness to Professor Jack, who has courteously revised for the purpose his appreciation of W. H. Hudson which was printed in the issue for October 1918 of the *University Extension Bulletin*.

Thanks are also due to the Registrar of the University Extension Board for permission to make use of the article by Professor Jack.

LIST OF WORKS BY W. H. HUDSON

The Philosophy of Herbert Spencer (Appleton, New York). 1894.

The Strange Adventures of John Smith. 1896.

Studies in Interpretation (Putnam). 1896.

The Sphinx and other Poems (Elder & Shepard, San Francisco). 1900.

The Life of Sir Walter Scott (Maclaren). 1901.

Rousseau and Naturalism in Life and Thought (T. & T. Clark, Edinburgh). 1903.

Herbert Spencer (Constable). 1908.

An Introduction to the Study of Literature (Harrap). 1910.

The Story of the Renaissance (Cassell). 1912.

Idle Hours in a Library (Doxey, San Francisco).

An Outline History of English Literature (Bell). 1913.

Representative Passages from English Literature (Bell). 1914.

A Quiet Corner in a Library (Rand McNally & Company, Chicago). 1915.

The Man Napoleon (Harrap). 1915.

France : The Nation and its Development from Earliest Times to the Establishment of the Third Republic (Harrap). 1917.

English Literature in the Nineteenth Century (Bell). 1918.

General Editor of the "Poetry and Life Series," many volumes of which he wrote himself (Harrap).

The Elizabethan Shakespeare (Harrap)—

 The Merchant of Venice.

 Love's Labour's Lost.

 The Tragedie of Julius Caesar.

 The Winter's Tale.

 A Midsummer-Night's Dreame.

CONTENTS

CONTENTS

CHAPTER I

THE MIDDLE AGES

1. INTRODUCTORY.—The French language, which was to form the vehicle of the great literature whose history we are to trace in the following pages, arose directly out of the popular Latin spoken by the Roman conquerors of Gaul. In the course of its development after the Frankish invasion of the fifth century—an invasion which contributed a good deal to its vocabulary but did not affect its fundamental characteristics—it broke up into two large geographical divisions: in the south, the *langue d'oc*, which had close affinities with the Italian and Spanish modifications of the original *lingua romana*; in the north, the *langue d'oïl*, the parent of modern French.[1] This *langue d'oïl* was itself subdivided into many dialects, the most important of which were those of Normandy, Picardy, Burgundy, and the Île de France. But the election to the monarchy of Hugh Capet, Duke of France, in 987, made Paris the capital of the kingdom and led to the ultimate triumph of the dialect of the Île de France. From this time on the other dialects of the north, and later,

---

[1] The terms *langue d'oc* and *langue d'oïl* are derived from the curious mediæval practice of describing a language by the word used for the affirmative. Thus Dante speaks of Italian as *la lingua di sì*.

the *langue d'oc*, or provençal, began to sink into mere *patois*, though it was not until the fourteenth century that, mainly as the result of the political unification of the country, a recognised standard French emerged out of the general linguistic anarchy, and not until the fifteenth that its stability and uniformity were definitely assured.

It is not necessary for us here to take any account of such experiments as were made in France, either in prose or in verse, before the time of the Capetian dynasty. The history of French literature really begins with the *Chansons de Geste* of the eleventh century, and these will be our own point of departure. But as the French literature of the Middle Ages—from the eleventh century to the fifteenth —though very rich, very varied, and in its own way very interesting, is itself a subject for the special inquirer rather than for the general student, a mere sketch of it, in its broader outlines, will for present purposes suffice.

2. THE MIDDLE AGES.—It would be an entire mistake to think of these five centuries as if they constituted a single period during which life was fixed, society underwent no change, and thought remained at a standstill, for they were in fact centuries of very great though very gradual transformation. None the less they were broadly characterised by certain common features which we have in mind when, generalising, we speak of them as the Middle Ages. Among these features one of the most important from the point of view of literature was the division of the French people into four sharply distinguished classes—the clergy, the nobility, the *bourgeoisie*, and beneath these, the great submerged masses, including the artisans of the towns and the peasants and villeins of the country. The clergy held almost unchallenged a

monopoly of the learning and intellectual culture of the time ; their principal interest was, of course, in theology and scholastic philosophy ; the language of their choice was their ecclesiastical Latin, but they had also a share, though a small one, in general vernacular literature, and in this their influence told naturally in the direction of didacticism. The nobles cared little for intellectual pursuits ; the feudal system, as it existed in France, made them largely independent of the central authority ; they spent much of their time in private warfare among themselves or in struggles with the crown ; their leisure was devoted mainly to martial exercises and the chase. Hence the literature which they inspired and which was produced for their amusement was fundamentally an aristocratic literature—a literature of fighting, of chivalrous sentiment, and, as time went on and the refinements of life began to affect them, of love in the peculiar romantic and courtly acceptation of the term. The temper of the burgher classes was strikingly different ; they represented the practical genius and sound good sense of the nation, its essentially Gallic qualities, its wit, its homely wisdom, its turn for satire. Necessarily, while the prestige of the Church and the power of the feudal system were at their height, the *bourgeoisie* played an insignificant part in the life of the country ; but as with changing conditions they began to gain slowly in wealth and the influence which wealth brings with it, they began to be a force in society, and the literature which resulted everywhere reflected their own modes of thought and feeling. Much of it is indeed pervaded by their direct hostility to the privileged orders, whose long-continued domination they were coming more and more to resent, while generally it is marked by a strong spirit of reaction against the romantic idealism of the nobility. It is thus, broadly speaking, a popular

as distinguished from an aristocratic literature—a literature in the main realistic in tone and tendency, coarse
in material, unconventional and vigorous in style.
As for the lower classes, their part was to provide
occasional subjects for literature, and chiefly, though
not entirely, for jest and satire. Otherwise they did not
count.

While, however, we are justified in speaking of the
Middle Ages in these general terms, it is necessary that
we should recognise the large changes which, as we have
noted, came over French life from the beginning of our
period till its close. The eleventh and twelfth centuries
embraced the ascendant stages of the mediæval order ;
feudalism and chivalry were now rising towards their
height ; in the intellectual sphere the supremacy of the
Church was complete. The thirteenth century, though
from one point of view it may fairly be regarded as the
golden age of mediævalism—for it was the age of Louis
IX., of Thomas Aquinas, of the Mendicant Orders, of the
great cathedral builders—was none the less profoundly
affected by the beginnings of many influences—social,
as in the growth of the *bourgeoisie* ; intellectual, as in the
spread of education among the laity and the first breath
of the spirit of humanism—which in the long run were
to sap mediævalism at its foundations. It may thus be
described as the springtime of the Renaissance. But the
disasters of the fourteenth century, and in particular the
desolating Hundred Years' War, and the disorganisation
and anarchy which ensued, were fatal to culture, and intellectual progress was for the time arrested. Then with
the fifteenth century France entered upon a period of
comparative calm. In large measure as the result of the
Hundred Years' War the power of feudalism was broken ;
with feudalism, the ideals and sentiments of chivalry

began to wane ; under Louis XI. an enormous step was taken towards the subordination of the nobles and the unification of the kingdom ; the *bourgeoisie* meanwhile continued to gain ground at the expense of the privileged classes. These general changes from century to century should be carefully marked, for their influence will become apparent as we pass the literature of the Middle Ages under brief review.

3. CHANSONS DE GESTE.—The *chansons de geste* (songs of deeds or exploits : Latin *gesta*), with which our survey begins, were originally composed for recitation, either by the poet himself (*trouvère*) or by a professional minstrel (*jongleur*), in the castles of the feudal nobility, and, taking their tone from the audience to which they were addressed, they dealt almost entirely with incidents of fighting and slaughter. By far the most famous of these is the *Chanson de Roland*, which probably dates, in the form in which it has come down to us (a form which, however, it reached only after a long course of development and amplification), from the second half of the eleventh century. Its very slight historical foundation was provided by Charlemagne's expedition against the Saracens in northern Spain, but the actual matter of the poem is pure legend. It tells how Roland, the greatest of Charlemagne's peers, while leading the rear-guard of the king's army through the narrow pass of Roncevaux in the Pyrenees, is, through the treachery of another peer, Ganelon, surprised by the enemy ; how he and his men withstand with desperate courage assault after assault ; how at length, when only two of his barons, Archbishop Turpin and Olivier, are left alive at his side, he consents to sound on his horn a last call for help ; how before help arrives first Olivier, then Turpin, and then Roland himself are slain ; and how Charlemagne afterwards

wreaks vengeance upon the Saracens and upon the traitor Ganelon. As in all such poems (and the remark may here be made once and for all), characters, sentiments, and manners are entirely mediævalised, and thus the poem presents a picture, not of the supposed period of its action, but of the chivalry of its own time. The hero himself, with his prodigious physical strength, his fantastic notions of courage, his keen sense of personal honour, his inordinate pride (dying he recites at length his conquests and triumphs), his devotion to his overlord, stands out in bold relief as an idealised type of mediæval knighthood in which those who listened to his stirring story would of course see a romantic image of themselves. A strong religious element is also introduced into the poem, in consonance with the spirit of the age : Charlemagne is divinely counselled in dreams ; a miracle is performed in his behalf when " the sun is stopped in heaven " ; angels descend to bear the souls of the dying heroes to paradise.

Though monotonous in matter and style, the *chanson* has a great deal of real vigour and a certain Homeric directness and simplicity, while in places it rises to genuine epic grandeur : as in the fine description of the strange darkness at midday and the prodigious storms which occur throughout France while the last great fight is raging, and in the scene of Roland's death, when, placing his sword Durandal and his *olifant* (ivory horn) beneath him, he lies calmly down, with his face towards Spain, and his right hand, grasping his glove, extended towards heaven in a final act of homage to God. Like all the oldest French poetry the *Chanson de Roland* is written in decasyllabic couplets linked not by rime but by assonance, or the similarity of sound between the last accented vowels of the adjacent lines without reference to the consonants (*bise, dire*; *albe, Carles*, etc.), as, *e.g.*, in the couplet :

> Sun destre guant en ad vers Deu tendut,
> Angle de l'ciel i descendent a lui.[1]

Numerous other *chansons de geste* survive from the eleventh, twelfth, and thirteenth centuries, but none of them compare for intrinsic value with this really remarkable poem. Many of them, however, resemble it in dealing with the legendary exploits and adventures of Charlemagne and his paladins, as, *e.g.*, the twelfth-century *Huon de Bordeaux*, which has a special interest because it introduces the fairy dwarf, Auberon or Oberon—"le roy du royaume de la féerie"—who afterwards figured so largely in romantic literature, and whom we remember of course particularly in connection with the *Midsummer Night's Dream*.

4. ROMANS ÉPIQUES.—In the formal classification adopted by many French writers on mediæval literature the *roman épique* is distinguished from the *chanson de geste* because, while the *chanson* is supposed to have a certain historical basis (how slight that basis was we have now seen), the *roman* is wholly legend or invention. The most important of the *romans épiques* belong to what is known as the Arthurian cycle ; that is, they are outgrowths from or graftings upon the ancient Celtic tradition, common to Wales and Brittany, of a certain Artus or Arthur, who like Charlemagne was mediævalised into a typical king of chivalry, and again like Charlemagne was the founder and head of an ideal order of knighthood. Among the special characteristics of these Arthurian stories are their free use of the marvellous and the

[1] " He holds out towards God his right glove ; the angels of heaven descend to him."

prominent place given in them to romantic love, a subject which was very much in the background in the earlier martial *chansons de geste*. As an example of a very large class we may here mention the famous *roman* (or, more correctly, the two connected *romans*) of *Tristan et Iseult*, the work of two Anglo-Norman poets, Béroul (about 1150) and Thomas (about 1170). Tristan, nephew of Mark, king of Cornwall, is entrusted with the mission of conducting from Ireland the beautiful Iseult la Blonde, who is to be his uncle's bride. They carry with them a powerful philtre, prepared by the bride's mother, the virtue of which is such that those who drink of it are inspired with a love "à toujours dans la vie et dans la mort." By accident, Tristan and Iseult themselves partake of this potion, and are thereby filled with a guilty passion. For a time they live together in a forest, where they are presently discovered by Mark, who, however, being touched with pity, consents to forgive Iseult on condition that Tristan shall give her up entirely. Tristan afterwards marries another Iseult—Iseult aux Mains Blanches —but is unable to forget La Blonde, who on her side never ceases to think of him. Wounded by a poisoned arrow, he sends a message to her to come to succour him, and lies impatient on his bed awaiting the returning vessel. The understanding is that if the vessel brings Iseult it will fly a white flag; if not, a black one. But his wife, who has surprised the secret, deceives him by telling him that the approaching ship is flying a black flag. Thereupon he dies in despair, and Iseult la Blonde, arriving too late, dies at his side.

The most celebrated of the poets who dealt with the *matière de Bretagne* is, however, Chrétien de Troyes, who wrote in the latter half of the twelfth century. His works, which are distinguished by considerable delicacy and a real quality of style, include *Le Chevalier de la Charette*, a tale of Lancelot and Guinevere ; *Le Chevalier du Lion*, which narrates the love and adventures of Yvain (Gawain), one of the knights of Arthur's court ; and the unfinished *Perceval* or *Le Conte del Graal*. The grail with Chrétien is only a talisman which confers happiness, but in the hands of his followers it soon became the mysterious Holy Grail, the quest for which developed into one of the principal episodes of the ever-expanding Arthurian cycle.

With these *romans épiques* we may also connect the *Lais*, or short stories in verse, written towards the end of the twelfth century by a certain Marie de France, of whom we know nothing except that she lived most of her life at the English Court and called herself Marie "de France" to mark her nationality. Her simplicity, tenderness, and skill in story-telling are well exemplified in such characteristic *lais* as *Le Chèvrefeuille* (on the love of Tristan and Iseult), *Les Deux Amans* (on a knight's devotion to his mistress), *Eliduc* (on a wife's sacrifice and her husband's infidelity and remorse), and *Lanval* (which tells how a knight was loved by a fairy who took him with her to the Island of Avalon).

Antiquity, or rather such confused and distorted memories of antiquity as survived during the Middle Ages, also provided material for a number of *romans épiques*, of which the best known is the *Roman d'Alexandre*, composed by Lambert le Tort and revised by Alexandre de Bernay (both twelfth century), and dealing in a most unhistorical and fantastic way with the birth of the Macedonian king, his education under Aristotle, his travels, his prodigious adventures, and his death. The most interesting thing about this poem is its form. Rime by this time had completely displaced assonance, but

to complete a typical work of mediæval and courtly idealism, it obviously represents the rising temper of revolt against that idealism. It is therefore significant that while the first part of the poem was extremely popular in aristocratic circles, this second part had an immense vogue among the middle classes. Taken as a whole the *Roman de la Rose* may thus be said both to sum up mediævalism and to mark the beginning of its end.

6. POPULAR AND SATIRIC POETRY.—The transition is therefore easy from the didactic poetry of the Middle Ages to a quite different kind of poetry—a poetry which, instead of painting fancy pictures of knights and ladies, and elaborating the subtleties of courtly love, set out to describe ordinary life and people very much as they actually were, and to turn the shafts of ridicule upon the absurdities and abuses of the time. This popular and satiric poetry was, as we have already indicated, *bourgeois* in origin, and in it we find all the essential character-istics—the gaiety, the wit, the shrewdness, the irreverence, the malice (" malice enveloppée de bonhomie ")—of the *esprit gaulois*. It is represented in perfection by the *fabliaux*, or short humorous stories in verse, of the thir-teenth and fourteenth centuries, with their animation, their comic verve, their piquancy of satire, their prevailing grossness. But its outstanding masterpiece is the beast-epic generally known as the *Roman de Renart*, but which is really a collection or aggregation of stories dating for the most part, in the form in which we now have them, from the twelfth and thirteenth centuries.[1] The hero of all these stories, and it is his personality which serves to bind them together and to give them a semblance of unity,

---

[1] This refers to what is distinguished as the primitive cycle. Further bulky additions were made to them in the fourteenth and fifteenth centuries.

is Renart the Fox, and their common though not their only theme is the cunning with which he contrives to get the better of his powerful enemies and to turn the weakness of those about him to his own advantage. All the characters—Noble the Lion (the king), Brun the Bear, Isengrin the Wolf, Grimbert the Badger, Tibert the Cat, Bernart the Ass (a priest), Chanticler the Cock, Copée the Hen, and the rest of them—are sharply defined and individualised (it is worth while to note that they figure under proper names),[1] and the comic situations and dialogues are, at least in the best of the stories, handled with extraordinary vigour. But the most important feature of the poem for us is its moral quality—its mocking spirit, its unabashed cynicism, its merciless satire of contemporary society and the chivalrous ideals of the aristocracy. Middle-class hostility to the privileged orders—to the powerful barons and the corrupt clergy—is manifest in it throughout, while the very fact that from first to last cleverness is exhibited as successful against all the odds of strength and position is itself suggestive of the writers' temper and aims. It is, indeed, a kind of anti-romance, in which the fashionable *chansons de geste* and *romans épiques* are burlesqued, sometimes even in a direct and specific way. It should, however, be added that the cunning Renart is not always successful ; while he beats the lion, the wolf, the bear, he is beaten in his turn by the cock, the titmouse, the raven, and the cat. But when he suffers defeat it is in all cases at the hands of those who are smaller and weaker than himself, and thus even in the hero's occasional humiliations the general thesis of the stories is clearly maintained.

[1] The popularity of the poem is curiously shown by the fact that Renart, or Renard, here the proper name of the particular fox which is its hero, soon became the generic word for fox, supplanting the original *goupil*.

7. LYRICAL POETRY. — Narrative poetry flourished most in the north ; in the south, and especially among the troubadours of Provence, it was lyrical poetry which was chiefly cultivated. These troubadours (the word is the southern form of the northern *trouvère*) were sometimes noblemen who devoted themselves to *lo gai saber* (the gay science), as the art of poetry was called, but more often court-poets who either wandered from castle to castle or lived for years in the household of a single patron —a Count of Provence, for example, or a Count of Toulouse. Upwards of three hundred and fifty of them are known to us by name, and though the larger part of their production has disappeared, a very great mass still survives. There is, however, a marked sameness in their poetry ; they sing of war, but more particularly of love and the casuistry of love ; but the individual note is almost entirely wanting in their verse, and while they are ingenious, delicate, and remarkably expert in form and style, to which they gave the most assiduous attention, they are eminently artificial. As on account of the language in which they wrote they do not really belong to the main stream of French literary history, their principal interest for us here lies in the fact that their influence presently stimulated the development of a somewhat similar poetry of courtly love (*amour courtois*) and conventional gallantry in the north. Thibaut IV., Count of Champagne (d. 1253), is regarded as the best of these courtly lyrists, but many other names—like those, for example, of Blondel de Nesle, who is traditionally associated with Richard Cœur de Lion, Conon de Béthune, and Gui II. of Conci, who took part in the fourth crusade, Jean Bodel of Arras, and Colin Muset, a humble dependant upon the generosity of various noble patrons —figure prominently in the annals of their school. Like

the troubadours they treated love, their chief subject, in
a purely romantic and artificial way ; like the troubadours
they cultivated many elaborate and intricate forms of
verse. Poetry of this courtly kind continued to be
written in the fourteenth and fifteenth centuries, as by
Guillaume de Machaut (1284–1370), Eustace Deschamps
(1328–1415), Christine de Pisan (1363–1431), Alain
Chartier (c. 1390–1441), and Charles d'Orléans (1391–1465);
but as by this time the old ideals and sentiments were
fast waning, it tended to become more and more unreal.
Hence the increasing devotion to mere form shown in
the evolution of complicated stanzas—the *chant royal*, the
ballade, the *rondeau*, the *rondeau double*, and so on—each
of which had its fixed rules of construction and riming.
Meanwhile, however, a change in the character of this
lyrical poetry—a change parallel to that which we have
already noted in narrative verse—was heralded in the
work of the *trouvère* Rutebeuf (d. 1280), whose obvious
personal sincerity is in striking contrast with the conventional make-believe of his contemporaries, and who,
though he maintains the established mechanism of verse,
takes for his themes his own struggles and misery, and
frequently turns his satire upon the actual topics of the
day. This break with tradition gives Rutebeuf a certain
historical importance. But it was not till nearly two
hundred years later that his real successor appeared in
the person of François Villon (1431–1465 ?), the greatest
French poet of the Middle Ages and one of the strangest
figures in any literature. Of Villon himself, perhaps,
the less said the better, for he was not only a Bohemian
and a debauchee but also an actual criminal, who in the
course of a stormy and errant life killed a priest in a
quarrel, was for a time a member of a gang of robbers
and cut-throats, underwent several terms of imprison-

ment, and on two occasions narrowly escaped hanging.
Yet vagabond and scoundrel as he was, he was a man of
real genius, deep feeling, and remarkable technical skill,
and he had moreover the rare merit, as M. Gaston Paris
has said, of putting his heart and his life into his verses.
The greater part of his work is comprised in two " testa-
ments "—an earlier *Petit Testament*, and a later *Grand
Testament*—in which, under pretence of bequeathing his
possessions, real or imaginary, he discourses about himself,
introduces character-studies of his friends and acquaint-
ances, and lampoons his enemies. These mock legacies
are undoubtedly very clever, but much of their wit is
necessarily lost on us to-day. The living Villon is rather
to be sought in his *ballades*, a number of which are included in the *Grand Testament* : among them, the most
famous of all, the *Ballade des Dames du Temps Jadis*,
with its haunting refrain, " Mais où sont les neiges
d'antan ? " Villon is never imitative or conventional ;
his verse has always the unmistakable ring of personality
and truth ; and his frequent touches of remorse, his
genuine emotional quality, his profound sense of the
beauty and brevity of life, the tender sadness with which
again and again he lingers over the thought of death—
a sadness shot at times with a spirit of macabre humour
—suffice to explain the unique appeal which, alone among
the poets of his age, he still makes to modern students.
He is, however, extremely difficult to read, for his language
is very archaic and he often indulges in slang.

But Villon was a solitary figure in the literature of the
fifteenth century, and he exerted no immediate influence.
The general tendency was rather away from the realism
which he represented towards increasing pedantry, affecta-
tion, and devotion to the mere mechanics of verse, as in
the writers known as the Grands Rhétoriqueurs, who

developed and extended the rules of versification, worked
in the most intricate forms of stanza, introduced strange
and bizarre methods of riming, and indulged in all sorts
of puerile tricks and eccentricities. Neither collectively
nor individually have they any real interest for us, and
historically they are little more than curiosities. We
need not therefore concern ourselves about them here.
But one of them—Jean Marot—may just be mentioned
by name because he was the father of the Clément Marot
with whom we shall have to deal in the next chapter.

8. THE DRAMA.—The drama in mediæval France, as
elsewhere in Europe, was in origin the offspring of the
Church. Its germ was the so-called *drame liturgique*,
which arose by the gradual dramatisation of important
incidents commemorated in the ritual of the Christian
year—those, for example, connected with the festivals of
Christmas and Easter—and which appears to have assumed
definite shape by the early part of the eleventh century.
In this primitive liturgical play the altar itself was the
stage, the priests were the actors, the language in the
main Latin.[1] The first real step in dramatic evolution
was the detachment of this play from the services of the
Church and its transference from the altar to the open
air ; and this change was soon followed by the great
amplification of the original material, the introduction of
lay actors, and the substitution of the vernacular for the
ecclesiastical tongue : as *e.g.* in *La Représentation d'Adam*,
of the twelfth century, which was performed before the
church doors, dealt in detail with the whole story of the
Fall, and was written in French, though its dialogue was
from time to time interrupted by Latin texts recited by

---

[1] Though not entirely so. In the eleventh-century liturgical drama
of *The Wise and Foolish Virgins*, for instance, there are occasional
passages in the vulgar tongue, in this case Provençal.

priests, who were still apparently the most important if not the only performers. This curious piece, which is the oldest extant example of its class, may be regarded as a connecting link between the liturgical play proper and the fully developed *mystère* [1] which ultimately evolved out of it. More than sixty *mystères* have come down to us, principally from the fifteenth century, most of the earlier specimens having been lost ; and these, which in the aggregate comprise something like a million verses, are usually grouped into three cycles according to the nature of their subject-matter : the Cycle of the Old Testament ; the Cycle of the New Testament and the Apostles ; and the Cycle of the Saints. A few surviving *mystères*, however, stand quite outside this classification ; like the *Mystère du Siège d'Orléans*, which deals with Joan of Arc, and the *Mystère de la Destruction de Troie* (written by Jacques Milet in 1452), both of which are of peculiar interest because of their non-religious themes. The *mystères* were, of course, designed primarily for edification, their express purpose being to instruct the people in the history and doctrines of the Christian religion ; their tone was therefore, in general, grave and serious ; but to strengthen their popular appeal comic scenes, often of a very gross kind, were freely introduced. At first they were performed by very miscellaneous bodies of actors, clerical and secular, but presently companies, or fraternities, as they were called, were organised to take charge of them ; the most famous of which was the *Confrérie de la Passion*, which acquired the monopoly of acting *mystères* in Paris under letters-patent from Charles VI. in 1402. For nearly one hundred and fifty

[1] Strictly *mistère*, from *ministerium*, office, representation. The form *mystère* arose from the confusion of this with the mysteries (*mysteria*) of religion. But though etymologically incorrect it is now sanctioned by usage.

years after this, this powerful company continued to give performances, now in one place now in another, but in 1548 it definitely established itself in part of the Hôtel de Bourgogne. This was the first regular theatre in France. That same year, as it happened, the Parliament of Paris prohibited the further representation of religious plays, and thereupon the Hôtel de Bourgogne became the first home of the secular drama.

Side by side with the *mystères* another form of religious drama flourished in the *miracles*, specimens of which have reached us from a period considerably earlier than that of the oldest surviving *mystères* themselves. The *miracle* is technically defined as a dramatic representation in which the Virgin or one of the saints intervenes miraculously in human affairs; as in *Le Jeu de Saint Nicolas*, by Jean Bodel, in the *Miracle de Théophile*, by Rutebeuf (both thirteenth century), and in the large collection of *Miracles de Notre-Dame* preserved in a manuscript of the fourteenth century. The specific character of these pieces is clearly indicated in the descriptive titles of some in this collection; as, *e.g.*, "Cy commence un Miracle de Nostre Dame, comme elle garda une femme d'estre arse [burnt]," and "Cy commence un Miracle de Nostre Dame, coment le roy Clovis se fist chrestienner [became a Christian] a la requeste de Clotilde, sa femme, pour une bataille que il avoit contre Alemans e Senes, dont il ot la victoire, et en le christienment envoia Diex [God] la Sainte Ampole [the phial of holy oil]." In general, however, the *miracles* were marked by a very free handling of their subjects, and by the expansion of the realistic and purely human interest of the story in hand at the expense of its religious significance; while for the rest the writers drew as they chose upon all sorts of sources, including not only the apocryphal gospels and the lives of the saints but also *chansons de geste*, *romans*, and tales of adventure. Hence the *miracle* at times lost all its distinctive quality and became entirely secular ; as in the *Histoire de Grisélidis* (fourteenth century), which simply dramatises the then very popular story of the Patient Griselda and her tyrannical husband.[1] Here it may be noted in passing that such terms as *mystères, miracles,* and the like were so loosely employed during the Middle Ages that exact classification is often quite impossible.

A third type of didactic play which was cultivated for a time with great industry was the *moralité,* which was the direct product of the mediæval love of allegory. Sometimes the *moralité* was specifically religious, as in *Bien Avisé et Mal Avisé,* which treats of the contrast— as old as the Choice of Hercules and as modern as Hogarth's picture-tale of the two apprentices—between the right and the wrong way in life. Sometimes the theme was of an everyday, practical character, as in *La Condemnation des Banquets,* by Nicolas de la Chesnaye (early sixteenth century), which, as the title suggests, is an object lesson on the evils of intemperance and gluttony. Sometimes the ethical intention is reduced to such extremely scanty proportions, as in *L'Aveugle et le Boiteux* (1496), that it is difficult to discover it at all. Here again classification fails us, for in France as in England the *moralité* soon broke through the conventional limits of its original form. Such so-called *moralités* as *Les Enfants de Maintenant, L'Enfant Ingrat,* and *L'Enfant Prodigue,* with their pictures of family life and their emphasis upon the domestic virtues, are really primitive examples of the type of play which centuries later was to be known as the *drame bourgeois.*

Meanwhile, and as early as the second half of the

---

[1] This is familiar to English readers through the *Clerk's Tale* of Chaucer, who took it from the *Decamerone* of Boccaccio, who in turn seems to have derived from an older French story, *Parement des Femmes.*

thirteenth century, a genuine comic drama began to
emerge in two singular plays by Adam de la Halle (1230?–
1288?), who, like Jean Bodel, was a native of Arras. The
first of these, *Le Jeu d'Adam*, or *De la Feuille*, is hardly
more than a satiric dialogue of Aristophanic quality, in
which the author makes free with himself, his wife, his
domestic troubles, and his friends. The second, *Le Jeu
de Robin et de Marion*, is a kind of *opéra-comique*, which
presents in dialogue mingled with lyrics a pretty story
of rustic love-making of the sort familiar in the *pastourelles*
of contemporary courtly poets. It can hardly be supposed
that these two plays were solitary specimens of real comic
drama in their time, though they are the only specimens
which we now possess. At any rate, by the fifteenth
century comedy was already well established and widely
popular in the two forms of *sottie* and *farce*. The *sottie*,
which was a short satiric piece, is often hardly distinguishable from the *moralité*, from which it frequently took the
machinery of allegory ; as in *Le Jeu du Prince des Sots*
(1512), by Pierre Gringore, or Gringoire, a violent attack
upon Pope Julius II. in which the king (in whose interests
the play was written) figures as the Prince des Sots, the
Church as Mère Sotte, the people as Sotte-Commune, and
so on. The *farce* may be roughly described as a dramatised form of the *fabliau*, which it resembled in its general
subject-matter and tone, its vivacity, its broad humour,
and its extreme coarseness. As an innocent example of
the class we may take the one entitled *La Cuvette*. In this
the wife of a certain Jacquenot draws up a list (*rollet*) of
the household duties which her hen-pecked husband is to
perform on pain of being beaten for the slightest omission.
While engaged in the family washing, however, the wife
falls into her tub and is in imminent danger of drowning.
She calls loudly to her husband to lift her out ; he con-

sults his list and replies that this is not in his *rollet* ; and though he finally consents to save her, it is only after he has put their marital relationship upon a new and more satisfactory footing.   But by far the most famous of all the old *farces* is that of *Pathelin*, a genuine masterpiece by some unknown writer of the fifteenth century, in which the various types of character introduced are sharply defined, the dialogue is racy and natural, and the situations as they arise are handled with a keen eye to theatrical effect.   It is not too much to say that in this brilliant little piece we have a first expression of that true comic spirit which in fulness of time was to culminate in Molière.

9. PROSE.—Prose developed much more slowly than verse in the French literature of the Middle Ages, and it was not till the beginning of the thirteenth century that it assumed any importance.   Then it began to be used by the chroniclers in place of the Latin which had hitherto been employed by the monkish writers of history.   In this new departure the honour of priority belongs to Geoffrey de Villehardouin (1164?–1213), who in his *Conqueste de Constantinople* wrote a simple and straightforward narrative of the principal events of the fourth crusade, in which he had himself taken part.   Among the many chroniclers by whom he was followed in the next two centuries three only call for attention here.   The first of these is Jean de Joinville (1224–1319), who when a very old man compiled, under the title of the *Histoire de Saint Louis*, a sort of anecdotal biography of the great king whose personal friend he had been and whom he loved with the most ardent devotion.   His narrative is artless and unmethodical, but his sympathy with his subject and the nature of that subject itself combine to make it very attractive.   Next comes Jean Froissart (1337–1410?), whose *Chroniques*, the composition of which extended

over many years, deal with the events of his own time (1325–1400) and particularly with the Hundred Years' War. Rambling and unequal, but often picturesque and sometimes wonderfully dramatic, this celebrated work reads more like a romance of chivalry than a piece of sober history ; indeed its actual value as history is often doubtful. But this is a matter which does not immediately concern us. The chief point for us to emphasise is the general character of Froissart's narrative. He opens his prologue with a eulogy of " prouesse," and specially invites young knights to read his book that they may learn from it how to become "preux chevaliers." This strikes the keynote. From first to last his discourse is of campaigns, expeditions, battles, deeds of daring, jousts, tournaments, brilliant festivities, the glory of arms. A writer of the Court for the Court, he is interested in such things and in such things only. He dwells with unflagging enthusiasm upon the pomp and circumstance of war ; the other side of war—the national ruin which it entailed, the misery which followed in its train—lies altogether beyond his purview. Hence his *Chroniques* belong entirely to the aristocratic literature of the time. But the social and political changes which, though he knew nothing of them, the events which he records were helping to bring about, are clearly reflected in the *Mémoires* of Philippe de Commines (1445 ?–1511), the last of the mediæval historians of any note, and who indeed takes us over into the sixteenth century. Commines, who for some years held important positions in the service of Louis XI. (a fact of significance in connection with the character of his work), conceived and treated history in a way very different from that of Froissart. There is no romantic colour, no chivalrous idealism, no picturesqueness in his writing, but if his pages lack grace and charm, they are on the other hand rich in ideas. He writes, not as a mere story-teller, intent upon the external life and movement of his narrative only, but as a shrewd and quite unscrupulous politician, whose primary interest is in the motives and characters of men and the causes and consequences of events. In reading Froissart we are in the Middle Ages. In reading Commines we feel that we are emerging into the modern world.

Outside the chronicles there is little of general interest in the French prose of the Middle Ages, and that little is in the form of fiction. This is the place to mention an example of hybrid composition — the anonymous " chantefable " of *Aucassin et Nicolette* (later twelfth century), a charming and tender love-story which is at once an offshoot from the *roman* in verse and a connecting link between this and the *roman* in prose. But it was not till towards the close of the Middle Ages that prose began to be used freely for fiction, and then it was mainly for short stories and adaptations of tales already told in verse. The principal name in this context is that of Antoine de la Sale (1398–1461), to whom are ascribed *Les Quinze Joyes du Mariage*, a bitter satire on women, *Petit Jehan de Saintré*, a tale of courtly love, and (probably in collaboration with several other writers) *Les Cent Nouvelles Nouvelles*, a collection of licentious stories, some imitated from the Italian, some taken from the old *fabliaux*, and some apparently original.

CHAPTER II

THE SIXTEENTH CENTURY

POETRY AND THE DRAMA

10. THE SIXTEENTH CENTURY.—The sixteenth century is the great age of the French Renaissance, which is commonly dated from the accession of Francis I. in 1515. As in all such cases where large and complex movements are in question, the assignment of a definite beginning is in the main a matter of convenience only. Yet the association of the Renaissance with the name of Francis has a certain historical justification, for though the new forces in life and thought had long been at work, it was not till the early years of his reign that their influence was generally felt, while by the time of his death in 1547 their triumph was so complete that all the traditions of the Middle Ages had practically disappeared. Hence his accession seems really to mark the opening of a fresh chapter in the history of French civilisation. Moreover, the part which he personally played in the great revival must not be overlooked. With all his vanity and vices he had a genuine love of learning and art, and as the munificent patron of scholars, painters, and men of letters he did much to encourage the new ideas and tastes.

With the sixteenth century, then, we enter upon an

age not only of immensely stimulated intellectual activity, but also of intellectual activity under totally changed conditions. It was an age which, in Michelet's phrase, discovered both the world and man—the world, with all its boundless interests and opportunities—man, with all his desires and appetites ; an age of reaction against the whole mediæval order, of general emancipation, of fresh departures in many things. The old repressive view of life, which had long crushed individuality, was now abandoned, together with the asceticism which this had entailed. The universal domination of the Church was challenged. Men sought to liberate themselves from the trammels of theology and effete scholasticism. The spirit of free inquiry and criticism spread far and wide. Philosophy, art, literature, even religion itself, emerged from the shadow of the cloister to unite themselves with all the living interests of the secular world. The intellectual horizon expanded on every side ; thought and imagination were dilated ; in France, as in England (to use Mr. Green's words), " the sphere of human interest was widened as it has never been widened before or since by the revelation of a new heaven and a new earth." [1] Hence arose a new literature, born of new impulses and answering to new needs.

Among the many forces which co-operated in the creation of the Renaissance spirit one of outstanding importance must be specially recognised—that of the printing press, which, introduced into France in 1470, was already active in the early years of the sixteenth century. It would be impossible here to consider in detail, as it would certainly be impossible to exaggerate, the many-sided and profound influence exerted by this " most formidable instrument of the modern reason."

[1] *Short History of the English People.*

On one point, however, stress must be laid. By popularising knowledge, disseminating facts, ideas, and speculations, and bringing an increasingly wide public into the great intellectual currents of the time, the press was the chief agency in breaking down the mediæval fabric of thought, destroying the practical monopoly of learning long enjoyed by the clergy, fostering the awakened lay spirit, and thus ensuring that general secularisation of life which was perhaps the central characteristic of the new age.

These intellectual changes were accompanied by fundamental changes in French society. The Hundred Years' War had, as we have said, struck a deadly blow at the old disruptive feudalism, and had thus prepared the way for Louis XI., whose one great aim it was to suppress the turbulent nobles, gather their scattered fiefs into a homogeneous kingdom, and make the monarchy supreme. His policy of concentration and unification was not to be carried to completion, it is true, till the time of Richelieu, but already under Francis I. the nobles were beginning to lose the semi-independence of their former state; already they were ceasing to be a feudal aristocracy and were becoming an aristocracy of the Court—an aristocracy in the modern as distinguished from the mediæval sense of the term. With Francis, indeed, the Court for the first time became the recognised centre of fashion and culture. Meanwhile a corresponding alteration was taking place in the private life and manners of the nobles themselves. An interest in intellectual things began to be regarded as a qualification of the new type of " gentilhomme." The gloomy old fortresses, whose one purpose it had been to provide defence in case of siege, began to make way for sumptuous palaces, the very architecture of which was an index of the modified tastes of the rising generation. At the same time, and largely as a result of the internal repose and prosperity which the country had enjoyed under Francis' predecessor, Louis XII., the *bourgeoisie* continued to advance, and during the sixteenth century they increased steadily in wealth, prestige, and power.

All these general movements necessarily affected the literature of the time in many ways. A more special factor in the development of that literature must also be noted—the influence of classicism. Charles VIII.'s invasion of Naples in 1494 had led to what Michelet called the French " discovery of Italy "—the country in which for nearly a century the great revival of classical learning, art, and taste had been at its height. Under the spell of Italy a similar revival now began in France. From this point on, the study of the classics was pursued in France with boundless enthusiasm ; French genius became saturated with ancient culture ; and the rise of the classical movement in French literature was the result. Steeped in the spirit of the new humanism, writers turned impatiently from the older literature of their own country to seek their inspiration, their models, their standards of judgment in the works of Græco-Latin antiquity.

It must finally be remembered that the sixteenth century in France was also the Age of the Reformation. In origin part of the general movement of emancipation from mediævalism, the great religious revival was at the outset warmly welcomed by many of the leading French humanists, who saw in it the promise of enlightenment and freedom of thought. But when they learned, as they soon did, that Calvinism meant, not enlightenment and freedom of thought, but gloomy fanaticism and the old tyranny of dogma under a different form, their sympathy changed into apathy or antagonism. Then

came the terrible Wars of Religion, which under Francis
II., Charles IX., and Henry III. aroused the fiercest
passions on one and the other side and drenched the
country with blood, and after these, the settlement
secured by Henry IV.'s abjuration of Protestantism in
1593. Such influence as the Reformation exerted on
French literature will be noted from time to time in the
following pages. Here it is necessary only to point out
that, though there are a few exceptions to be allowed for,
the rupture between humanism and Protestantism was
practically complete long before the century reached its
close. The difference in literary significance between the
Reformation in France and the Reformation in England
thus becomes apparent. In England the religious revival
was one of the chief forces in Elizabethan literature. In
France its direct effect on literature was on the whole
slight and temporary.

11. MAROT.—As we are now prepared to learn, the
poetry of the first half of the sixteenth century was largely
a poetry of the Court, but as such it was associated not
only with Francis I. himself, but also with his sister,
Margaret of Angoulême (1492–1549), afterwards Duchess
of Alençon and Queen of Navarre. She was herself a
poet of some little pretension, though her *Marguerites de
la Marguerite des Princesses*, with their mystical piety and
allegorical machinery, belong entirely to the outgoing
Middle Ages ; and she is also known as the author of the
Heptaméron, a collection of seventy-two prose tales in the
style of the *Decamerone*, in which, however, the licentious
stories themselves are curiously turned to purposes of
moral edification.[1] But it is as a patroness of letters that

[1] How much of this work was actually from her pen is a matter of
controversy. It seems probable that a good deal of it at least was
contributed by her courtiers, notably by the free-thinking Bonaventure
des Périers.

she is chiefly held in remembrance. She gathered about her many humanists, and gave protection in particular to those who were interested in religious reform. Among these was the writer who occupies the chief place in the poetry of his time.

Clément Marot, son of Jean Marot, the *rhétoriqueur*, was born at Cahors in 1496. In 1519 he became *valet de chambre* to Margaret, but later entered the service of the king, whom he accompanied on his ill-fated expedition to Italy. Wounded and captured at Pavia, he was soon allowed to return to France (1525), where, however, his Protestant sympathies got him into serious trouble, for he was twice imprisoned on charges of heresy, and finally compelled to seek safety in flight. After making public recantation of his religious errors (1536) he once more appeared at Court ; but his translation of some of the Psalms into French verse, though encouraged by the king, was condemned by the Sorbonne, and again he hastened to place himself beyond the reach of the long arm of ecclesiastical authority. He first made his home in Geneva, but finding the austere atmosphere of Calvin's little republic intolerable, he went on to Turin, where he died in poverty in 1544.

Marot wrote much in many forms, in some of which, as in his *ballades* and *rondeaux*, he was simply following the traditions of the Middle Ages, while in others, such as his *épigrammes*, *épîtres*, *éclogues*, and *élégies*, he worked on classic models. He thus represents the transition in taste from the old to the new, but on the whole he belongs mainly to the old. A man of facile and rather frivolous nature, he had little strong passion to express in his poetry, and though sometimes he strikes a genuine note of pity or indignation, he rarely succeeds when he attempts the higher style. This is shown even in his fifty Psalms, which, though harmonious in versification, have very slight poetic merit. But his charming ease—the ease not of mere " happy negligence," but of conscious art—his delicate irony, his badinage, his light but certain touch, combine to give him special excellence in the less ambitious and more informal style of verse. His *chansons* (*e.g.* " Qui veult avoir liesse ") and *rondeaux* (*e.g.*, *De sa Grande Amye*) are marked by exquisite grace, and some of his *épigrammes* and *satires* deserve high praise. But perhaps he is at his very best in his *épîtres*, familiar, lively, witty, tender, as, *e.g.*, *Adieu aux Dames de la Cour*, and the two addressed to the king—*Pour avoir esté derobé* and *Pour le délivrer de Prison*. The description in the former of these of his valet, who was a gourmand, a drunkard, a thief, a liar, and various other things, but for the rest the best fellow in the world, is justly famous, while equally good is the conclusion of the latter in which, writing from prison, he gravely apologises to his royal patron for not presenting his petition to him in person. The historical significance of Marot's work as a whole lies in the fact that he abandoned the pedantry and affectations of the *rhétoriqueurs*, in which he was bred, and introduced a manner of writing at once natural and courtly.

Marot for a short time exercised a considerable influence over the poetry of the Court, but those who belonged to his school were only minor poets. Perhaps the most important of his followers was Mellin de Saint-Gellais (1486?–1558), who gained success with the lighter forms of verse, and is credited with the introduction of the Italian sonnet into France. He may be regarded as a link between the poetry of the earlier and that of the later fifteenth century ; in other words, between the school of Marot and that of Ronsard.

12. RONSARD AND LA PLÉIADE.—Marot's poetry, as we

now see, was in various ways representative of the transitional taste of his time, but it was little touched by that enthusiasm for classical antiquity which was a leading characteristic of the literature and art of the Renaissance. Such enthusiasm, on the other hand, was the principal motive-force behind the work of the group of writers collectively called La Pléiade, whose deliberate attempt to revolutionise French poetry is the most noteworthy feature in the history of that poetry during the second half of the sixteenth century.

Pierre de Ronsard, the leading spirit in the revolution, and " the Prince of Poets," as his contemporaries called him, was born in 1524 in the château of La Poissonnière in the valley of the Loire, near Vendôme. As a boy he became page to the Dauphin, on whose death he passed into the service first of the Duke of Orléans and afterwards of Madeleine of France, whom he accompanied to Scotland on her marriage with James Stewart ; and he was later in the suite of the French Embassy at Spiers and at Turin. His career as a courtier was, however, cut short by a serious illness, which left him deaf (1543). Upon this he resolved to devote himself to scholarship and literature, and for the next seven years gave himself up entirely to the study of Greek and Latin under the direction of the well-known humanist, Jean Dorat (or Daurat), Principal of the Collège Coqueret in Paris. It was then that he gathered about him a number of congenial young spirits— Remi Belleau, Étienne Jodelle, Joachim du Bellay, and Pontus de Thyard—who united themselves into a literary fellowship which was at first called La Brigade ; but when they were presently joined by Jean Antoine de Baïf, and their number (with the elderly Dorat as the "dark star " of the constellation) was thus raised to the mystic seven, they changed the name to La Pléiade, in imitation of the

Seven Poets of Alexandria in the time of Ptolemy Phila-
delphus. Ronsard's first book, a volume of *Odes*, appeared
in 1550, and though it encountered violent opposition
from adherents of the older school, it gave him at once
the premier place among the poets of the day. The rest
of his life was uneventful. He enjoyed the special favour
of Charles IX. and a position of high distinction at the
Court, but after that king's death he retired in failing
health to the Abbey of Croix-Val in his native countship,
where he passed his remaining years in lettered ease, and
where, still at the height of his reputation, he died in
1585.

The manifesto of La Pléiade is contained in a small
volume of great historical interest, *La Deffense et Illustration de la Langue Françoyse*, published by Du Bellay in
1549–50, which lays down the programme of the school.
In respect of language, a strong protest is made against
those pedants who, like the extreme classicists in Italy,
despised the vernacular tongue and regarded it as unworthy of consideration beside Latin and Greek. At the
same time Du Bellay argues that if native French is to
be raised to a plane of equality with Latin and Greek, it
must be enriched in various ways, and particularly by the
free importation of words and idioms from old French,
from the French dialects, from the vocabularies of the
arts and sciences, and from the classic languages. In
regard to literature the writer undertakes to prescribe
" quelz genres de poèmes doit élire le poète françois."
He should leave entirely alone all the popular forms of
old French poetry—the *rondeau*, the *ballade*, the *chant
royal*, the *virelai*, and the rest of such trifles (*épiceries*),
and should write epigrams in imitation of Martial, elegies
after the fashion of Ovid, Tibullus, and Propertius, epics
like the *Iliad* and the *Æneid*, eclogues like those of Theo-

critus and Vergil, odes attuned to the sound of the Greek and Latin lyre, sonnets in the manner of the " learned " and " fluent " poets of Italy, tragedies and comedies having the ancient tragedies and comedies as their " archetypes." Such were the principles which guided the members of La Pléiade in their work, and the result was, of course, a great deal of lifeless imitation and not a little absurd pedantry. Yet on the whole the poetry of the Brotherhood is by no means so dry and barren as might have been expected, for notwithstanding their theories they were still touched by the native spirit, and the personal note is often strong in their writings.

In accordance with the programme of his school, Ronsard himself made an heroic attempt to naturalise in French literature some of the " great forms " of ancient poetry. He did this in his *Hymnes*, many of which are on the Homeric model, though others, like the *Hymne de l'Éternité* and *Hymne de la Mort*, are independent developments of the type. He did it in his *Odes*, which are fashioned on those of Pindar. He did it in his unfinished epic, *La Franciade*, the theme of which is the exploits of Francus, son of Hector, and the legendary founder of France, and in which all the conventions of the classic epic are laboriously reproduced.[1] But these ambitious experiments, with their parade of erudition, their mythological embroidery, and their overwrought and pedantic style, have only an historical interest. Ronsard's real qualities as a poet must be sought in his minor writings, as in his sonnets (*e.g.*, *Sonnets pour Hélène*) and his informal

---

[1] It should be noted that this is the last important poem in decasyllabic verse. In his preface Ronsard says that though he had formerly thought the alexandrine the finest measure in the language, he had changed his opinion and adopted decasyllabics as the best suited to heroic purposes. Yet he used alexandrines in much of his other work.

odes and lyrics (*e.g.*, *À Antoine Chasteigner, De l'Élection de son Sépulchre*), which are remarkable for their tenderness of feeling and their charm of versification.

After Ronsard the only really important poet of La Pléiade is Du Bellay (1525–1560), whose sonnet-sequences, *Les Ruines de Rome* (translated by Spenser) and *Les Regrets*, are grave and lofty in tone and deeply imbued with romantic melancholy, and who is also the author of one most delightful lyric, *D'un Vanneur de Blé aux Vents*.

13. OTHER POETS OF THE SECOND HALF OF THE SIXTEENTH CENTURY.—Ronsard's most dangerous rival, however, was not a poet of his own fellowship, but an independent disciple who in a general way accepted his principles but adapted them to his own purposes. This was the Protestant Guillaume du Bartas (1544–1590)—the " divine " Du Bartas, as our Gabriel Harvey called him— who achieved a fair measure of success with a Biblical epic *Judith* (1573) and gained enormous popularity with *La Sepmaine* (1579), an account of the work of creation which at once went through many editions and was translated into many languages (into English by Joshua Sylvester). In the selection of such scriptural subjects we note the influence of the writer's Calvinism. Du Bartas had a bold imagination and considerable poetic power, and in working out his grandiose scheme he occasionally reaches real sublimity (*e.g.* the opening lines of Livre IV., in which the Deity is compared with a painter contemplating a just-finished landscape). But his style is often vicious, and in particular he goes far beyond the Pléiads themselves in the Latinisation of the French language and the employment of monstrous compound forms (*e.g* " Le feu donne-clarté, porte-chaud, jette-flamme "). Another Protestant poet who may

conveniently be mentioned here, though his work actually belongs to the early years of the next century, is Théodore Agrippa d'Aubigné (1550–1630), who was one of the leaders of the Huguenot party under Henry IV., and wrote, along with much prose, a poem entitled *Les Tragiques* (1616), in which, in very unequal verse—now strong and supple, now rugged and contorted—he describes the persecutions of his co-religionists and the horrors of civil war.

14. THE DRAMA.—The reformation of the theatre by the substitution of a drama based on classic models for the *mystères*, *moralités*, *sotties*, and *farces* of the mediæval stage was, as we have seen, one part of the programme of La Pléiade. The way for this new movement had to some extent been prepared during the first half of the sixteenth century by numerous translations of Greek tragedies and Latin comedies, by imitations of these in Latin for performance by students in universities and colleges, and by occasional experiments in French verse like the *Abraham Sacrifiant* (1547)—a hybrid piece, but more mystery than tragedy—of the Protestant humanist, Théodore de Bèze. But the foundations of the new drama were laid by Ronsard's young disciple, Étienne Jodelle (1532–1573), in a couple of tragedies—*Cléopâtre Captive* (1552) and *Didon se Sacrifiant* (1558), and a comedy —*Eugène* (1552). The titles of the two tragedies indicate their subjects : the former (which was performed with great applause before Henry II. and his Court) deals with the suicide of the Egyptian queen ; the latter is a close dramatic rendering of the well-known episode in the fourth book of the *Æneid*. They both make desperately dull reading and their intrinsic merit is very small, though *Cléopâtre* is on the whole rather the better of the two. But the position which they occupy as the first

works of the classic school—the school which was to flourish almost unchallenged in France for nearly 300 years—makes them historically important, and from this point of view the principal thing to emphasise is the fact that in their simplicity of subject and treatment, the extremely limited range of the characters, their preservation of the unities of plot, time, and place, their entire repudiation of action on the stage, the highly rhetorical quality of their dialogue, and their use of a regular chorus, they reproduce all the structural features of the Senecan drama on which they are modelled. As a point of detail it may be noted that while *Cléopâtre* is written in a combination of decasyllabics and alexandrines, *Didon* is throughout in alexandrines with a regular alternation of masculine and feminine rimes. This latter play is therefore additionally interesting because it introduced what was thereafter to be accepted by French dramatists as the one proper measure for tragedy.

Though in the prologue to *Eugène* Jodelle expressed his contempt for the older forms of comic drama, his innovation in comedy has little importance. *Eugène* owes something indeed both in structure and in characterisation to Plautus and Terence, but it is substantially a development of the mediæval farce ; its comic spirit is of native growth ; its principal figures—the abbé Eugène himself, his factotum Messire Jean, Guillaume the stupid husband, and Alix his frivolous young wife—are all obviously taken from the social world of the time. The contrast at this point between the new tragedy and the new comedy in France should be carefully marked for its bearings upon the subsequent history of the drama. Tragedy at its rebirth was wholly scholarly and imitative, and scholarly and imitative it remained. Comedy, on the other hand, had its roots in the popular stage, and however much it was afterwards affected by classic influences, it never lost the traces of its origin.

Jodelle's lead in tragedy was followed by numerous other writers of the later sixteenth century, the most important of whom was Robert Garnier (1535–1601). Garnier's plays have not much more dramatic quality than those of Jodelle, but they are greatly superior to these in poetic power and in style. Two of them, however, possess a certain independent interest : *Les Juives* because of its Biblical subject ; *Bradamante* because, like this, it is upon a non-classical theme (from Ariosto's *Orlando Furioso*), because it is an early example of that mixed form of drama, the *tragi-comédie*, or tragedy with a happy ending, and because it omits the chorus. The best writer of comedy during this period was Pierre Larivey (1540–1611), who, himself the son of an Italian father, produced comedies of intrigue (*e.g.*, *Le Laquais*, *La Veuve*, *Les Esprits*) adapted or imitated from Italian models, though the scenes are laid in France and the characters and manners adjusted to native conditions. At one point he made a significant innovation ; following his Italian originals he adopted prose in place of verse. This change he explains and justifies in a letter to a friend in which he expresses some misgiving as to its success, since his " nouvelle façon d'escrire " had not thus far been much employed "entre noz François." But largely owing to the popularity of Italian comedy at the time, prose had established itself as a medium for comedy by the close of the century.

CHAPTER III

THE SIXTEENTH CENTURY (*concluded*)

PROSE

15. THE PROSE OF THE SIXTEENTH CENTURY.—Down to the close of the fifteenth century, as we have seen, prose had progressed very slowly in France. In the sixteenth century its development was rapid. This was in the main the natural result of the extension of literary culture and the study of the classics. But social conditions had also much to do with it. In the first place, since excitement about theological questions was now general, writers on both sides were prompted to adopt the language in which they could address the largest audience, and thus the religious controversies of the time contributed greatly not only to the displacement of Latin by French, but also to the establishment of a clear, direct, and unacademic style. Here in particular Protestantism counted, for from the first the reformers were inspired by democratic aims and an earnest desire to reach down to the common man. Secondly, the spread of intellectual interests among the middle classes was a potent factor in the evolution of the new prose. Poetry remained essentially aristocratic. A very considerable portion of the public to

which the prose writers appealed was composed of the educated members of the *bourgeoisie*.

During the sixteenth century, therefore, prose was used for many different purposes. It was used by translators, whose work opened up the treasures of classic literature for those to whom the originals would have remained sealed books; as by Jacques Amyot (1514–1593), whose version of Plutarch (*Vies des Hommes Illustres*, 1558) enjoyed an immense and well-deserved popularity.[1] It was used to disseminate knowledge in many learned and scientific writings. It was used for biographies and memoirs, the composition of which (in part owing to the enthusiasm for Plutarch) now became popular (*e.g.*, *La Vie de Bayard* by " Le Loyal Serviteur " ; the *Commentaires* of Blaise de Montluc) ; for history (*e.g.* the *Histoire Universelle* of D'Aubignac) ; and for political speculation (*e.g.* the republican tractate, *Discours de la Servitude Volontaire*, by Montaigne's friend, La Boëtie). It was used for religious argument and appeal, as in two acknowledged masterpieces of their respective schools, *L'Institution Chrétienne* by Jean Calvin,[2] and *L'Introduction à la Vie Dévote* by Saint François de Sales : [3] the one remarkable as literature for the severe simplicity of its style, the other for its poetic beauty. Most of this activity was, however, as will be seen, in fields which lie outside our present inquiry. In the general prose literature of the sixteenth century two names stand out supreme, one in the first, the other in the second half. They are those of Rabelais and Montaigne.

[1] It was in Sir Thomas North's English translation of this that Shakespeare found the material for his Roman plays.

[2] Calvin first published this work in Latin in 1535. His translation of it, which appeared in 1541, is regarded as one of the first monuments of modern French prose.

[3] This was not published till 1608, but it is always classed among the prose works of the sixteenth century, to which the writer belonged.

16. RABELAIS.—François Rabelais was born at Chinon in Touraine, probably in 1490, though the actual date is uncertain. He was educated at the convent school of La Baumette near Angers, and about 1509 entered the Franciscan monastery of Fontenay-le-Comte in Poitou. There his enthusiasm for scientific and humanistic studies, and especially for Greek learning, which was then closely associated with heresy, brought him into trouble with the authorities, and in 1524, having obtained permission to transfer himself to the milder rule of St. Benedict, he left the Franciscans, carrying with him that hatred and scorn of monks and monasticism which was afterwards a dominant note of his writings. About 1530 he abjured the religious life altogether and went to Montpellier, where he devoted himself to the study of medicine and lectured on Galen and Hippocrates, returning thither in 1537 to take his doctor's degree. In the meantime he settled in Lyons, then famous as an intellectual centre, where he found congenial companions, pursued his studies in the hospital, edited a number of medical works, and gained a sound reputation in his profession. But he was too restless in temper to remain long in one place. At different times he wandered much about France; he was in Italy in the suite of Cardinal du Bellay in 1533 and 1536, and again in 1549; in 1546–47 he was town-physician at Metz ; in 1550 he was appointed to the cure of Meudon, which he held for two years, though it is not certain that he ever performed any of its duties. Resigning in 1552 he went the following year to Paris, where, it is supposed, he died soon after his arrival.

Rabelais' one great work in literature consists of the chronicles of two fabulous giants—*La Vie très Horrifique du Grand Gargantua* and *Pantagruel, Roy des Dipsodes*, *avec ses Faicts et Prouesses Espouvantables*—which he produced at intervals in the midst of his other occupations.[1] So far as they can be classified at all, these chronicles may be said to form a kind of burlesque prose *roman d'aventures*, though even this description scarcely suggests their entire want of system or sequence. Rabelais wrote on from chapter to chapter in complete indifference to anything like general plan or even consistency, and the result was a mere shapeless mass of episodes and digressions. There is little that is absolutely original in his raw material. He did not invent his gigantesque machinery, which belonged to the folk-lore of his native Touraine, and most of his incidents may be traced back now to one and now to another of the many sources which lay open to a man of his omnivorous reading. But he allowed his wit and fancy to play unchecked upon his material, and the amazing product is entirely his own. His characteristics are so varied that they defy formal analysis. At times he indulges in the wildest extravagances — as when Gargantua very nearly swallows half-a-dozen pilgrims with his salad, one of whom sticks in a hollow tooth and sets up a raging toothache. At times he revels in the discovery of some utterly absurd idea, which he pursues through pages of reckless nonsense. His enormous vocabulary is full of bizarre words fabricated at will to suit his purpose or caprice. In his verbal jugglery and innumerable tricks of style he exhibits himself as a learned mountebank of infinite resources ; he gives us immense strings of words—as in his description of Demosthenes

---

[1] These comprise five books in all, the first being devoted to Gargantua, the remaining four to Pantagruel. The fifth book, however, was not published till twelve years after Rabelais' death, and there has been much controversy concerning its authenticity. It seems probable that it was made up out of notes and fragments which he left behind him in manuscript.

rolling his tub (Liv. iii., Prologue), in which we count sixty-one verbs in unbroken succession ; and enormous catalogues, like that of the games of Gargantua (i. 32) which contains no fewer than 195 items, and that of the books in the Library of St. Victor (ii. 7) which runs to 140 titles. Above all we have to recognise his outrageous grossness. Licence of language was very great at his time, and he took full advantage of it. The result is that his fun often degenerates into a riot of indecency.

The abounding humour, the sheer extravagance, and the frequent foulness which are thus among the most obvious features of Rabelais' work are doubtless in a measure to be explained by reference to the promptings of his own nature, for though the legendary distortion of his character into a hard-drinking wastrel and practical joker is now known to be absolutely devoid of foundation, it is still true that he was a lover of broad laughter in whom the old *gaulois* spirit was strong. But there was, after all, an underlying method in his absurdities. He was not only a great humorist, he was also an earnest and independent thinker, whose whole philosophy of life was in conflict with the orthodox teachings of his age. But it was very dangerous at the time to challenge these teachings openly, and even the suspicion of heresy might easily lead a man to the dungeon or the stake. In these circumstances Rabelais took the one course which seemed open to him. He used his extravagances as a cloak for his opinions of men and things. In his assumed rôle of irresponsible buffoon he was able to speak his mind freely about many subjects which otherwise he would hardly have dared to touch.[1] But though he thus sought

[1] None the less he stirred up a host of powerful enemies among the theologians and other supporters of the old ideas. His fourth book, though he obtained the royal sanction for it, was condemned by the Sorbonne and prohibited by the Parliament of Paris.

to provide himself with a safe cover in case of emergency, he did not fail to give the judicious reader due warning of his ultimate intentions (Liv. i., *Prologue de l'Auteur*).

It is true that the tendency of modern criticism has been to see more systematic philosophy in Rabelais' pages than he himself ever dreamed of putting there. Thus, for example, to say that he designed to typify in Grandgousier (Gargantua's father) the whole Middle Ages, in Gargantua the transition from the Middle Ages to the Renaissance, and in Pantagruel the Renaissance itself, is to attempt to reduce his random ideas to too formal a scheme. Yet a certain fairly well-defined theory of life runs through and animates all his work. This theory rests on the principle of the absolute goodness of nature and the excellence of whatever is natural, as it is specifically set forth in the allegory of Physis and Antiphysis, the former of which gives birth to beauty and harmony, the latter to excess and discord (iv. 32). Such belief in the goodness of nature, with its necessary corollary, belief in intellectual and moral liberty, brought Rabelais into sharp antagonism with Calvinism on the one hand and with the entire system of mediæval Christianity on the other, for disbelief in nature, asceticism, and dogmatic tyranny were common features of both the theological schools. His own position in religion was thus that of an independent outsider, whose simple creed was summed up in the doctrine " to serve, love, and fear God." But though he does not spare the Protestants (*e.g.* iv. 45-47), it is rather against the Catholics, their superstitious practices (*e.g.* iv. 29-32), the entire system of ecclesiasticism (v. 1-6), the pretensions of the papacy (iv. 48-53), and so on, that his most vigorous satire is directed. In particular, he is never weary of pouring ridicule upon monasticism and everything which it stood for and symbolised — its repudiation of the natural instincts, the spirit of servile obedience which it inculcated, the barren scholasticism which had been fostered by it. Here we have the text of his famous programme of educational reform as outlined in the chapters on Gargantua's early training (i. 21, 23, 24, and cp. Gargantua's letter to his son in ii. 8), and in his great Utopian dream of the Abbey of Thelema (i. 52-57), an institution which was to be dedicated to the cultivation of a life of freedom, cleanliness, and right reason, and which was therefore to represent the opposite in every respect of the pinched, anæmic, and unnatural ideals of the religious orders. Furthermore, in his satire upon many things by the way, Rabelais is always the apostle of nature, good sense, and liberty against convention, superstition, and artifice—as in his frequent attacks upon the scholastic philosophers, upon the absurdities of the law (*e.g.* iii. 39-43, v. 14), upon the Latinised French of the Pléiade (ii. 6). Another aspect of his work which must not be overlooked is the excellence of some of the character-drawing. Pantagruel is an admirable portrait of the ideal king ; Frère Jean des Entommeures is a vigorous sketch of the practical man of action ; while in Panurge, the clever, shifty, unscrupulous adventurer, we have a humorous creation which deserves a place not far below Sancho Panza and Falstaff.

17. MONTAIGNE.—Though Rabelais was a product of the early Renaissance, the roots of his genius were in the Middle Ages. The great essayist who comes next on our list was, on the other hand, wholly a man of the new time.

Michel Eyquem was born in 1533 in the Château of Montaigne, in Périgord, which his great-grandfather had purchased out of money made by commerce in Bordeaux. He was the third child of Pierre Eyquem de Montaigne, a man of independent views and not a few eccentricities, who was much in advance of his day in many ways, and notably in respect of education—a matter of special interest on account of the lasting influence which at this point he exerted over his son's mind (for Montaigne's own educational theories see *Essais*, i. 25, and incidentally i. 24, ii. 8, 10, 31). After six and a half years of thorough classical training at the Collège de Guienne in Bordeaux, then one of the best schools in the country, he entered at thirteen on the study of law, and in due course became successively member of the Cours des Aides of Périgord and Counsellor to the Parliament of Bordeaux. He did not like his profession, and afterwards wrote with contempt of the wranglings of the lawyers and the abuses which then too often disgraced the administration of justice, but he seems to have performed his duties punctually enough for the sixteen years during which he was occupied with them, though in the meantime he made frequent journeys to Paris and was in occasional attendance at the Court. In 1565 he married the daughter of one of his fellow-counsellors, but his marriage has far less importance in his biography than his friendship (which is one of the great friendships of literature) with another of them, Étienne de la Boëtie (1530–1563), whom he loved with the deepest devotion, and whose memory he cherished tenderly till the very end of his own life (see, *e.g.*, *Essais*, i. 27, ii. 8). On the death of his father in 1569 (his two elder brothers having died some time before) he succeeded to the family estates and became Sieur de Montaigne. Resigning his official position, he thereupon settled down to the quiet life of a country gentleman, looking after his property, enjoying a certain amount of outdoor exercise, but most at home in the library which he had arranged for himself in the round tower of his château (see iii. 3).

Here, surrounded by his books and with his favourite cat as his companion, he passed his days reading, dreaming, writing, in a kind of busy idleness which exactly suited his disposition, and of which the *Essàis* were presently the fruit. This delightful routine of existence was twice interrupted : once by a long journey in Germany, Switzerland, and Italy, undertaken in part from his curiosity to see other countries, in part in the hope that the medicinal waters of certain foreign health-resorts might afford him relief in the painful malady from which he was suffering (1580–81) ; [1] and again, far less pleasantly (for public duty always went against the grain with him), by his election to the mayoralty of Bordeaux, an office which he filled for two terms (1581–85). After this he returned to the retirement of his château, and there he died in 1592.

Montaigne's work in literature is relatively small in bulk and is throughout in a single form, for it is comprised entirely in three books of *Essais* (the first two published in 1580, the third in 1588), varying greatly in length and numbering 107 in all. He was not, as he is very anxious to insist, an author by profession (see Letter to Mme. de Duras, ii. 37), and there is nothing of the professional quality in his pages ; he began to write because he wanted occupation and found pleasure in expressing himself ; and though it is fairly evident that as he went on he came to regard his production more and more seriously, his desultory and haphazard manner remained unchanged to the end. He had read much, and what he read suggested many thoughts and questions to him ; he had seen life and had formed his own judgment of men and affairs ; and it was his aim to set down these results of his studies, his experiences, and his meditations for his own entertain-

---

[1] The record of this journey is provided by a diary which he meant for his own eye only, and which in fact was not published till 1774.

ment and the benefit of his readers. But this he did
without method, without plan, without regard even for
consistency. The stated text of one of his *Essais* is
scarcely more than a point of departure for miscellaneous
speculations on all sorts of things ; he wanders from
it into bypaths of reminiscence, anecdote, quotation,
theory ; he indulges perpetually in digressions ; having
once allowed himself to be diverted from the topic nominally in hand, he rarely gets back to it again. The very
title which he chose for his discourses, *Essais* (a word
which he employs in its original etymological sense), is
itself indicative of their character. Moreover, the style
which he adopts is in perfect harmony with his manner.
In its ease, spontaneity, and entire freedom from bookish-
ness and convention, it is a style as far as possible removed
from that of formal composition. It is rather the style
of good, racy, vigorous conversation. Montaigne cared
nothing for the dignity which writers in general were so
solicitous to maintain. There are many grave and noble
passages in his *Essais*, but there is nothing forced or
strained in them ; their eloquence is simply the eloquence of sincere emotion expressing itself in appropriate
phrases. As he himself declared, he loved homely and
natural speech and style, which were the same on paper
as they were in the mouth.

The absolutely personal quality of the *Essais* is,
therefore, their outstanding characteristic. Wide as is
their range and varied as are the subjects with which they
deal, they form in their entirety a body of literature of
the most intimately confidential kind, for their beginning,
their middle, and their end is always the writer himself.
Montaigne's avowed purpose, and it is this which gives them
their substantial unity, was indeed to produce in them a
portrait of himself which should be faithful in its minutest

particulars to the original from which it was drawn. On this point he is clear and emphatic. " C'est ici un livre de bonne foy, lecteur," he writes in his preface. " Je veux qu'on me voie en ma façon simple, naturelle et ordinaire, car c'est moy que je peinds. . . . Je suis moy mesme la matière de mon livre." And again and again in the *Essais* themselves he strikes the same note, as, *e.g.*, " Ce sont icy mes fantasies, par lesquelles je ne tasche point de donner a cognoiser les choses, mais moy " (ii. 10), and " Le monde regarde toujours devant soy ; moy, je regarde dedans moy ; je n'ay affaire qu'a moy ; je me considère sans cesse, je me controulle, je me gouste . . . je me roule en moy mesme " (ii. 17). In carrying out this purpose of self-delineation Montaigne often loaded his pages with private and trivial gossip which is sometimes otiose and occasionally rather unedifying (for autobiographical details see in particular ii. 6, 7, iii. 3, 13). Such details may be disregarded by readers who are not so much interested in Montaigne *chez lui* as Montaigne was himself. The essential feature of the *Essais* is the perfect frankness with which the writer depicts his character and lays bare his mind ; and at this point his inconsistencies assume a special importance. His intellect was singularly open, flexible, and *ondoyant*—an intellect " toujours en apprentissage et en espreuve " (iii. 2) ; he saw many sides to most questions ; he dealt freely now with one side and now with another ; and he never sought to resolve the resulting contradictions of his thought or to gather his opinions into a coherent whole.

Montaigne's egotism, however, had far wider bearings than might at first sight be supposed. His infinite curiosity about himself was indeed only one aspect of his infinite curiosity about life in general. " Chaque homme porte la forme entière de l'humaine condition," he writes

(iii. 2), and his preoccupation with himself was at bottom preoccupation with himself as a sample of humanity. In the words of one of his favourite mottoes (the well-known phrase from Terence), as he was a man nothing human was foreign to him. Hence his fondness for travel and his insistence upon it as a means of education (i. 25), and his devotion to history which he conceived, in a singularly modern way, as " l'anatomie de la philosophie " (*ibid.* and ii. 10). His *Essais*, therefore, are something more than a study of himself ; they are a repertory of observations of life and judgments upon it. There is nothing in the least systematic about his philosophy, it is true, for system-building was impossible to a man of his mental habits ; but his insight, his sagacity, and his honesty combine to make his discursive theorisings wonderfully pregnant and suggestive. At the root of his thought lies his profound and persistent scepticism—the scepticism so well indicated by his device—a pair of scales—and his motto— " Que sçay-je ? " Amid the fierce conflict of creeds which raged at his time and the unmeasured dogmatism of the contending schools he stood apart, the very incarnation of the anti-dogmatic spirit. Wherever he turned he found himself confronted by uncertainties ; all his inquiries led to the one conviction that nothing is so hopeless as the quest for absolute truth. He dwells upon the contradictions in human nature itself and the bewildering variety of opinions which results from these (i. 22) ; upon the purely subjective character of all our thinking (i. 26, 40) ; upon the inability of the mind to discover any firm footing for itself either in the wisdom of the past or in the facts of experience (for the fullest expression of his scepticism see ii. 12). His philosophy, therefore, acts as a universal solvent, yet it should be carefully noted that in matters of religion he found an escape from his own logic in the authority of the Church. As a moralist he is usually described as an epicurean, but his epicureanism (see particularly iii. 13) was touched and modified by the stoicism of some of his beloved classic authors, notably Plutarch and Seneca, for whom he had the deepest admiration (ii. 32). The charge often brought against him on ethical grounds is that his teaching makes for laxity, indifference, and selfishness, and there is a certain amount of justification for it. On the other hand, we have to recognise the marvellous sagacity with which he often discourses on the conduct of life ; the practical helpfulness of his thoughts by the way ; his absolute honesty and truthfulness ; the frequent nobility of his temper, as in his many fine passages on death (*e.g.* i. 19) ; his large tolerance and sympathy ; and the humane spirit which runs through all his *Essais* and which led him, always by their general tone and again and again by specific utterance, to condemn the bigotry, the ferocity, and the cruelty of his age. Taken in their entirety, the *Essais* may without exaggeration be described as the most vital book in the European literature of the sixteenth century, and their influence has been continuous from that time to our own. Such vitality and such influence have to be explained by reference, not to Montaigne's greatness as a thinker, or to the originality of his ideas, but to the whole tone and character of his mind. He wrote as one who had emancipated himself from all retrospective habits of thought, and who, instead of relying on the past, subjected all questions anew to reason and common-sense, and every sentence which comes from his pen is instinct with his own individuality. Hence his astonishing freshness after the lapse of more than three hundred years ; hence his continued power of stimulating and fertilising other minds.

CHAPTER IV

THE SEVENTEENTH CENTURY

POETRY

18. THE SEVENTEENTH CENTURY.—The "grand siècle," as French historians call the seventeenth century—though for purposes of literary classification this must be understood to extend till the death of Louis XIV. in 1715—saw the consolidation of the power of the crown by Richelieu, the last struggles of the feudal nobility in the disturbances of the Fronde, their final subjugation by Mazarin, and the culmination of absolute monarchy under the Roi-Soleil. These political movements have a direct importance for the student of literature. Centralisation in government was accompanied by centralisation in culture, and this in turn was largely responsible for the triumph of classicism. The literature of the sixteenth century had been essentially individualistic ; with few exceptions its writers had followed their own bent and had gone their own way, and little had been accomplished towards the establishment of any general standard of judgment and taste. The outstanding feature of the seventeenth century in literature, as in politics, was the reduction of chaos to order and the achievement of unity under authority, and in the one

case as in the other liberty and personality were alike sacrificed.

When, the Wars of Religion over, peace and prosperity were restored to the distracted country, social evolution began afresh on the lines which have already been indicated, and the transformation of the feudal nobility into a *noblesse de cour*, which had commenced under Francis I., was now carried to completion. One conspicuous result which attended the formation of this new *société mondaine* was the popularity of those reunions of " honnêtes gens " which flourished in large numbers in Paris and in the more important provincial cities during the first half of the century, and played so prominent a part in the social history of the age. The most celebrated of these *salons*, as they came to be called, was that of the Hôtel de Rambouillet, which for more than thirty years (roughly, from 1610 to 1645) was the principal centre of the literary life of the metropolis ; but there were others which sprang up in imitation of or in rivalry with it, of scarcely less note. At first the influence of these coteries in refining manners and speech, and fostering the arts of polite intercourse, was very much for good. As time went on, however, they brought themselves into well-merited contempt by the monstrous affectations which they encouraged in their dread of vulgarity and desire for distinction, and, in particular, by their spirit of extravagant gallantry, the artificiality of their tone and tastes, and the " preciosity " which turned their conversation into a jargon intelligible only to the initiated. As they gave women an easy ascendancy in all social affairs, they helped to feminise literature as well as manners ; hence their general tendency was towards the elimination not only of the pedantry and coarseness, but also of the vigour and raciness of the sixteenth-century writers. In this way they left their mark on literature. Otherwise their direct influence upon it was neither deep nor lasting. It was confined in the main to the lighter kinds of poetry and prose (*e.g.* the *vers de société* of Vincent Voiture, 1598–1648), and to the romance (see *post*, pp. 110-115).

Incidentally the *salon* led, or at least contributed, to the establishment of an institution of far greater importance than itself, for out of a small and select circle, this time of men of scientific and artistic interests, emerged the Académie Française, organised, though not originated, by Richelieu, and incorporated by royal letters-patent in 1635. The Academy carried yet one step farther that movement towards the centralisation of culture which had already appeared in the *salon* ; as, in Matthew Arnold's words, " a supreme court of literature " and " a sovereign organ of the highest literary opinion," it was in fact a logical development of the great cardinal's policy of absolutism. It meant that in intellectual matters, as in political, a central authority had been set up which was henceforth to be supreme in all questions falling within its jurisdiction.

This movement towards absolutism in culture was not, however, completed till, on the death of Mazarin in 1661, Louis XIV., then a young man of three-and-twenty, took the reins of government into his own hands. At this point the influence of the *salons* finally disappeared before that of the Court, which now gave the law in literature as in everything else. The king's personal taste in art is sufficiently indicated by Versailles : it was a taste for the elegant, the grandiose, the correct ; and in literature his taste was the same. Under his autocratic sway it was this taste which now prevailed.

Yet though an artificial unity was thus secured, disturbing forces were at work which in the long run were to prove fatal to its continuance. From quite early in the century onward we can trace the influence of the *bourgeois* spirit making in many ways against the spirit, first of the *salons*, and afterwards of Versailles, and this influence gained in strength when, amid the disasters of the closing decades of Louis' reign, the centre of intellectual power shifted from the Court to the capital. The results of this change we shall have to consider when we pass on into the eighteenth century. Our present concern is with the poetry of the classical period.

19. MALHERBE.—François de Malherbe, with whom our study begins, was born at Caen in 1555. His father belonged to the magistrature, and he himself first sought a career in the law, but he presently abandoned the gown for the sword and fought in the Wars of Religion. Though he had already written verses before the close of the sixteenth century, most of his poetry, and all that is at all valuable in it, was produced after 1605, when he settled in Paris and attached himself to the Court. He died in 1628. Malherbe paid for the favours which he received from his royal patrons and others in authority by many poems of a servile character, but he also wrote *odes* and *stances* on public occasions (*e.g.*, *Sur l'Attentat commis en la Personne de Henri le Grand*, 1605 ; *Ode à la Reine Mère du Roi sur les heureux Succès de sa Régence*, 1610 ; *Ode au Roi Louis XIII allant châtier les Rochellais et chasser les Anglais*), which, though frigid, are not wanting in strength and dignity. Such poems give him a certain place in the history of his time as the poetic exponent of those ideals of government which it was Richelieu's great work to realise. Otherwise they have little interest for the modern reader. Nor do the rest of his writings make much appeal to us ; in fact

there is perhaps only one of them which can be said really to live, and that is the *Consolation* which he addressed to M. du Perier on the death of his daughter Rose—a touching poem specially remembered for the often-quoted stanza :

> Mais elle était du monde, où les plus belles choses
> Ont le pire destin ;
> Et rose, elle a vécu ce que vivent les roses,
> L'espace d'un matin.

Malherbe is indeed one of those writers whose historical importance is wholly out of proportion to their intrinsic merits. He was in no sense a great poet ; he had neither imagination, nor vision, nor deep feeling, nor any magic of style ; and his verse, though highly finished, is in general prosaic and cold. But he came at a time when critical ideas were changing in the direction of his own taste ; he had thus the peculiar good fortune to identify himself with the movement of his generation, and his influence helped that movement to prevail. Boileau's famous " enfin Malherbe vint," it is true, over-emphasises his personal part in the reform of French poetry in the early seventeenth century. Yet he certainly did lay down the lines which that poetry was to follow for the next two hundred years, and for this reason he deserves more attention than we should otherwise bestow upon him.

His poetic principles were largely negative, and were chiefly concerned with matters of technique. He set out to clear the language from the archaisms, provincialisms, and neologisms of the Pléiade, and from the affectations and conceits which had been introduced into French poetry under Italian influences. He rejected entirely the theory of Ronsard that poetry should use a specialised kind of diction : the diction of poetry should be just pure French, like that of the best prose. He thus restricted and impoverished the language of poetry as Ronsard had attempted to enlarge and enrich it, and by eliminating the personal factor turned it into a language of mere convention. " Le tyran des mots et des syllabes," as he was called,[1] he gave the most scrupulous attention to the minutest grammatical details, and corrected and re-wrote with such laborious care that, the legend ran, he would use a ream of paper to produce a single stanza. In regard to versification he prescribed many exacting rules, and in particular regulated the alexandrine by banishing *enjambement*, or the running on of the sense from one couplet to another. Thus by precept and example, as Boileau said, " il réduisit la Muse aux règles du devoir," and became the chief power in the formation of that classical school of poetry of which he is recognised as the first master—the school which, repressing entirely the individual element and sedulously avoiding everything savouring of extravagance in thought or style, was to take as its watchwords, lucidity, correctness, good sense, elegance, and propriety.

20. RÉGNIER. — " Tout reconnut ses lois," Boileau declares in his too sweeping estimate of Malherbe's influence. As a matter of fact, though the general current of critical opinion was in his favour, and though a few avowed disciples—the most prominent of whom was Honoré de Buet, Marquis de Racan (1589–1670)— soon gathered about him, his laws for the moment were by no means universally accepted. There were those indeed who, in the interests of personal freedom, protested against them, like Théophile de Viau (1596–1626), who in his poem, *Sur Malherbe et ses Imitateurs*, while

---

[1] " Vous vous souvenez du vieux pedagogue de la cour qu'on appelait autrefois le tyran des mots et des syllabes " (Balzac, *Socrate Crétien*, x.).

he acknowledges the skill of the master, refuses to be
bound by his rules :

> Imite qui voudra les merveilles d'autrui,
> Malherbe a très bien fait, mais il a fait pour lui . . .
> J'aime sa renommée et non pas sa leçon . . .
> Je veux faire des vers qui ne soient pas contraints.

Of these independent writers, who represent the last
efforts of the older poetic spirit against the new classical
creed, the most important is Mathurin Régnier (1573–
1613), a poet of real genius and originality, the author
of some minor poems of great beauty and pathos, but
best known by his sixteen satires, which easily rank
among the finest things of the kind in French literature.[1]
It is therefore to be regretted that, himself a loose liver,
his ·verses too often (in Boileau's words) " se sentaient
des lieux où fréquentait l'auteur." His essential greatness lies in the breadth and vigour of his characterisation ;
as Boileau justly said, it was he who " du consentement
de tout le monde a mieux connu avant Molière les mœurs et
les caractères des hommes." Historically he is interesting
because of his uncompromising antagonism to Malherbe
and his doctrines. In his ninth satire he ridicules those
who devote all their study to petty details of syntax and
versification (" car s'ils font quelque chose, c'est proser
de ·la rime et rimer de la prose ") and think there is
nothing good " s'il n'est pas fait à leur mode," and for
himself boldly advocates liberty and the rights of genius,
which, he declares, are above all the mere rules of art.

---

[1] The most interesting of these are : II. *Les Poètes*, a vivid description of the literary world of the time ; IX. *A Nicole Rapin*, an attack
on Malherbe ; XII. *Son Apologue*, which contains his theory of satire ;
XIII. *Macette*, a powerful study of a hypocritical old woman—Régnier's
masterpiece, but to be read only by those who are willing to accept its
extreme grossness ; and XV. *Le Poète malgré soi*, an account of his own
manner of writing and of the qualities of his character.

His own style is strong and free, but often loose and even incorrect, and whether we agree with him or not in his statement that "les nonchalances sont ses plus grands artifices," we must admit that his "nonchalances" are very numerous. In his management of the alexandrine he again defies Malherbe by his continual use of *enjambement*.

21. BOILEAU.—Despite the insubordination of Régnier and a few other poets here and there, however, Malherbe's influence increased steadily after his death, and nearly half a century later his work was completed by a writer who holds an assured place in the history of French literature as "the lawgiver of Parnassus" and the authoritative exponent of the classical creed. The son of a registrar to the Parlement, Nicolas Boileau-Despréaux was born in Paris in 1636. In youth he was destined for the Church, but he soon gave up theology and took to the law, which in turn he abandoned for literature when on his father's death he inherited a fortune which, though small, sufficed to make him independent. Henceforth his life was that of a typical man of letters, who lives for literature and cares for little else. By his outspoken criticism he made many bitter enemies among the writers of the day, but on the other hand he enjoyed the friendship of Molière, Racine, and La Fontaine, and the patronage of the king, and he was long the ruling spirit of the Academy. In his closing years he retired to Auteuil, where he died in 1711.

Boileau's works include twelve satires which are closely fashioned on classic models ; [1] twelve *épîtres*, in the ninth of which he discourses on his favourite text, " Rien n'est beau que le vrai " ; a number of *odes*,

---

[1] *E.g.*, II. *Accord de la Rime et de la Raison*, addressed to Molière ; and IX. *À son Esprit*, which is specially important as an exposition of his aims as a satirist and a defence of his severity in the treatment of bad literature.

épigrammes, and minor poems ; and in prose, a *Dialogue sur les Héros de Romans* and *Réflexions sur Longin*, both of which are of some interest on the critical side, and will be referred to again later. But for present purposes we need consider only two of his writings which, each in its own way, possess a special importance—*Le Lutrin* (1672–83) and *L'Art Poétique* (1674).

Le Lutrin, which was one of Pope's models in *The Rape of the Lock*, had its origin in an " assez bizarre occasion "— a quarrel between the *chantre* and the *trésorier* of the Sainte-Chapelle about the position of the reading - desk and the lawsuit which followed. This incident Boileau takes as the foundation of a " poème héroï-comique," a new kind of burlesque in France, though Italy had already produced a well-known specimen in Tassoni's *La Secchia Rapita*, or *Rape of the Bucket* (1614). Formerly the method of the burlesque writer had been to select an heroic subject and to turn it into ridicule by treating it in a commonplace and vulgar way,[1] as Scarron had done in his *L'Énéide Travestie* (1648–53). Boileau reverses the process by choosing a trivial subject and treating it with epic dignity : · the essence of the " mock heroic " being this calculated and sustained discrepancy between matter and style. " C'est un burlesque nouveau, dont je me suis avisé dans notre langue," he writes in his address to the reader ; " car au lieu que dans l'autre burlesque Didon et Énée parloient comme des harengères et des crocheteurs, dans celui-ci, une horlogère et un horloger [2] parlent comme Didon et Énée." Nor is this all ; for not only are the epic tone and manner adopted throughout, but the poem is laid out on the regular epic plan, with the " supernatural

[1] Cp. " Le Parnasse parla le langage des halles " (*L'Art Poétique*, i.).

[2] In the final revision of the poem a *perruquière* and *perruquier* take the places of the *horlogère* and *horloger*.

machinery " which was then regarded as indispensable in the epic—dreams, omens (in accordance with classic tradition), and (in Chant IV.) a battle in the approved Homeric style. *Le Lutrin*, though it falls far short of *The Rape of the Lock* in delicacy of fancy and lightness of touch, may still be read with amusement. In dealing with it historically we must remember that it was the product of an age when the " rules " of the epic were much discussed and numerous bad epics were being written (*e.g.*, *La Pucelle d'Orléans*, 1656, by one of the principal butts of Boileau's satire, Jean Chapelain).

Far more importance, however, attaches to *L'Art Poétique*, a didactic poem in four cantos, in which Boileau formulates his critical creed, and which was long accepted as the great text-book of classicism. This essay in verse —and in verse which is on the whole very mechanical and pedestrian—is offered as a manual of instruction to the would-be poet who, convinced to begin with that he really *is* a poet by right of birth (a point upon which, it must not be forgotten, Boileau lays the utmost stress), wishes to use his powers to the best advantage. In the first canto general rules are given of a purely technical character, and a short history of French poetry from Villon to Malherbe is introduced ; in the last, the moral aspects of the poet's life and work are considered ; the intervening cantos are devoted to a discussion (by no means exhaustive) of the *genres* of poetry and the special laws which govern each. Boileau's central doctrine is that the poet should follow nature, or, as he otherwise expresses it, take reason as his guide : thus—

> Jamais de la nature il ne faut s'écarter,

and

> Aimez donc la raison ; que toujours vos écrits
> Empruntent d'elle seule et leur luxe et leur prix.

This doctrine really means that the poet should avoid extravagances, eccentricities, and the cultivation of personal idiosyncrasies of all kinds, and keep steadily to what is natural and reasonable, that is, to what belongs to the normal and general course of experience. In this sense we have to interpret the principle that

> Rien n'est beau que le vrai, le vrai seul est aimable,

from which all the alleged rules of poetic art are supposed to be derived. But it is important to notice that while Boileau ostensibly rests his case on pure reason, his argument leads to classicism of the narrowest kind. For how are we to know what is natural and reasonable ? how are we to distinguish between what is general and what is particular ? between what is true and what is merely factitious ? The answer is that such knowledge and enlightenment are to be acquired only in the great school of the classics who have provided us with permanent standards and models. This theory of the dependence of modern literature upon that of the ancients runs through the entire essay, and lies at the root of all its special precepts.[1]

As a piece of constructive criticism *L'Art Poétique* strikes us now as singularly jejune, uninspired, and insufficient. Boileau was thoroughly honest ; he was sincerely solicitous for the interests of literature ; and it must be acknowledged that he did good service by clearing away the affectations which infested the minor poetry of his time, and by his constant, though often rather brutal, attacks upon second- and third-rate writers. But his views were narrow, his judgment hard, and the

---

[1] Pope took over the whole argument about following nature, with its corollary regarding the supremacy of the classics, and applied it to the problem of judgment in literature in his *Essay on Criticism*, 68-140.

tone of his mind dogmatic. Entirely wanting in the historical sense and in any feeling for the natural and spontaneous growth of literature, he regarded the types of poetry, with all their rules and conventions, as definitely established once and for all, and treated them accordingly in terms of fixed formulas. Moreover he was very inadequately equipped for his task, for his knowledge of literature was extremely circumscribed, his training in the classics was practically confined to the Latins, he was almost entirely unacquainted with contemporary foreign authors, while his blunders of statement reveal a surprising ignorance even of the earlier poetry of his own land. But the limitations of outlook and false conceptions of poetic excellence which resulted from such deficiencies were not perceived at the time, nor indeed for more than a century afterwards. Boileau's right to reign over Parnassus was almost universally acknowledged,[1] and under his rule poetry broke finally with the great national tradition, lost all life, freedom, and spontaneity, and became stereotyped, artificial, formal, and colourless.

22. LA FONTAINE.—Among the forms of poetry overlooked by Boileau in his classification was the fable. Such omission was the more curious because of the pre-eminence achieved in this particular field by one of his closest friends.

Jean de La Fontaine, the prince of fabulists, was born in 1621 at Château-Thierry in Champagne, where his father was *Maître des Eaux et des Forêts*. His education was sadly neglected, but he early began to browse among the old books in his grandfather's well-stocked library, and thus gained a familiarity, rare at the time, with the

---

[1] " And Boileau still in right of Horace sways " (Pope, *Essay on Criticism*, 714).

works of Marot, Rabelais, and other sixteenth-century writers. After studying first for the Church and then for the Bar he was appointed in succession to his father to the rangership of his district, and continued to perform, though very indifferently, the duties of the office for nearly ten years. Meanwhile he was reading widely and dabbling in composition, though it was not till 1654 that he took his first real step in authorship with a translation of Terence's *Eunuchus*. Then he drifted to Paris, where he soon became popular in society, and where the rest of his life was spent. A man of easy-going disposition, egotistical and self-indulgent, though with many lovable qualities which made those about him blind to his faults, he was happy in finding patrons on whose bounty he lived, a detached, amused spectator of the world ; in his naïveté, irresponsibility, and frankness very much of a child, but with a shrewd insight into character and an infinite sense of the absurdity of things. Towards the end, as the result of a long illness, he was converted, expressed regret for what was objectionable in some of his writings, made his peace with the Church, and died " très chrétiennement " in 1695.

Though he wrote a couple of comedies (*Le Florentin* and *La Coupe Enchantée*) and a number of miscellaneous poems, La Fontaine's fame rests entirely upon his *Contes* (1664, 1667, 1671, 1675) and his *Fables* (Livres I.-VI., 1668 ; VII.-XI., 1678 ; XII., 1694 — 241 in all). The *Contes*, which are versions of stories from Boccaccio, Ariosto, Machiavelli, Rabelais, the *Heptaméron*, the *Cent Nouvelles Nouvelles*, and various Greek and Latin writers, are little masterpieces of sparkling and delicate art ; but they are marred by a licentiousness so great that though they were extremely popular for that very reason in the libertine society of the time, the last volume was actually suppressed by the police. It is fortunate, therefore, that all their finest qualities—their skill in narrative, their wit, irony, and fancy, the grace, variety, and suppleness of their versification, and their peculiar personal charm—are to be found without any taint of their lubricity in the *Fables*, which have certainly never been surpassed in any literature, and which still make so universal an appeal because, as Silvestre de Sacy has well said, " the child rejoices in the freshness and vividness of the story ; the eager student of literature in the consummate art with which it is told ; the experienced man of the world in the subtle reflections on character and life which it conveys." In the composition of these *Fables* La Fontaine rarely invented his subject ; occasionally he took some current anecdote (*e.g.*, VII. 2 ; VIII. 7) ; but in general he borrowed his material, and the extent of his reading is shown by the range of his sources, which are sometimes oriental, sometimes classical, sometimes mediæval, sometimes modern. Yet his indebtedness to others began and ended with his material ; by his way of using it he makes it his own ; " son originalité," as Sainte-Beuve pointed out, " est dans sa manière, non dans sa matière." According to his view, a fable is compounded of two parts —the body and the soul : the body being the story, the soul the interpretation or moral (see his Preface) ; though it should be noted in passing that many of his own *Fables* are not really fables at all, but simply humorous tales admirably told (*e.g.*, *Le Dépositaire Infidèle*), or pretty little idylls (*e.g.*, *Les Deux Pigeons, Tircis et Amarante*). The story itself he conceives as a comedy in narrative ; hence he describes himself as making of his work

Une ample comédie à cent actes divers.
(*Le Bûcheron et Mercure.*)

The actors in this comedy, in harmony with the long-standing tradition of the fable, are most often animals, whose characters are presented with extraordinary insight and precision ; and it is worth while at this point to remember that La Fontaine was a warm lover of animals and a close observer of their habits. He is, however, equally successful when he works with human figures instead (*e.g.*, *L'Enfant et le Maître de l'École, Le Savetier et le Financier, Le Bûcheron et la Mort, La Laitière et le Pot au Lait*). It is indeed all one whether he uses beasts or men ; whichever method he adopts, he portrays with such vividness the outstanding types of the contemporary world—king and courtiers, clergy, lawyers, financiers, the *bourgeoisie*, the peasantry—that his *Fables* as a whole rank second only to the comedies of his friend Molière as a picture of the society and manners of the seventeenth century. It should also be observed that at times he sets his drama against a background of landscape, and that when he does so, it is a bit of real nature that he gives us, not the artificial decoration which did duty in most of the poetry of his time. As for the " soul " of his *Fables*, it is a mistake, not the less serious because it is so common, to assume that the morals which he elicits from or appends to his stories are necessarily meant for guidance. He has been condemned, for instance, because he is supposed to teach in *Le Chêne et le Roseau* the wisdom of bending to circumstances instead of standing up against them, and to inculcate in *La Chauve-souris et les Deux Belettes* the arts of the time-server and trimmer. But in such cases he is merely generalising experience, not laying down rules of conduct, and it is obviously unfair to find fault with him because he depicts the facts of life as he had himself observed them. Dogmatism was indeed quite foreign to his genius and aims, and the relative slightness of the direct didactic element in his work is a significant point of contrast between his method and that of such older fabulists as Æsop and Phædrus. His philosophy as a whole is that of a shrewd, kindly, but rather cynical spectator of life, who has a quick eye for the vices, follies, and affectations of the world about him and satirises these, severely, but good-humouredly, throwing his own stress upon the supremacy of nature and the virtue of common-sense.

Irrespective of his intrinsic merits, La Fontaine is interesting on account of the position which he occupies in the literature of his time. French critics claim him as a classicist because of his avowed admiration of the ancients (see his *Épître à Huet*), the fine sense of unity which governs his work, his careful craftsmanship, his restraint. But the popular element in his writings, his *gauloiserie*, and the freedom and variety of his style give him a place by himself among the poets of the seventeenth century.

23. LA QUERELLE DES ANCIENS ET DES MODERNES.— It was not till the end of the eighteenth century that any attempt was made to repeal Boileau's laws of poetry, and not till the time of the Romantic Movement that they were finally discarded. But during his own lifetime one essential part of his doctrine—that regarding the supremacy of the classics—was definitely challenged in the controversy known as La Querelle des Anciens et des Modernes. In part under the influence of René Descartes, who in his *Discours sur la Méthode* (1637) had built up a system of thought on a basis of pure reason and in entire independence of scholastic and theological dogma, a spirit of defiance against the authority of the past had arisen in science and philosophy which little by little spread to other subjects. Of this spirit the controversy in question was one expression. Though there had

already been a few preliminary skirmishes, the battle began in earnest with a poem, *Le Siècle de Louis le Grand*, which Charles Perrault [1] read at a session of the Academy on January 27, 1687. As the object of this poem was to flatter the king, who had just recovered from a serious illness, the poet allowed himself to be carried away by his enthusiasm even to the extent of instituting a comparison between the Age of Louis in France and the Age of Augustus in Rome :

> La belle antiquité fut toujours vénérable,
> Mais je ne crus jamais qu'elle fut adorable.
> Je vois les anciens sans plier les genoux ;
> Ils sont grands, il est vrai, mais hommes comme nous.
> Et l'on peut comparer, sans craindre d'être injuste,
> Le Siècle de Louis au beau Siècle d'Auguste.

Such was his bold thesis, which shocked some of his hearers, among them Boileau, and in support of which he proceeded to maintain in detail the superiority of contemporary art and literature to the art and literature of the past. The poem dropped like a bomb into the literary world, and the discussion which followed divided the critics for some eighteen years into two hostile camps. The cause of the moderns was supported in particular by Fontenelle (*Digression sur les Anciens et les Modernes* in his *Discours sur l'Églogue*, 1688) and Perrault himself (*Parallèle des Anciens et des Modernes*, 1688–97),[2] whose arguments, often sound, sometimes fantastic, rested

---

[1] Best known as the author of a delightful collection of prose fairy tales, *Histoires du Temps Passé*, or *Contes de ma Mère l'Oye*, 1697.

[2] The best contribution to the discussion was, however, made by Saint-Evremond in his brief essay, *Sur les Poèmes des Anciens* (1685), which reveals an admirable balance of judgment and a quite modern sense of development in literature. Saint-Evremond was then living in exile in England, whither the controversy soon spread, and where it inspired Sir William Temple's worthless *Essay on Ancient and Modern Learning* and, indirectly, Swift's *Battle of the Books*.

ultimately upon the general theory of progress in literature as in civilisation at large. The great champion of the ancients was Boileau, who replied indirectly to Perrault in his *Réflexions critiques sur quelques Passages du Rhéteur Longin* (1693). On the whole, Boileau attacks the question on its minor issues only, and does not seem to appreciate its fundamental principles. On one point, however, he meets his adversary quite fairly. Perrault had insisted that the current admiration of the ancients was largely superstition. Boileau appeals to the permanence of taste : " L'antiquité d'un écrivain n'est pas un titre certain de son mérite ; mais l'antique et constante admiration qu'on a toujours eue pour ses ouvrages est une preuve sûre et infaillible qu'on les doit admirer."

By the early years of the eighteenth century the quarrel had died down, leaving behind it little in the way of definite result. Nor in the circumstances was definite result to be expected. The discussion was vitiated by uncritical extravagances on both sides, and even more by the fact that modernists and classicists alike approached the question in a dogmatic spirit and without the slightest sense of the historical meaning of literature and its necessary dependence at all times upon the civilisation and culture of the age out of which it springs.

CHAPTER V

THE SEVENTEENTH CENTURY (*continued*)

THE DRAMA

24. TRAGEDY BEFORE CORNEILLE.—Jodelle and his immediate followers did little to create a living form of tragedy. Even Garnier's merits were rhetorical rather than dramatic, while the six tragedies of Antoine de Montchrestien (1575 ?–1621)—of which *L'Écossaise, ou Marie Stuart,* is accounted the best—though they have some pathos and a real lyrical note in the choruses, are scarcely more than literary exercises : in fact, it is not certain that they were ever put on the stage. The first step towards vitalising the serious drama was taken by Alexandre Hardy (1569?–1631 ?), a prolific writer of plays for the theatre of the Hôtel de Bourgogne, who in the course of thirty years is said to have produced several hundred pieces, of which forty - one survive. In his tragedies (*e.g., Marianne, Didon se Sacrifiant, La Mort d'Achille*) Hardy adopted the classic form in broad outline, though he eliminated the chorus and dealt very freely with the unities. In his tragi-comedies (*e.g., Gésippe ou Les Deux Amis, Frégonde*), with their large cast of characters and the variety and complexity of their plots, he approached much more nearly to the romantic type of

play. In them, indeed, he shows the strong influence of the Spanish romantic drama. Hardy had, what his predecessors had not, a genuine sense of the stage, and his merits were those of the practical playwright. Unfortunately, he was a very poor writer, and if his pieces possess a strong histrionic element they are entirely destitute of the higher qualities of art. It is, I think, generally recognised that had he been a man of real genius and power he might conceivably have changed the course of French tragedy by deflecting it into the romantic channel. But though he was popular he carried no weight. In the critical discussions which were meanwhile going on about the principles of dramatic art the *réguliers* (as the supporters of classicism were called) finally triumphed over the *irréguliers*, and some three years after Hardy's death the *Sophonisbe* (1634) of Jean de Mairet (1604–86) definitely established the form which was at once to be adopted by " le père du théâtre français," Corneille.

25. THE PRINCIPLES OF CLASSIC TRAGEDY.—Though the underlying principles of this form of tragedy have already been indicated by the way, a succinct statement of them is desirable. Nominally founded upon the practice of the Greeks and the teachings of Aristotle, classical tragedy was really shaped upon the Latin plays which have come down under the name of Seneca, and which present the type in its severest and stiffest form. At two points the new poets departed from their model : they gave great prominence to the love interest, which had been conspicuous by its absence from the serious drama of antiquity, but had come to be a chief motive in modern literature ; and they dropped the chorus, which they finally felt to be a useless encumbrance, though they retained a kind of attenuated survival of it in the con-

fidant who is so prominent a figure on their stage. Otherwise they followed the Senecan drama very closely. Their
plays were, to begin with, entirely aristocratic in theme
and quality ; their subjects were drawn from the great
pages of history or legend (by preference from the history
or legends of Greece or Rome) ; their actors, whether
good or bad, were at least "illustrious," in accordance
with the doctrine afterwards enunciated by Voltaire,
that "tragedy always requires characters raised above
the common plane." [1] In harmony with their matter
their manner and style were uniformly dignified and
heroic ; their diction was kept throughout at the ideal
pitch of stately nobility ; nothing suggestive of collo-
quialism or familiarity was allowed ; while long rhetorical
speeches took the place of dramatic dialogue, and declamation was substituted for natural talk. Action, and
especially violent action, was practically banished ; a
classical tragedy might have plenty of stirring incidents
in the ground-work of its plot, like *Le Cid*, with its two
duels and big battle ; but such incidents were not represented ; they were merely reported to the audience in set
narratives : a method which inevitably tended to the
further amplification of the rhetorical element at the
expense of the really dramatic. Unity of tone was
strictly enforced ; tragedy was wholly and consistently
tragic ; no variety was introduced into it ; no touch of
humour was ever permitted to mar its sustained solemnity.[2]

---

[1] *Remarques sur le Second Discours de Corneille.*

[2] Already in the seventeenth century there were a few *irréguliers*
who protested against this dogma of the unity of tone on the ground
that since the drama should reflect life, and life itself is made up of
tears and laughter, variety and not unity should be the rule (see, *e.g.*,
François Ogier's preface to the *Tyr et Sidon* of Jean de Schélandre,
1628). The tragi-comedy, which was a play of tragic quality but happy
ending, and the heroic comedy, in which comedy itself rose to something approaching tragic seriousness, were attempts to break down the

Finally, in regard to construction, the utmost importance was attached to the three unities—of time, of place, and of action. The compactest definition of these unities is that given by Boileau in his instructions to the tragic poet :

> Qu'en un lieu, qu'en un jour, un seul fait accompli
> Tienne jusqu'à la fin le théâtre rempli ;

which means that the entire plot of a play was to be confined to a single scene, and within a single day, and that it should be composed of a single story without sub-plots or minor incidents of any kind. In practice, it is true, these rules were not always adopted according to the letter ; occasionally the scene shifted from room to room of the same palace, or from street to street of the same city, while the theoretical day of twenty-four hours was stretched to include two days and the intervening night. But into such attempts of dramatists here and there to elude the literal requirements of the law, and the discussions which grew up about these, we need not now enter. The bearings of the unities upon the composition of the drama at two points must, however, be noted. In the first place, simplicity of subject brought with it limitation of character scheme : hence the very small cast of actors in a classical tragedy and the resulting concentration of attention upon them. Secondly, as under the rule of time the dramatist was unable to represent the whole of his action from its rise to its completion, he was forced to confine himself to its closing portions : hence in turn the expansion which these closing portions undergo in his hands. Joined with the almost entire absence of action from the stage, these two features help to explain why classic

---

formal divisions between the two types of drama ; but at a time when all literary *genres* were treated as fixed and permanent, they were not regarded with favour.

tragedy is essentially a tragedy of character, though necessarily of character conceived and treated in a static rather than in a dynamic manner.

That all these arbitrary and pedantic laws of construction resulted in a type of drama which, while wonderfully perfect in form, was essentially artificial, it is not now to the point to insist. The whole system of classic tragedy has long since been abandoned as an outworn academic superstition, and its supposed æsthetic foundations have little or no meaning for us to-day. But within its cramping limitations some great and lasting work was produced, as we shall see on turning at once to its two supreme masters, Corneille and Racine.

26. CORNEILLE. — Pierre Corneille sprang from a Norman " famille de robe," and was born at Rouen in 1606. He was educated at the Jesuit College of his native city, studied law, and became an advocate; and though he soon abandoned his profession, it has often been suggested that the influence of his legal training and the forensic habit of his mind may be recognised in the arguments and pleadings which are so prominent in his plays. His heart was, however, already given to the stage, and the success of his comedy of intrigue, *Mélite* (1629), encouraged him to devote himself to the drama, though it was not till after numerous experiments that he discovered his proper way. Meanwhile he attracted the attention of Richelieu and became one of his " five poets," whose business it was, taking an act apiece, to carry out the designs which the great cardinal put into their hands. But Corneille had the temerity to criticise one of his patron's plots, and their relationship came to an end. This was in 1634. The next year he produced his first tragedy, *Médée*, and in 1636 took Paris by storm with *Le Cid*, the first masterpiece of the classic school. This

brilliant play is founded upon a long rambling Spanish drama by Guillem de Castro, *Las Mocedades del Cid*, which with its crowd of characters, its constant bustle of action, and its total disregard of the unities, is a representative example of the Spanish romantic stage. In order to reduce his materials to the forms of classic tragedy Corneille prunes away the secondary interests with which the main theme was complicated, discards all the characters that are not absolutely necessary to the working out of his subject, removes the action from the stage (thus, *e.g.*, substituting the Cid's descriptive oration of seventy-three lines for the representation of the battle with the Moors), and confines the plot within the required limits of time and place. Yet, technically, *Le Cid* is by no means perfect as a classic drama, and the newly established Academy in passing judgment upon it had no difficulty in laying bare its defects. The fact that the blow which is given by the heroine's father to the hero's father is actually given on the stage, was pronounced a breach of decorum ; the love of the Infanta for the Cid was censured as providing at least the rudiments of a sub-plot ; while, as is very obvious, the unity of time, though nominally accepted, is really broken by the impossible concentration of so many events within the period prescribed. This official condemnation of his licences did not, however, interfere with the success of the play, and so far as popular suffrages were concerned, the " Querelle du *Cid* " ended in his favour. But he had learned his lesson, as we can see from the structural regularity of the plays which followed, notably the four great tragedies—*Horace* (1640), *Cinna* (1640), *Polyeucte* (1643), and *La Mort de Pompée* (1643). These, with *Nicodème* (1651), represent his powers at their highest, though mention must also be made of *Le Menteur* (1643), the best comedy of the French stage before Molière. In 1647 his triumph had been completed by his admission to the Academy ; but in 1652 the failure of *Pertharite* discouraged him, and he retired to Rouen, where he busied himself with a critical edition of his writings and a translation into verse of the *Imitation of Christ*. He returned to the theatre in 1658, but, though he wrote much during the next twelve years, he never repeated his former successes. After the fiasco of his *Suréna* in 1674 he gave up playwriting entirely, and passed quietly out of the public eye. He died in 1684.

Though Corneille is properly regarded as the real father of French classic tragedy, the natural bias of his genius was undoubtedly towards the romantic. This is shown not only in *Le Cid*, but also in some of his later plays, like the heroic comedy *Don Sanche d'Aragon*, the tone and manner of which remind us in advance of Hugo's *Ruy Blas*. After the strictures of the Academy upon *Le Cid* he made, it is true, submission to the classic doctrine, yet he always chafed under the restraints which it imposed upon him. Thus in the extremely interesting *examens* which he prefixed to his plays in the edition of 1661, and in his three *Discours* on the art of the drama, we find him advocating the most generous possible interpretation of the rules, and pleading specifically for " quelque élargissement " in the matter of the unities of place and time. The modern reader will, in fact, feel that Corneille was sadly hampered, and that he knew that he was sadly hampered, by the limitations of the artificial form in which he was compelled to work, and that his opulent genius would have found greater scope and a more congenial medium in the romantic drama. Yet notwithstanding his restiveness he brought his energies under such thorough control that in *Horace, Cinna*, and *Polyeucte* he produced dramas which will endure the test of the most rigorous canons of the classic school.

In one way in particular he gave a splendid demonstration of what classic tragedy is capable of accomplishing within its limitations, and he did this by focussing his attention upon the psychological significance of his subjects. He did not neglect external incident, as did his younger contemporary Racine ; indeed many of his plays abound in incident and are marked by a strongly melodramatic strain. But his primary interest was in the emotional experiences of his characters and their inner conflicts, and especially in the conflict of passion and duty, and the triumph of duty over passion. This motive, in the working out of which he displays his finest qualities, appears in his plays under a variety of forms ; as in *Le Cid*, in which the pivot of the plot is the successful struggle of honour against love ; in *Horace*, in which we have the glorification of the old Roman patriotism rising superior to the closest domestic ties ; in *Cinna* and *Nicodème*, which in different ways illustrate the power of a man over himself ; in *Polyeucte*, which is a tragedy of Christian faith crowned by martyrdom. Corneille's plays are a school of noble if at times fantastic sentiment. His characteristic note is the note of high courage ; his favourite theme, the supremacy of the individual will. All his typical figures, good and bad alike, are conceived on the grand scale, and are lifted far above the common plane of humanity by their essential greatness of soul. Extraordinary in themselves, they are, moreover, placed in extraordinary situations, with the result that the emotional conflicts portrayed also assume extraordinary proportions. Romantic exaggeration was thus an outstanding feature of Corneille's art. As his mental bias was thus towards the strong and heroic he was naturally more at home with men than with women, and was in general out of his proper element in the treatment of love. His women—his " adorable furies " as a contemporary called them—with their pride, ambition, and domineering spirit, are indeed more masculine than feminine, while love itself, being commonly employed, not for its own sake, but to create the crisis in which it is to be overcome, is, on the whole, rather ineffectively handled by him. Corneille was a most unequal writer ; many of his plays are far below the level of his best ; and even in his best we come from time to time upon passages of dreary rhetoric or bombastic declamation which have neither poetic value nor dramatic truth. His tendency to degenerate into the mere special pleader and to indulge in fine-spun disquisitions and dialectical subtleties which are singularly inappropriate to the characters on whose lips they are put, is generally recognised as a conspicuous weakness of his work. His greatness in his own chosen field of heroic passion is, however, indisputable, and no one who reads him attentively can fail to admire his tremendous energy, the sweep and vigour of his versification, and the frequent splendour of his style.

27. RACINE.—Corneille's one rival, Jean Racine, was thirty-three years his junior, for he was born in 1639 at La Ferté-Milon in Champagne. He came of a family closely connected on both sides with the Jansenists, and was educated in their well-known schools at Beauvais and Port-Royal. Thoroughly indoctrinated with their moral and religious ideas, he left the latter institution at nineteen to pursue his studies in the Collège d'Harcourt. At this time or a little later, however, he began to evince a taste for worldly society and decided leanings towards the stage, and misunderstandings with his old teachers, which were presently to develop into an open quarrel, were the result.

Meanwhile he dabbled in literature, produced some verses on the king's marriage, which, though of slight value, secured for him a place on the royal pension list, and became intimate with Boileau. His first tragedies, *La Thébaïde ou les Frères Ennemis* and *Alexandre le Grand*, which were produced by Molière's company in 1664 and 1665 respectively, were so obviously reminiscent of Corneille and Quinault (see p. 83) that no one perceived in them the slightest signs of a fresh and original power. But in *Andromaque* (1667), which, according to Perrault, created as much excitement as *Le Cid* had done thirty-one years before, all the writer's distinctive qualities were fully revealed. This was followed by a comedy, *Les Plaideurs* (1668), a pungent satire on the law, after which came six more tragedies—*Britannicus* (1669), *Bérénice* (1670), *Bajazet* (1672), *Mithradite* (1673), *Iphigénie en Aulide* (1674), and *Phèdre* (1677). By this time, however, the influence of his early training was reasserting itself ; he began to be troubled with scruples about the theatre ; and the momentary failure of *Phèdre*, which greatly irritated his extremely sensitive nature, seemed to him a warning voice from heaven. He accordingly made his peace with Port-Royal, gave up playwriting, married, and for more than twenty quiet years divided his time between his family and his duties as one of the king's historiographers royal. His only remaining dramas were two of a religious character, which he wrote at the request of Mme. de Maintenon, for performance by her young ladies at Saint-Cyr—*Esther* (1689) and *Athalie* (1691). He died in 1699.

The first point to emphasise in the study of Racine is his admirable craftsmanship. In construction and composition—in the laying out of his plan and in the filling in of its details—he is a consummate master. The exigent

rules under which Corneille fretted, fit Racine's genius to
a nicety ; indeed, he seems to obey them naturally and
spontaneously, not as rules imposed upon him from
without, but as conditions involved in his own fundamental
conception of dramatic art. Plot, intrigue, action, as
ordinarily understood, hardly exist in his plays, and he
never allowed himself to be embarrassed by wealth of
material. The ideal at which he aimed was concentration
of interest through the utmost possible simplification of
subject. The invention of a large number of incidents as
a means of holding the attention of the spectator was for
him a sign not of fertility but of poverty of genius ; the
true poet ought to be able to keep attention alive through
the five acts of his tragedy " par une action simple,
soutenue de la violence des passions, de la beauté des
sentiments, et de l'élégance de l'expression " (*Préface* to
Bérénice). True to this conception he reduces his drama
to a single moral crisis, selecting by preference that final
point in the ascending scale when, the passions of his
characters being at their highest tension, the smallest
event will suffice to precipitate a catastrophe. Even
more, then, than the drama of Corneille that of Racine is
purely psychological—a drama of endless talk, introspec-
tion, discussion. Mere external incident has in itself no
interest for him ; he treats it as cause or effect only of his
real tragedy, which is the tragedy of emotional disturbance and conflict in the souls of his characters. As a
psychological dramatist, however, he is sharply divided
from Corneille, because while he deals at times with other
passions, such as loyalty and ambition, he makes love,
which with Corneille had been of secondary interest, his
central motive. Some problem of love lies indeed at the
heart of all his plays. As a French critic has said :
" Dans toutes les tragédies de Racine on trouve un per-

sonnage qui aime un autre, et n'en est pas aimé ; mais cet autre aime un troisième qui (le plus souvent) lui rend son amour."[1] The tragical consequences arising from this complex emotional situation provide him with his dominant theme ; but this theme he elaborates under so great a variety of aspects that though his plays resemble one another in data they differ widely in details. In general, however, it may be remarked that, again in contrast with Corneille, he is most successful with his women characters. Love is more powerfully, and, it is commonly agreed, more truthfully depicted in his women than in his men.

It remains for us to emphasise one aspect of Racine's art which, though of great importance, is likely to escape the notice of the English reader. That he is a typical classicist is easily perceived ; that his classicism involves a distinct tendency towards realism is not so apparent. Indeed, his world is avowedly so remote from that of everyday life (see *Préface* to *Bajazet*), his art is so entirely ideal, the dignity of tragedy is so scrupulously maintained by him, and his tone is throughout so obviously that of conventional gallantry and the etiquette of the Court, that the frequent use of the word realist by his French critics may well cause us some surprise. The nature of his so-called realism will, however, become apparent if we put ourselves at the historical point of view. The bent of Corneille's genius had led him to exploit the exceptional. Racine keeps to what is broadly human in character, sentiment, theme. This is his classicism. But where Corneille had placed persons in themselves extraordinary in extraordinary situations, Racine, repudiating his great forerunner's romantic exaggeration, deals with men and women who masquerade under antique names, it is true,

---

[1] Petit de Julleville, *Le Théâtre en France*, p. 163.

but in whom, none the less, we recognise the qualities, passions, and weaknesses of the human nature with which we ourselves are familiar, and these men and women he places in situations which might arise, and which indeed do often arise, in the common course of life. This is what we mean by his realism.[1] Beneath the highly conventional machinery of his tragedies, therefore, we often seem to touch the real springs of motive and action, and even his artificial diction has, in comparison with Corneille's, a frequent note of naturalness and simplicity.

28. OTHER TRAGIC POETS OF THE SEVENTEENTH CENTURY.—However little personal enthusiasm we may be able to feel to-day for Corneille and Racine, they will always remain interesting to us as great masters in their own particular sphere of dramatic art. Their contemporaries have nothing more than a purely historical significance, but three of them deserve passing mention. Jean de Rotrou (1609–50), the oldest and most important of these, and for a time one of Richelieu's " five poets," was a fertile though unequal writer of comedies, tragicomedies, and tragedies. His best work is to be found in two plays of the last-named class—*Saint-Genest* (1646), a tragedy of martyrdom, derived from a Spanish drama of Lope de Vega, but in treatment reminiscent of *Polyeucte*, and *Venceslas* (1647), also Spanish in origin, but with unmistakable resemblances here and there to *Horace*. Thomas Corneille (1625–1709), a younger brother of Pierre, was a successful playwright, distinctly clever in matters of mere technique, and, as we can see in such re-

---

[1] Though he does not mention Corneille by name, it is clear that he has him in mind when in the first of his two prefaces to *Britannicus* he writes contemptuously of those tragic poets who abandon the natural to throw themselves into the extraordinary, fill their pages with surprising incidents, and put into the mouths of their characters declamations which are inappropriate to their personalities and circumstances.

presentative plays as *Laodice* (1668), *La Mort d'Hannibal* (1669), *Le Comte d'Essex* (1678), and the tragi-comedy of *Timocrate* (1656), with a strongly romantic turn of mind. This is one of several points of contact between him and his greater brother. On the other hand, Philippe Quinault (1635–88), though now best known as a writer of operas, the work of his later life, anticipated Racine in various ways, and notably in his treatment of love, in his earlier tragedies, of which *La Mort de Cyrus* (1656) and *Astrate* (1663) may be cited as examples. After Racine's time tragedy declined, and in the hands of his younger contemporaries became more and more anæmic. Between his retirement from the stage and the close of the century, indeed, no new writer appeared who calls for even formal recognition.

29. COMEDY BEFORE MOLIÈRE. — In the earlier decades of the seventeenth century the comic stage, still asserting its independence of academic influences, was largely occupied with farces which carried on the popular traditions of the Middle Ages. The stock characters which figured prominently in many of these, like the resourceful valet and the jealous pedant, were also utilised in comedies of a somewhat higher class and with greater literary pretensions, such as *Jodelet ou le Maître Valet* (1645), a brisk play of double disguise, by Scarron (see p. 117), and *Le Pedant Joué* (1654), by Cyrano de Bergerac (see p. 117, n. 1). Comedies of intrigue, with complicated plots, in the fashion either of the Italian or of the Spanish stage, were also popular ; as, *e.g.*, *La Sœur* (1645) of Rotrou, *Les Ennemis Généreux* (1654) of Scarron, and the *Mélite* and *Menteur* of Corneille. Meanwhile, the real comedy of manners began to emerge, giving at times distinct promise of the greater things which were soon to come, as in Corneille's *La Veuve* (1633) and *La Galerie du*

Palais (1634), his brother's *L'Amour à la Mode* (1651), and *La Belle Plaideuse* (1654) by Bois-Robert. Thus, though nothing of permanent importance had yet been accomplished, considerable progress had been made along many lines—in the management of plot, in the portrayal of character, in the representation of social life and manners—in the years immediately preceding the rise of the greatest comic dramatist of France and of modern times, Molière.

30. Molière.—Jean Baptiste Poquelin was born in Paris in 1622. His father, who was a tradesman in easy circumstances and *valet tapissier de chambre du roi* (or general superintendent of the royal furniture), gave him an excellent education in the Jesuit Collège de Clermont, where he was thoroughly grounded in the classics. He also studied philosophy under Gassendi, one of the boldest and most advanced thinkers of the time, to whose influence, which seems to have stimulated his natural tendency towards free thought, we may perhaps trace his fondness for touching on philosophical questions and for ridiculing (as, *e.g.*, in *Le Mariage Forcé*) the controversial subtleties and jargon of the schools. He was destined either for his father's calling or for the law, but the stage early began to exert an irresistible fascination over him, and when on coming of age he received his share in the small fortune left by his mother, he abandoned all idea of a commercial or legal career, became an actor (under the name of Molière, which he now assumed), and in association with a family of comedians, the Béjarts, hired a tennis court, and started a dramatic enterprise which he called the Illustre Théâtre (1643). This, however, failed, and in 1646 he and his company were forced to leave Paris and take the road. For twelve years they toured the provinces, during which time Molière saw much of life under many aspects, laid up a rich store of experiences and observations, and

learned the business of playwriting by practical work done not for the critics but for the stage. Of his early essays as a dramatist two only survive—*La Jalousie du Barbouillé* and *Le Médecin Volant* : farces of the broadest kind, crude as a whole, but with prophetic touches here and there.[1] But towards the end of his period of apprenticeship he produced two other plays (both imitated from the Italian), which, though still experimental, properly belong to the body of his work—*L'Étourdi* (1655) and *Le Dépit Amoureux* (1656). In 1658 he was back in Paris, where he performed before the king in Corneille's *Nicodème* (as an actor he was ambitious of succeeding in tragic *rôles*, though his genius was unmistakably for comedy), and in a farce, *Le Docteur Amoureux*, now lost ; and having gained the royal favour he became head of a company known as the " Troupe de Monsieur," with an assured position both at the Court and in the capital. The next year he opened his real career as a dramatist with *Les Précieuses Ridicules*, a brief but brilliant satire on preciosity and the *salons*, then already in their decline. Henceforth his life was one of enormous activity ; but though he was the chief actor in his company, and though upon his shoulders as its manager rested the entire burden of its responsibilities, he produced in his remaining fifteen years no fewer than twenty-eight plays small and great, or, on an average, nearly two each year. There is no doubt that this incessant strain was too much for his frail physique, and we cannot wonder that he broke down prematurely under it. His splendid fight against the steady encroachments of disease ended with tragic suddenness one night in February 1673, when, performing

[1] It is not, indeed, absolutely certain that these are his, but it is in the highest degree probable that they are. Details from the former reappear in *George Dandin*, of the latter in *L'Amour Médecin* and *Le Médecin malgré lui*.

the part of the hypochondriac in his last play, *Le Malade Imaginaire*, he was seized with convulsions on the stage and carried home to die.

Two facts in Molière's biography must be emphasised on account of their direct bearing upon his work—his marriage and his relations with the king. His marriage with Armande Béjart, which took place in 1662, was an unhappy one, and though in his case, as in the case of all dramatists, we must be on our guard against the tendency to read too much of the man himself into his work, there can, I think, be no question that the conduct of his beautiful but frivolous young wife and his own jealousy have left their mark in the bitterness which often characterises his treatment of women, as notably in the case of the coquette, Célimène, in the most personal of his plays, *Le Misanthrope*.[1] His relations with the king, which were very close, affected him for good and evil. On the one hand, the royal protection provided him with a defence against the many enemies whom he stirred up about him by his bold and pungent satire, and thus enabled him to carry on his mission as the social censor of his time. On the other hand, the king's command compelled him occasionally to turn aside from his proper line to manufacture *divertissements de circonstance* for the amusement of the Court, and as a result his genius was sometimes wasted in hasty and trivial work (*e.g.*, *La Princesse d'Élide*, *Les Amans Magnifiques*).

Ignoring such work, as having no independent interest for us to-day, we may divide the bulk of Molière's plays into two groups—the lighter plays, which for the most

---

[1] Alceste, the hero of this play, is undoubtedly drawn from one side of Molière's own character. How far Célimène was fashioned upon his wife is a problem much discussed by the specialists. It is at any rate known that he described her as Lucile in *Le Bourgeois Gentilhomme*, iii. 9.

part are broadly farcical, and the great comedies of character. This classification, however, is not absolutely exact, because there are a few plays, like *George Dandin* and *Le Bourgeois Gentilhomme*, which are on the border-line between the two divisions, and a couple which lie outside them entirely—*La Critique de l'École des Femmes* (1663) and *L'Impromptu de Versailles* (1663) : brilliant and extremely original little pieces, of polemical intention, in which Molière replies to his critics and carries the war into their camp, and which are therefore of great importance for the information which they give us about his dramatic theories.[1] Of his farces (*e.g.*, *Le Mariage Forcé*, 1664 ; *Le Médecin malgré lui*, 1666 ; *M. de Pourceaugnac*, 1669) it is enough to say, first, that they overflow with fun and gaiety ; secondly, that if their exuberant jesting is at times a little too coarse for modern taste,[2] the laughter which they arouse is nearly always as wholesome as it is hearty ; and, finally, that amid their riotous and apparently irresponsible mirth, the serious purpose of the social satirist and reformer is often clear. But delightful as these farces are in their own way (and no lover of rich, broad humour would wish for a moment to depreciate them) it is in the great comedies of character—and pre-eminently in *L'École des Femmes* (1662), *Tartuffe* (1664–1669),[3] *Don Juan* (1665), *Le Misanthrope* (1666), *L'Avare*

[1] Another play, the quite unsuccessful heroic comedy, *Dom Garcie de Navarre*, also has no place in the general scheme.

[2] The charge of coarseness was brought against Molière by some of his contemporaries, especially among the *précieuses*; on which point see his defence in *La Critique de l'École des Femmes*. As in the case of our own older writers, as, *e.g.*, Shakespeare and Fielding, the matter must be regarded from the historical point of view. It is, I think, generally admitted that in fact Molière did a great deal to purify the comic stage.

[3] This tremendous attack on religious hypocrisy created so great a disturbance that it was twice prohibited, once immediately on its production in 1664, and again when Molière attempted to revive it in

(1668), and *Les Femmes Savantes* (1672)—that Molière's powers are to be found in their full perfection, and it is by virtue of these that he holds his place secure in the front rank of the dramatists of all the world. In tone these plays differ fundamentally from those of the other group. Life is still regarded in them, it is true, from the comic side, but their ground-work is serious, they carry with them a heavy burden of thought, and in their emotional intensity they often rise to the point at which comedy passes insensibly into tragedy. Moreover, they are all *pièces à thèse*—plays with a strongly marked didactic purpose. Molière saw the superficial absurdities of the society about him and delighted to make merry over them ; but he saw too, and through the medium of a temperament deeply tinged with melancholy, the more dangerous evils which were gnawing at the heart of it ; and though he never forgot that the first business of comedy is " de faire rire les honnêtes gens " (*Critique de L'École des Femmes*), he held that " le théâtre a une grande vertu pour la correction " (*Préface* to *Le Tartuffe*), and true to this conception he deliberately turned his stage into a school for moral reform.

Naturally, as a comic dramatist, he used by preference the great instrument of ridicule, and the range of his satire is wonderfully wide—as wide almost as the society to which he held up the mirror. Foolish ideas about education—*mariages de convenance*, made for wealth or position instead of love—the levity of fashionable men and women —the affectations of the blue-stockings—the empty pretences of would-be poets and critics, philosophers,

---

1667. It was not till 1669 that it was definitely authorised on the public stage. The reader of *Don Juan* must never forget that that powerful study of the libertine who at the last turns hypocrite, was written when *Le Tartuffe* was under the ban, and was designed by Molière as a reply to his enemies.

lawyers, doctors—religious hypocrisy—the ambitions of the *nouveaux riches* who aped their " betters " and were determined to push their way into society—the shameless manœuvres of the aristocracy, who, despising the *bourgeoisie*, made free with their money and laughed at them up their sleeves: such were some of the subjects and people dealt with by him, with a courage which often seems surprising ; indeed, his lash fell upon almost every form of charlatanism and unreality conspicuous in the metropolitan world of his day. There is nothing particularly original, and certainly nothing idealistic, about his criticism of life, but it is essentially healthy and bracing. He is pre-eminently the representative of the *bourgeois* spirit and the very incarnation of the sanity, the downright practical temper, the sterling good sense of the class from which he sprang. He has a hearty contempt of artifice, convention, the romanesque, and nonsense of all kinds, and like Rabelais, like his own friend La Fontaine, he believes implicitly in liberty, and throws his stress upon nature and the natural. Hence his lifelong hostility to the doctors, whom in no fewer than five plays (*Don Juan*, *L'Amour Médecin*, *Le Médecin malgré lui*, *M. de Pource-augnac*, and *Le Malade Imaginaire*) he held up to ridicule as pedants who set up to be wiser than nature and as charlatans who concealed their ignorance in mists of pompous phrases. In religion, though there was not the slightest ground for the allegations of impiety made against him by the " devout," he certainly leaned strongly towards free thought.

As a dramatist Molière everywhere shows his inside knowledge of the stage and his practical grasp of the principles of stage technique. " On sait bien," he declares in his prefatory note to *L'Amour Médecin*, " que les comédies ne sont faites que pour être jouées," and his own plays are devised primarily and expressly to meet the requirements of representation. At the same time, he was habitually indifferent in the matter of construction. His plots are carelessly put together ; their conclusions are often forced or lame, as in the case of *Le Tartuffe*, or brought about by some familiar device, like the discovery of a lost child or the sudden reappearance of some one supposed to be dead. But his intrigues, such as they are, serve his purpose, in his farces for the introduction of effective imbroglios and situations, in his great comedies as machinery for the exposition of character. And exposition of character was his strongest point. Important and unimportant, his men and women stand upright on their feet ; he has the vitalising touch which gives life to even his minor figures. The most significant feature of his characterisation on the critical side, however, is that it tends always to the typical. Disregarding adjuncts and mere idiosyncrasies, he fastens upon central qualities and dominating motives—" humours " as Ben Jonson called them—and builds entirely with these. Thus, for example, his Tartuffe is *the* hypocrite rather than *a* hypocrite, Harpagon *the* miser rather than *a* miser. This method of artificial simplification places him among the classicists who, as we have seen, sought not what was peculiar to the individual as individual, but what was general in humanity. Its disadvantages are obvious, but his genius enabled him to transcend them and to create types which are none the less living people, and which, while necessarily embodying much that was local and temporary in seventeenth-century France, remain fundamentally true for all places and all times. As La Harpe admirably said, " ses comédies . . . pourraient suppléer à l'expérience, non parce qu'il a peint des ridicules qui passent, mais parce qu'il a peint l'homme qui ne change point."

31. COMEDY AFTER MOLIÈRE.—Molière had many followers, but of those who can properly be included within our present period two only are important enough to merit reference here—Regnard and Dancourt. Jean François Regnard (1655–1709) belongs very clearly to the school of Molière, whom he often imitated closely, but he had nothing of his master's depth and was entirely wanting in his moral earnestness. He was, however, a clever writer, with a happy knack of hitting off superficial peculiarities in dialogue which is witty and pointed, and his verse runs with delightful ease. *Le Légataire Universel* (1708) is the most amusing of his plays, though its fun is little more than buffoonery. His masterpiece, *Le Joueur* (1696), deals with the passion for gaming which then infested all ranks of society, but without a trace of that moral purpose which Molière would have imported into his theme. Some of his slighter plays may still be read with pleasure ; as, *e.g.*, the really charming little one-act comedy in prose, *Attendez-moi sous l'Orme* (1694). Florent Carton Dancourt (1661–1725), who was, like Molière, an actor as well as a dramatist, has far less claim than Regnard to literary distinction, but his numerous and lively comedies (*e.g.*, *Le Chevalier à la Mode*, *La Maison de Campagne*, *Les Bourgeois de Qualité*, *La Loterie*) caught the taste of the hour and enjoyed a great popularity. He was particularly successful in delineating the manners of contemporary society, and if his plays have lost much of their original interest because they were purely topical, they are for that very reason valuable as documents for the student of French life during the period of that widespread moral disorganisation which began in the last years of Louis XIV.'s reign and culminated under the Regency.

CHAPTER VI

32. THE PROSE OF THE SEVENTEENTH CENTURY.—The forces which we have noted at work in the transformation of poetry in the seventeenth century, and which, while they helped to clear away the pedantry and conceits of earlier writers, destroyed its freedom and spontaneity, also affected prose, but much more favourably. Here the new tendencies were on the whole for good. The purification of the language was, it is true, attended by considerable loss of picturesqueness and variety, but it was still a gain when the rule of " le bel usage " was accepted as the governing principle in taste, and when the long trailing sentences of the sixteenth century, with their innumerable conjunctions, relative pronouns, and subordinate clauses, were broken up and reduced to order. Prose now indeed assumed its distinctively modern form, and became for the first time a perfectly adequate medium of communication among educated people on subjects of interest to all. This change in the quality of prose can be traced directly to the influence of the new *société mondaine*, the *salons*, and the Academy, but it is not so closely associated with any one writer as the corresponding reform of poetry is with Malherbe. One name is, however,

always mentioned in connection with it—that of Jean Louis Guez de Balzac (1594–1654), who is chiefly known by his letters, nominally addressed to many of the great persons of the day, but really intended for general perusal. Both before and after their publication they were read with boundless enthusiasm by a wide circle of admirers. In themselves they possess but little interest for us to-day, for they are essays rather than letters, and while they lack the familiar charm which belongs to the genuine letter, their value as essays is very small. But their importance on the side of style must not be overlooked. Balzac led the way in the new prose, and his two special qualities emphasised by Boileau—propriety of diction and skill in sentence-construction—give him historically a certain claim to distinction.

33. THE MORALISTS : PASCAL.—It has been justly said that " tout grand écrivain du XVIIe siècle est doublé d'un moraliste." [1] Preoccupation with moral considerations is indeed one of the most noteworthy features of the literature of the age. We see this in the tragedies of Corneille and Racine and in the comedies of Molière. We see it even in the *Fables* of La Fontaine. In these writers, of course, the prevailing " tendance moraliste " expressed itself only indirectly and under the conditions imposed by their different forms of art. There were, on the other hand, many among their contemporaries who were, as we may say, moralists by profession, and who, to use Nisard's distinction, treated ethical questions " non parmi d'autres choses, mais à part, et comme sujet unique." The majority of them—and their name is legion—have little interest for the general reader, but three at least belong to the history of literature as such—Pascal, La Rochefoucauld, and La Bruyère.

[1] Lintilhac, *Précis de la Littérature française*, ii. 100.

Blaise Pascal was born at Clermont-Ferrand in 1623, and was one of the three children of Étienne Pascal, President of the Cour des Aides of Montferrand, and a man of fine character and great intellectual powers. A precocious child, he early showed an astonishing genius for mathematics ; at seventeen he wrote a treatise on conic sections ; at eighteen he invented a calculating machine. In 1646 the whole Pascal family fell under the influence of Jansenism, to which they became converts. Blaise none the less continued his scientific studies and experiments till a breakdown in health in 1652 compelled him to desist. For the next two years he frequented worldly society, and during this period, it would appear, his religious fervour somewhat waned. Then, whether or not, as is often supposed, as the result of a carriage accident, in which he nearly lost his life, he passed through a spiritual crisis during a night of strange mystical ecstasy, the experiences of which he commemorated in a few broken sentences and ejaculations upon a paper which thereafter he always carried sewn in his clothes. After this he renounced the world (1654) and spent the rest of his life in retirement, partly at Port-Royal, partly in Paris. His health had always been poor, and the extreme austerities to which he subjected himself in his endeavour, as his sister Gilberte puts it, " de se perfectionner de plus en plus," told sadly upon him. Worn out with severe and incessant sufferings, borne with saintly resignation, he died in Paris in 1662.

Pascal's character must always remain something of an enigma, for it was compounded of contradictions. To discuss it here is impossible, but stress must be laid upon the fact that he was at once a scientist and a mystic, a logician and a visionary. He had in a supreme degree what he himself calls the "geometric mind" (" l'esprit de la géometrie "), but his ardent faith and his intense imagination carried him far beyond the regions of exact reasoning ; and it is precisely this rare combination of massive intellectuality and high spiritual power which gives their specific quality to his writings. Of these, two, notwithstanding the highly special nature of their subjects, must always be included in any survey of seventeenth-century French literature—his *Provinciales* and his *Pensées*.

The *Lettres écrites par Louis de Montalte à un Provincial de ses Amis et aux Révérends Pères Jésuites, sur la Morale et la Politique de ces Pères*—commonly known for the sake of brevity as *Les Provinciales*—are eighteen controversial tractates in the form of letters, which were published at intervals in 1656 and 1657. They had their origin in a great theological controversy which was raging at the time between the Jansenists and their orthodox opponents on the true nature and action of Divine Grace, Pascal's primary purpose in writing them being to defend his friend, the Port-Royalist Arnauld, against the Sorbonne, which had condemned him for heretical opinions on the points at issue.[1] To this special subject the first four letters are mainly devoted, and to it the writer returns in the last two. But in the intervening twelve—V. to XVI. inclusive—he substitutes offensive for defensive tactics, and deals at large with the whole question of Jesuit theory

[1] The religious movement known as Jansenism took its name from the Dutch theologian Cornelius Jansen (1585–1638), whose *Augustinus*, a commentary on the writings of St. Augustine, published two years after his death, gave rise to a long and acrimonious controversy between those who adopted his views on the doctrine of Grace and other subjects, and those who held them to be heretical. These views were in opposition at several important points to the teachings of the Jesuits, who therefore pursued their supporters with unrelenting bitterness. The principal centre of the movement was the lay community established at Port-Royal, near Versailles, the members of which gave their lives to the work of education and the practice of the most austere piety.

and practice ; and this he does with such tremendous power that this part of his work remains the most formidable attack ever delivered upon the principles of the Order. That the *Provinciales* rank among the masterpieces of polemical literature is universally acknowledged. Unfortunately, since we cannot now be expected to take the faintest interest in the verbal squabbles of Jansenists, Jesuits, New Thomists, and Molinists about Efficacious Grace, Sufficient Grace, and Proximate Power, their subject - matter is against them. Yet their greatness merely as literature must be apparent to any one who dips into their pages. Pascal is not only a mighty controversialist ; he is also a consummate literary artist, and his skill in conducting an argument and in driving it home, his irony, now delicate and now scathing, the sparkling comedy of the earlier letters and the vehement eloquence of the later, are an unfailing source of delight even to those who have no taste for theological discussion as such. It is not without justice that he has been compared for dramatic quality with Plato, for humour with Lucian and Molière, for rhetoric with Cicero and Bossuet. In particular, we must recognise the excellence of his style. His purpose being to appeal not to theological experts but to the educated general public, he wrote in a language which, as he declared, he meant to be " intelligible aux femmes mêmes"; and his lucidity, brilliancy, strength, and grace combine to make his work one of the landmarks of French prose. As Sainte-Beuve said : " Ce n'est que vers le milieu du XVIIe siècle que la prose française, qui avait fait sa classe de grammaire avec Vaugelas,[1] et sa rhétorique avec Balzac, s'émancipa tout d'un coup et devint la langue du parfait honnête homme avec Pascal."

For some years before his death, as his nephew Étienne

---

[1] The author of *Remarques sur la Langue Française*, 1647.

Périer tells us, Pascal had cherished the ambition of writing a great work in defence of Christianity, and had carried the subject about with him continually in his mind; but ill-health prevented the systematic prosecution of his design, and all that he left behind as a contribution towards it was a mass of notes, which were published in 1670 under the title of *Pensées*. These notes are in a chaotic state, and though modern editors have attempted to arrange them upon some definite plan, their efforts, which by no means correspond with one another, can be regarded as tentative only. Thus the *Pensées* are inorganic as well as incomplete and fragmentary; yet even so, they take a high place in religious literature by reason of the depth and pregnancy of their thought, their psychological penetration, and the concentrated vigour of their expression. It would appear to have been the apologist's intention to meet the " libertins," or free-thinkers, on their own ground—that of human nature itself—and to build upon this his demonstration, first of natural religion, and then of Christianity. It has been observed by many critics, and must indeed be obvious to every reader, that there is a profoundly sceptical quality in much of his speculation. In exposing the pretensions of the intellect and the weaknesses and inconstancy of mankind he not only follows Montaigne in his most pyrrhonist moods, but often repeats him, for it is noteworthy that he was a great admirer of the sixteenth-century essayist and was evidently much influenced by him.[1] Moreover, his attitude towards life was uncompromisingly pessimistic. But if he seeks to overthrow the entire structure of thought which the intellect of man has painfully erected, and to

[1] See *Entrétien avec M. de Saci*, in which he contrasts two types of philosophy—stoicism and pyrrhonism (the philosophy of doubt)—taking Epictetus as his representative of the former, Montaigne of the latter.

exhibit the pettiness and misery of the common human lot, it is only that he may clear the way for a reconstruction on the basis of religious faith and hope. Man is a mystery; he is feeble and wretched; yet he has the noblest aspirations; though a single drop of water may destroy him, his capacity for thought makes him greater than the entire universe. Science and philosophy seek in vain to explain this contradiction; deism is insufficient to account for it; but Christianity, with its doctrine of the Fall and its promise of salvation through Christ, meets the problem and solves it. Christianity cannot be proved by the intellect only; its proof lies in its correspondence with the whole nature of man and in the way in which, alone of all systems of thought, it satisfies the totality of his needs. This seems to be the foundation of Pascal's apologia. It may be pointed out that by far the most interesting and suggestive of his *Pensées* are those which deal with psychological and moral questions; those which are concerned with the special evidences of Christianity contained in the Bible and the Fathers are necessarily more limited in their appeal.

34. LA ROCHEFOUCAULD.—A scion of one of the noblest families of France, François, Duc de la Rochefoucauld, was born in Paris in 1613, and was thus ten years Pascal's senior. In early manhood he took part in a plot against Richelieu, and later was prominent in the Fronde. Severely wounded at the battle of Porte Saint-Antoine (1652), in which the insurgents under Condé were defeated by the Government forces under Turenne, he retired from public life, and after spending some years in the country to restore his health, shattered by the long-continued strain of excitement and adventure, he settled in Paris, where he became a familiar figure in some of the great

salons, notably that of Mme. de Sablé.   His closing years were uneventful and sad, and he died in 1680.   By temperament La Rochefoucauld was predisposed to pessimism : " pour parler de mon humeur," he wrote of himself, " je suis mélancholique " (*Portrait fait par lui-même*) ; and the knowledge of the world and of men which he had gained in the course of his political intrigues, and the bitterness of his own thwarted ambitions, combined to deepen his natural gloom into the most pronounced misanthropy.   Hence the unrelieved cynicism of his reading of life in the remarkable little book on which his fame securely rests, his *Maximes et Réflexions Morales* (1st edition, 1665 ; 6th edition, greatly enlarged, 1678).   The writing of *Pensées*, or brief detached apothegms on moral questions, was much cultivated in Mme. de Sablé's *salon*, and other frequenters of it, besides La Rochefoucauld, sedulously practised the art of packing the utmost amount of meaning into the fewest possible words.   But no one among them approached him, and few writers of any time or country ever have approached him, in the power of concentrated expression.   As a stylist he is indeed a master.   As a moralist he is acute, independent, and penetrative, but one-sided and narrow. He traverses a fairly wide field of experience, it is true, but his thought is everywhere dominated by a single purpose—to lay bare the actual principles by which, however loth we may be to admit it, we actually govern our lives.   Under his remorseless analysis all conduct is reduced to modes of self-interest : " Les vertus se perdent dans l'intérêt comme les fleuves se perdent dans la mer " ; and again, " L'intérêt parle toutes sortes de langues et joue toutes sortes de personnages, même celui de désintéressé."   *Amour-propre*, though it may disguise itself in a thousand cunning ways, he finds the real motive force

behind all our actions, great or small, heroic or trivial ;
even what passes current as virtue is vitiated at its source ;
our very humility is only a subtle form of vanity, for " le
refus des louanges est un désir d'être loué deux fois," and
"on aime mieux dire du mal de soi que de n'en parler."
Though here and there a different note is struck, as in the
finely generous saying, " C'est se donner part aux belles
actions que de les louer de bon cœur," the tone of his
thought is on the whole profoundly misanthropic, and it is
not surprising that he has often been accused of maligning
humanity. It must, however, be acknowledged that he
told many unpalatable truths, which are not the less true
because they are unpalatable. His radical fault was that
he dwelt persistently upon certain facts only, to the total
exclusion of all other considerations, the result being that
his criticism of life is perverted by his omissions. But
it should be noted that by the frequent use of such qualify-
ing words as "souvent," "presque," and the like, La
Rochefoucauld in the later editions of his book to some
extent mitigated the sweeping severity of his judgments.

35. LA BRUYÈRE.—Jean de La Bruyère belonged to
the "petite bourgeoisie" of Paris, and was born in that
city in 1645. He was educated at the University of
Orléans, studied for the Bar, and became an advocate,
but he never practised, choosing rather, as he himself
says, to live "dans la solitude de son cabinet" and to
spend his days in the study of Plato. In 1684, on the
recommendation of his friend Bossuet, he was appointed
tutor to the young Duke of Bourbon, grandson of the
Great Condé, and remained in the household of Condé
till his death in 1696. A spectator and student of life,
he began to write late, and put all his observations and
judgments into the one book by which he is remembered,
Les Caractères ou les Mœurs de ce Siècle (1688), which he

published in the first instance as an appendix to a translation of the *Characters* of the Greek philosopher, Theophrastus. This book has neither system nor plan ; it is, in fact, a kind of medley, made up of many things ; but reflections and portraits, or character-studies, are the principal elements in its composition. " Tout l'esprit d'un auteur," he declares, " consiste à bien définer et bien peindre " ; and in this phrase he provides a key to his own method, for in the main he defines and paints. As a maxim-writer he rarely equals La Rochefoucauld either in the penetration of his thought or in the vigour of his expression, though his criticism of life is often very shrewd if seldom very deep, and his style, which was the product of constant care and labour, is one of the best examples of the new seventeenth-century prose. His great success, however, was achieved with his character-studies, in which (as he explained in the *Discours* which he delivered on his admission to the Academy) he combines a multitude of individual traits, taken now from this side now from that, into composite portraits representing some of the outstanding types in contemporary society. From this point of view his book possesses, over and above its intrinsic literary value, a permanent historical interest as a vivid picture of the men and manners of the day. But he was not merely a painter ; he was also, and indeed primarily, a moralist, who in writing sought, what he insists the true philosopher should always seek, not the empty praise of his readers, but " un plus grand succès," which is " de les rendre meilleurs." While not a misanthrope, like La Rochefoucauld, he had a keen eye for the social evils of his time, which often stirred him to generous indignation. The boldness of some of his opinions indeed surprises us when we come upon them amid his more conventional generalisations. He did not hesitate to touch upon the wrongs which were being done by men of rank and power, upon the evils of war, upon the abuses of absolutism. "Le peuple n'a guère d'esprit et les grands n'ont point d'âme," he writes in his chapter, *Des Grands* ; "celui-là a un bon fonds et n'a point de dehors ; ceux-ci n'ont que des dehors et qu'une simple superficie. Faut-il opter ? Je ne balance pas ; je veux être peuple." This is a remarkable statement to come from the pen of any man of La Bruyère's position, and I quote it because it illustrates a quality in his thought which has led many French critics to speak of him as a precursor of the democratic writers of the eighteenth century. Still more remarkable and more prophetic is the sympathy which he occasionally showed with the miserable down-trodden masses, as in the famous and often-quoted passage in his chapter, *De l'Homme*, in which he describes the wretched peasantry, who to the ordinary observer may seem little better than beasts, and yet "quand ils se lèvent sur leurs pieds, ils montrent une face humaine, et en effet, ils sont des hommes."

36. RELIGIOUS WRITERS.—From these lay moralists we turn naturally to those among their contemporaries within the Church who, though wholly or chiefly theologians, have still to be included in any survey of seventeenth-century literature. The most important of these is Bossuet, the greatest of the pulpit orators of an age particularly rich in pulpit oratory. Like nearly all the notable men of letters of the time, Jacques Bénigne Bossuet sprang from the middle classes. He was born at Dijon in 1627, educated at the Jesuit school of his native city, and at the Collège de Navarre in Paris, and becoming in 1652 a canon of Metz early made his mark as a preacher and as a polemical writer against the Protestants. In 1659 he created a sensation by his first sermon in Paris,

after which he was soon recognised as the leader of the devout party at Court. In 1669–70 he was Bishop of Condom ; from 1670 to 1681 tutor to the dauphin ; and on resigning his position was appointed Bishop of Meaux. During the last period of his life he was specially active as a controversialist, championing the royal authority and the liberties of the Gallican Church against Rome and the Ultramontanes, and doing battle both with the Protestants and with the doctrines of Quietism as interpreted by Fénelon. He died in 1704. Bossuet was a man of strong convictions and intense religious feeling ; narrow and intolerant ; a pronounced conservative and an ardent supporter of the fixity of dogma and of absolute authority in Church and State. Three of his principal writings are devoted in particular to an exposition at large of his political and theological doctrines : his *Politique tirée de l'Écriture Sainte* (published 1709), which is an elaborate argument on Biblical grounds for the theory of the divine right of kings in its extremest form ; his *Discours sur l'Histoire Universelle* (1681), prepared in the first instance for the dauphin as a demonstration of the workings of providence in human affairs ; and his *Histoire des Variations des Églises Protestantes* (1688), in which he endeavours to establish the supremacy of the one undivided Church by exhibiting the hopeless want of unity among the schismatics. In other works he upholds the authority of the Church against licence in morals and heretical tendencies in thought, as in his *Maximes et Réflexions sur la Comédie* (1694), specially remarkable for its bitter attack on Molière ; and in his *Rélation sur le Quiétisme* (1690) ; while in others again, as, *e.g.*, the *Traité de la Connaissance de Dieu et de Soi-même* (published 1741), he devotes himself to the task of building up the faith of believers. As an historian and controversialist, Bossuet, though not a great or original thinker, has been much praised for his thorough grasp of his subjects, his dialectical skill, and the purity of his style, but his sermons, upwards of 200 of which survive, after all constitute the real corner-stone of his fame. Some of these, as, *e.g.*, those *Sur l'éminente Dignité des Pauvres, Sur la Providence,* and *Sur la Mort,* are sermons in the usual sense of the term ; others, of which those on Henriette of France, Henrietta of England, and the Prince de Condé are the most celebrated, are funeral orations. As an orator he reveals all his gifts in full perfection—his argumentative power, his fervour, his imagination. His style is deeply coloured by the influence of the Bible and the Fathers, in the study of which he was steeped. His avowed purpose being only to move and convince, he did not aim at, but rather avoided, mere literary ornament and grace. He is indeed often simple with a kind of Hebraic simplicity ; sometimes he is even rugged ; but what impresses us most in reading him is the stately splendour of his eloquence.

Bossuet's principal rival as a preacher was the Jesuit, Louis Bourdaloue (1632–1704), a man of extraordinary honesty and courage, whose special characteristic was his logical power, and who in contrast with Bossuet threw the stress of his teaching on the moral rather than on the doctrinal side ; while a little later the reputation of both these great orators was overshadowed by that of their younger contemporary, Jean Baptiste Massillon (1663–1742), who is now remembered chiefly for his funeral oration on Louis XIV., and for the series of Lenten sermons (*Petit Carême*) which he preached before Louis XV. in 1718.

But after Bossuet the foremost place among the religious writers of the seventeenth century must be

assigned to Fénelon. Born in 1651, in the Château de
Fénelon in Périgord, François de Salignac de la Mothe
Fénelon took holy orders in 1675, was tutor to Louis XIV.'s
grandson, the Duke of Burgundy, from 1689 to 1695, and
was then presented by the king to the archbishopric of
Cambrai. Already he had formed a friendship with the
celebrated Quietist, Mme. de Guyon, whose defence he·
undertook against those who pursued and persecuted her
for heresy. This brought him into collision with his old
friend Bossuet, and a conflict ensued, conducted on
Bossuet's side with great acrimony and on Fénelon's
with remarkable dignity and tact. In the end, Bossuet
triumphed and Fénelon was condemned by Rome (1699).
About the same time he also drew down upon himself
the anger of the king by his political views. Henceforth
he lived and laboured entirely in and for his diocese, and
died, still under a cloud, in 1715. Fénelon was a very
voluminous writer, and his works embrace a great variety
of subjects—theology, ethics, education, philosophy, history, literary criticism. But he is best known by his
Télémaque (1699), which, like his *Fables* and his *Dialogues
des Morts*, he designed for the use of his royal pupil.
Starting from the fourth book of the *Odyssey*, to which it
forms a kind of sequel, *Télémaque* recounts the further
adventures of the young Prince of Ithaca in search of his
father. But it is not merely a story; it is a *roman
pédagogique*, the narrative of which is simply a vehicle
of instruction on the conduct of life, the faithful Mentor
being always at hand to point the moral of every incident.
It was on account of the enlightened political views
expressed in it that the work aroused the wrath of the
king.

37. LETTERS AND MEMOIRS.—The same social conditions that favoured the development of the art of polite

conversation also stimulated that of letter-writing, and
the *littérature épistolaire* of the seventeenth century is
very large and very varied.[1]   Many of the most prominent
professional authors of the time, like Racine, Boileau, and
La Fontaine, were also industrious correspondents by the
way ; others, like Balzac and Voiture, adopted the form
of the letter, though nothing but the form, as their principal mode of expression ; but the art was cultivated in
particular by leisured men of society and by women,
and with pre-eminent success by the latter.   One of
these was the "incomparable épistolaire," who not only
holds an easy supremacy among her contemporaries, but
has also her niche in the temple of literary fame.   Marie
de Rabutin-Chantal was born in Paris in 1626, and at
eighteen became the wife of the handsome, dissipated
Henri, Marquis de Sévigné, whose death in a duel in 1650
left her a widow with two young children, a daughter and
a son.   The former, who in 1669 married the Comte de
Grignan, Governor of Languedoc, was the principal re-
cipient of her letters, though she also carried on a fairly
regular correspondence with a few intimate friends.   She
died while on a visit to Grignan in 1696.   Mme. de
Sévigné's abilities were of such a high order that both
surprise and regret have sometimes been expressed that
she did not, like so many other women of the time, devote
herself to the composition of some sustained work.   We
may, however, safely assume that, as M. Gaston Boissier
has suggested,[2] the letter-writing which for more than a
quarter of a century fully satisfied all her cravings for
self-expression, also offered a more congenial field for her
peculiar talents than she would have found even, let us

[1] The vogue of letter-writing is incidentally illustrated in an interesting way by the prominence of letters in the fashionable romances dealt
with in the next chapter.

[2] *Mme. de Sévigné* (in *Les Grands Écrivains Français*), Part II. iv.

say, in the romance. Her letters have the superlative merit of being real letters, not essays or treatises in disguise, and they possess all the freedom, expansiveness, and spontaneity which are the special charm of real letters when the writer has interesting things to talk about and knows how to talk about them in an interesting way. Living as she did at the centre of things, at the Court, in the capital, in the *salons*, she had always an abundance of excellent material for her ready pen, and her keenness of observation, her sound judgment, her never-failing wit and humour, and the ease and naturalness of her style, give vitality and point to everything she touches. Nor is her familiar gossip about domestic affairs less interesting, or for that matter of less value historically, than what she has to tell us about public events and people. But the ultimate secret of the enduring attraction of her letters is after all to be found in their continual revelation of the writer's own personality—her warm-heartedness, her gaiety, her unconventional piety, her devotion to her children and grandchildren, her loyalty to her friends. As a point of detail it may be added that, like La Fontaine, whom she greatly admired, she had a genuine feeling for nature. This comes out in particular in the letters written from her beautiful estate of Les Rochers in Brittany.

With the letter-writers of the seventeenth century we may naturally connect the writers of memoirs, who were also numerous, and who collectively left behind them a vast amount of material of great importance to the student of the politics and social conditions of the time. While their interest is in the main purely historical, two of them have an incontestable right to inclusion here—De Retz and Saint-Simon.

Jean François Paul Gondi, Cardinal de Retz (1614–79),

was a fiery, ambitious intriguer, who made himself
notorious in many ways during the civil war of the Fronde,
and who, as his implacable enemy, La Rochefoucauld,
said of him, stirred up the greatest disorders in the State
without knowing how to profit by them. His *Mémoires*,
which deal with the stormy years 1643–55, are prolix
and rambling, but they are marked by picturesqueness
of narrative, a strong dramatic quality, and much power
of character-drawing. At these and all other points,
however, they yield to those of Louis de Rouvray, Duc de
Saint-Simon (1675–1755), who is indeed as clearly the
first among the memoir-writers as Mme. de Sévigné is
among the letter-writers of French literature. Composed
after his retirement from public affairs on the death of
the Duke of Orléans in 1723, and covering as they do the
thirty-one years between 1691 and 1722, they really, of
course, fall outside our present period, but they are always
included in it because the author so distinctly belonged
to the older generation. Saint-Simon was a man of
many and violent prejudices, a good hater, an obstinate
partisan of the aristocracy, an equally obstinate opponent
of the *bourgeoisie*, whose political and social influence
was a source of perpetual irritation to him ; but he was
at the same time honest, independent, benevolent, and
sagacious, and in such matters as the persecution of Port-
Royal and the revocation of the Edict of Nantes he took
a firm stand against the forces of reaction. With all his
vanity and all his fads he had, moreover, the instincts of
the statesman, and he saw quite clearly, what most of
his contemporaries never saw at all, that under the
reckless follies of its government the country was drifting
to certain disaster. If, therefore, the amplest allowance
must be made for the continual perversion of his judgments by animus and passion, his *Mémoires* are none the

less valuable for the lurid light which they throw upon the men and movements of the calamitous closing years of Louis XIV.'s reign and period of the Regency.   Though written with total disregard of all considerations of literary art, they are also in their way a masterpiece of literature.   With ruthless realism Saint-Simon lays bare before us the baseness and pettiness which were concealed just beneath the pompous masquerade of the Great Monarch's court ; his graphic touch gives dramatic interest to every scene he describes ; the men and women who cross his pages, from the Roi-Soleil himself downward, have the substantial quality of actual humanity ; while his style, though careless, feverish, contorted, and incorrect, is remarkable for its energy and animation.

CHAPTER VII

THE SEVENTEENTH CENTURY (*concluded*)

PROSE FICTION

38. THE ARISTOCRATIC ROMANCE.—Prose romance, in the form in which it flourished greatly in France during the first three-quarters of the seventeenth century, was, like letter-writing, a creation of the new *société mondaine*, and as it reflected the manners, expressed the sentiments, and took the tone of that society, the general epithet, aristocratic, may appropriately be used to describe it. The first stage in its evolution is represented by the *roman pastoral*, which derives in part from the dramatic pastorals of Italy (*e.g.* Tasso's *Aminta* and Guarini's *Pastor Fido*), but in the main from the immensely popular Spanish romance, the *Diana* of Montemayor, which, published in 1558, quickly made the tour of Europe and was translated into French twenty years later. As the name implies, this type of fiction belongs to the great arcadian tradition in literature, which originated with the *Idylls* of the Syracusan poet, Theocritus, and Vergil's imitation of these in his *Bucolica*, and the revival of which at the time of the Renaissance was one result of the enthusiastic study of the classics. Like the pastoral poem and the pastoral play, the pastoral romance had nothing whatever to do with the crude realities of country

110

life; it was pastoral only in the accepted conventional sense; that is, its writers, ignoring all homely details, spent their efforts (as Southey said of our own Sir Philip Sidney) in

> Illustrating the vales of Arcady
> With courteous courage and with loyal loves.

Thus in the earliest and most representative example of its class in French literature, the *Astrée* (1610–27) of the ex-leaguer, Honoré D'Urfé (1568–1625),[1] we are concerned, as the author himself is at pains to inform us, not with " bergères nécessiteuses," who made their living by the care of their flocks, but with refined ladies who had become shepherdesses " pour vivre plus doucement et sans contrainte," and with gentlemen of the same rank and ideals. The main interest of the narrative is provided by the love of two such transfigured specimens of rusticity, Céladon and Astrée, who are separated by jealousies and misunderstandings, but who after many adventures and innumerable difficulties, perplexities, dissensions, and reconciliations, are—as the reader will find who has patience to reach the concluding volume—happily united at the end. The supposed period of the story is the fourth century of our era, but there is, of course, nothing to remind us in it of the social dissolution of that troublous time; and though its nominal scene is the region of D'Urfé's own beloved " belle et agréable rivière du Lignon," on the banks of which, as he tells us, " j'ai passé si hereusement mon enfance et la plus tendre partie de ma première jeunesse," the country of his imagination is inhabited, not only by the arcadians themselves, who play at simplicity with a pretty grace,

[1] Of the five parts of which this romance is composed, the first three were published during D'Urfé's lifetime, the remaining two after his death, by his secretary, who appears indeed to have been largely responsible for the fifth part.

but also by cavaliers of a quite modern pattern, nymphs, druids, and vestals. It is probable that such fancy pictures of rural life made a peculiar appeal to readers whose minds were still agitated by memories of the long and cruel Wars of Religion. At any rate, the taste of the age for artificial pastoralism of this description is attested not only by the immense and, to us, amazing popularity of this particular work among " polite " readers, but also by the praise which it long continued to receive from such competent judges of literature as Mme. de Sévigné, La Fontaine, and even Boileau. But though the vogue of *Astrée* endured for many years, and though it gave birth to a large number of imitations, the *roman pastoral* was soon succeeded by a somewhat different type of fiction, the *roman d'aventures*, otherwise known as the *roman précieux* or *roman chevaleresque*. The principal difference between these two types lies in the fact that, as Boileau put it, the pastoral romancer had taken as his heroes " des bergers occupés du seul soin de gagner le cœur de leurs maîtresses," while the writers of the *romans d'aventures* selected, " pour leur donner cette étrange occupation, non seulement des princes et des rois, mais les plus fameux capitaines de l'antiquité " ;[1] but a great expansion of the element of intrigue was also one of their distinguishing features. The lead in this new form was taken by Marin le Roy de Gomberville (1600–74), one of the first members of the Academy, whose *Polexandre* (1632) recounts the astonishing exploits of a king of the Canary Isles in quest of Queen Alcidiane, whom he pursues over a considerable portion of the world. Then came Gautier de Costes, Seigneur de La Calprenède (1610–63), whose fertility of invention has earned for him the nickname (which, however, must not delude the

---

[1] *Discours*, prefixed to *Les Héros de Romans*.

modern reader into any false anticipations regarding the interest to be found in his writings) of " le Dumas père du dix-septième siecle," and whose pseudo-historical *Cassandre* (1642–45), *Cléopâtre* (1647), and *Faramond* (1661) delighted " an infinite number of admirers." But even these were outdone in popularity by the romances which the famous *précieuse*, Madeleine de Scudéry (1607–1701), produced with some assistance from her brother Georges, who, it is supposed, provided the battles and the duels while she was responsible for the characterisation, the psychological analyses, and the interminable moral disquisitions : *Ibrahim, ou l'Illustre Bassa* (1641) ; *Artamène*, better known as *Le Grand Cyrus* (1649–53)— the typical work of the entire school ; and the scarcely less representative *Clélie* (1654–61). These works, as has been well said, form " le dernier terme du roman gallant, qui, après beaucoup d'excursions en sens divers, revient sur lui-même, et se consume dans l'analyse minutieuse et stérile de la gallanterie elle-même." [1]

It would be out of place here to undertake any detailed examination of these aristocratic romances, to which few but the very special students of the period or of the history of fiction are likely now to turn, but one or two of their general characteristics must be indicated. First among these to impress, and to terrify, the modern reader is their enormous bulk : *Astrée* runs (or, more strictly speaking, crawls) to 5500 pages ; *Polexandre* to nearly 6000 ; *Cléopâtre* appeared in twelve volumes ; *Cassandre* and *Le Grand Cyrus* each in ten.[2] This appalling prolixity

---

[1] Morillot, *Le Roman en France*, p. 3.

[2] For the encouragement of any adventurous student who may feel disposed to embark upon the perusal of one of these *romans à longue haleine*, it may, however, be said that the type used in them was large and the lines well spaced. In *Le Grand Cyrus*, for example, I find on a rough average from 140 to 150 words to a page. But then each volume contains something like 1500 pages !

is due in part to the leisurely character of the narrative and the inordinate elaboration of the descriptions ; in part to the immense space given to the dissection of motive and passion, soliloquies, discourses, and *disquisitions amoureuses* ; in part again to the everlasting complication of the main intrigue by innumerable episodes and subordinate actions, nearly every fresh individual introduced, either in the central plot itself or in any offshoot from it, persisting in telling his own story at enormous length.[1] In the second place, stress must be laid upon the fantastic nature of the materials of which these romances are composed. The unreality of D'Urfé's pastoral has already been noted. The unreality of the historical machinery of his successors is equally flagrant. Considerations of place and time are utterly ignored by them. In *Ibrahim* we are in Turkey ; in *Clélie* in the Rome of the kings ; in *Cassandre* in the Persia of Darius ; *Cléopâtre* deals with the love of the great queen's daughter and Juba, Prince of Mauritania ; *Le Grand Cyrus* is concerned with the gallant adventures of that famous conqueror in his wooing of his cousin, the " incomparable Mandane." But it is all one: Greeks, Romans, Egyptians, Persians, Knights of the Round Table, Paladins of Charlemagne, Peruvian Incas, are only aristocratic men and women of seventeenth-century France, with the manners of the Court in every detail of their behaviour, and the language of the *salons* perpetually on their lips. Though this total defiance of historical truth was one ground of Boileau's charge against the romances, it must be re-

---

[1] Morillot (*op. cit.* p. 4) states that there are forty-five " *histoires incidentes* " in *Astrée* ; Le Breton (*Le Roman au XVIIe Siècle*, p. 15) puts the number at " seventy or eighty " ; but I have not myself attempted to check the figures. Other romancers were quite as great sinners in this respect. The result of such abuse of the " story-within-story " device is a complexity which is absolutely bewildering.

membered that no such truth was ever aimed at in them, and that if their writers sinned grievously in this respect they did so openly. Here, in fact, we touch upon one of their chief sources of interest for their first readers, who recognised in them, as they were intended to recognise, idealised transcripts from contemporary society. Indeed, some of them at least, and notably those of Mlle. de Scudéry, were *romans à clef*, in which, as was well understood, the leading characters stood for famous persons of the time. Finally, one of their most important general features is their essentially romantic quality. Their plots are compounded of the most extravagant incidents ; their heroes are transcendent types of chivalry and courtesy ; and they are full of high-flown sentiment and over-strained gallantry. These were among the common characteristics of much of the literature produced by the ardent and spirited generation of the Fronde, as we can see even in the tragedies of Corneille. At the same time they reflect the taste of the *salons* in their fondness for dealing with the refinements of amorous passion and the casuistry of love. It is on this point in particular that Molière raised the laugh against them in his *Précieuses Ridicules*.

39. THE REALISTIC REACTION AND THE BEGINNINGS OF THE MODERN NOVEL.—With the general change of spirit in the third quarter of the century and the final triumph of classicism the aristocratic romances began to lose their vogue, while Boileau's pungent *Dialogue sur les Héros de Romans* (which circulated in the *salons* as early as 1664, though it was not printed until after Mlle. de Scudéry's death) did much to discredit them even in the circles out of which they had grown and in which they had found their special public. But even in the heyday of their popularity they had called out against

them that perennial *esprit gaulois* which long before had played havoc with romance in the *Roman de Renart* and *Pantagruel*. While D'Urfé's pastoral was still, in Perrault's phrase, " les délices et la folie de toute la France," Charles Sorel (1599–1674) poured ridicule upon it in his mock-pastoral, *Le Berger Extravagant* (1627), which narrates the history of a young student named Lysis, whose wits are turned by much reading of *Astrée*—as those of Don Quixote had been by his books of chivalry—who becomes a shepherd for the sake of love, and whose attempt to emulate the performances of Céladon results in a series of ludicrous misadventures. This, however, was not Sorel's first attack upon the vagaries of the romantic school. Five years before he had published his *Vraye Histoire Comique de Francion*, a work of much greater general interest because, instead of being a mere parody, it is a tale of manners and intrigue, in which a faithful reproduction of vulgar reality is offered as a substitute for the fine-spun unrealities of poetic fancy. As in *Le Berger Extravagant* the influence of Cervantes is very apparent, so *Francion* is evidently in large measure inspired by the picaresque novel of Spain, a form of realistic and satiric fiction which about the middle of the sixteenth century had followed close upon the romances of chivalry and the pastoral romances of that country.[1] The hero of this amusing little book is no amorous prince who conquers imaginary kingdoms in the name of his mistress and fills hundreds of pages with his courtly wooing. He is a shrewd young fellow of the world—a

[1] This was essentially a novel of low life, and it had a sharper or rascal for its central figure ; hence its name *picaresco*, from Spanish *picaro*, a rogue. The first of these picaresque novels was the anonymous *Larazillo de Tormes* (1554) ; the most celebrated, Mateo Aleman's *Guzman de Alfarache* (1599), later translated into French by Le Sage, whose indebtedness to the Spanish " rogue-novel " will be noted in its proper place.

sort of " frère ainé de Gil Blas," as M. Le Breton has
happily called him ; and his adventures are all on a very
common plane and lie among very commonplace people
—college pedants, lawyers, vagabonds, robbers, country-
folk. With all its defects—and it is often coarse in
matter and crude in style—*Francion* has a good deal of
boisterous humour, and its immense success (it was
reprinted sixty times within a few years) is at least easier
for us now to understand than the popularity of the
literature against which it raised the standard of revolt.

Next in order of time among the important contributions to the realistic reaction—and it is of important
contributions only that we can here take any account
—comes Scarron's *Roman Comique* (1651–57).[1] Paul
Scarron (1610–60) was a deformed cripple who for the
last twenty years of his life was the victim of terrible
diseases, but his physical sufferings did not repress the
natural gaiety of his disposition, which sustained his
courage and inspired his pen to the very end. His
humour took, in the main, the form of burlesque, as in
L'Énéide Travestie already mentioned, and the spirit of
burlesque pervades the work now in question, which,
instead of detailing the sentimental experiences of love-
lorn princes and princesses, describes in brisk and racy
fashion the doings of a company of itinerant actors on
their way through Le Mans. The *Roman Comique* is
ill-constructed and shapeless, and its fun too often depends
upon the kind of horse-play of which we have a foretaste
in the second chapter, when the tragedy of *Marianne* is

---

[1] Mention may here be made in passing of the *Histoire Comique des
États et Empires de la Lune* and the *Histoire Comique des États et Empires
du Soleil* of Savinien Cyrano de Bergerac (1619–55). But these are
satirical extravaganzas, in which the influence of Rabelais is very
apparent, and which in turn gave hints to Swift for his *Gulliver's
Travels*, and they hardly belong to the history of the novel.

interrupted by " mille coups de poing, autant de soufflets, un nombre effroyable de coups de pied, des juremens qui ne se peuvent compter." But the characters of the actors themselves and of the provincials with whom they mingle are handled with abundant vigour, those of the old comedian La Rancune and the little *avocat* Ragotin being indeed genuine creations of a farcical kind, and the successive scenes, though loosely strung together, are full of life. Hence any reader of fairly robust taste may still find plenty of amusement in the book.

Less vivacious than this, but historically of greater importance, is *Le Roman Bourgeois* (1666), by Boileau's friend, Antoine Furetière (1620–85), whose special power lay in his domestic realism. " Je vous raconteray sincère-ment et avec fidélité," he announces, at the outset, "plusieurs historiettes et galanteries arrivées entre des personnes qui ne seront ny héros ny héroïnes, qui ne dresseront point d'armées, ny ne renverseront point de royaumes, mais qui seront de ces bonnes gens de médiocre condition, qui vont tout doucement leur grand chemin, dont les uns seront beaux et les autres laids, les uns sages et les autres sots ; et ceux-cy ont bien la mine de composer le plus grand nombre." Such is the author's programme, and he carries it out in a series of vivid pictures of middle-class life, done with an accumulation of precise detail which anticipates the method of the " naturalistic " novelists of two centuries later. All through Furetière indulges in gibes at the fashionable writers, and draws out the contrast between romance and reality. At the same time, as with Molière, his satire has a double edge, for while he ridicules the aristocracy as seen from the point of view of the *bourgeoisie*, he is even more severe upon the *bourgeoisie* themselves, poking fun alike at their boasted domesticity and at the social ambitions which led them to ape the manners of the aristocracy and even to set up *salons* of their own in imitation of those of the *précieuses*. Thus, for example, one of his principal figures is an " amphibious " young man named Nicodème, an *avocat* by day, but a *courtesan* when his day's work is over, for he is one of the many of his class who " veulent passer pour des gens de bel air." This Nicodème makes love to a certain Javotte, the daughter of a *procureur*, according to the approved methods of "galanterie": that is, as love is made in *Cyrus* and *Clélie* ; but Javotte is a simple - minded young person of sound practical common-sense, and " je n'entends point tout ce que vous dites " is her discouraging reply to his flowery speeches. This same Javotte is presently introduced into one of the *salons* just referred to, where she creates great merriment by her total ignorance of literary matters, and especially by talking about a poem of four hundred lines as a sonnet. In such scenes we realise the close connection between the satire of *Le Roman Bourgeois* and that of *Les Précieuses Ridicules*.

In the works thus far mentioned, and pre-eminently in this of Furetière, we can trace the early evolution of the novel under the influence of the bourgeois spirit in its reaction against the aristocratic romance. But we have also to note the transformation of the aristocratic romance itself in the hands of a woman who was herself a representative of the society by which it had been fostered. Mme. de La Fayette (1634–93), the writer in question, was in earlier life a prominent figure in the Hôtel de Rambouillet, and she had already written a sentimental story, *La Princesse de Montpensier* (1662) and a *roman d'aventures* in the current style, *Zayde* (1670), before she broke fresh ground with her one important contribution to literature, *La Princesse de Clèves* (1678).

The scene of this short, simple, and touching tale is the Court of Henry II., though the historical background is evidently studied from that of Louis XIV. The heroine is a woman who having for some years been the wife of a man whom she esteems but does not love, has her affections suddenly engaged by the Duke of Nemours, whom she happens to meet one night at a ball at the Louvre. Faithful to her duty, yet fearing the strength of her newly-awakened passion, she determines to defend herself against herself by making a full confession to her husband. This she does. The prince is deeply touched by her devotion, but he none the less suffers from the pangs of jealousy, and he is presently seized with a fever and dies. Believing herself to have been the cause of his death, his widow refuses the suit of her lover, and ultimately retires to a convent. Such is a bare outline of this remarkable little book. In matter and tone, as will be seen, it is entirely aristocratic, but it is at the same time intensely human. Its emotional tragedy is treated with great delicacy and skill ; its characters are portrayed with fine insight and a firm touch ; and the power of psychological analysis which had hitherto been wasted on hopelessly impossible subjects, is for the first time directed in it to the problems of actual life. For these reasons it is rightly considered as marking a distinct stage in the development of the prose fiction of its time.

CHAPTER VIII

THE EIGHTEENTH CENTURY

GENERAL PROSE

40. THE EIGHTEENTH CENTURY.—What for the purposes of literary classification is known as the eighteenth
century is really the period extending from the death of
Louis XIV. in 1715 to the outbreak of the Revolution in
1789. In the literature of the earlier part of this period
premonitions of approaching change were already apparent, though as yet there was no conscious rupture
with the preceding generation. In the second half of
the century the new spirit became marked and general.
Even then the classical tradition was still largely maintained, amongst its most strenuous theoretical supporters
indeed being some of those who in practice were helping most to undermine it. But if the doctrines of the
classical school continued to receive a certain amount of
lip-service their vitality was fatally impaired. In fundamental character literature now underwent an entire
transformation.

Among the forces which were at work in bringing about
this transformation the first place must be given to
political and social changes. The "grand siècle" had been

an age of strong centralised government, of discipline and order in the State, and, superficially at least, of internal repose ; the eighteenth century was a period of disruption, disorganisation, and ever-growing unrest ; and as the unity of classicism had been a result of the one set of conditions, so the break-up of that unity was an inevitable consequence of the other. The later years of Louis XIV.'s reign—years of disaster abroad and reaction at home— had already heralded the decline of absolute monarchy in France. Then came the moral corruption of the Regency (1715–23), the utter degradation of royalty through the shameless debaucheries of Louis XV. and the pitiable weakness of his ill-starred grandson and successor, the appalling abuses of long years of reckless misgovernment, and, stimulated by these things, the spread of that spirit of discontent which was presently to find vent in the Revolution. This spirit was further strengthened by the rapid growth of science and the critical temper fostered by it. At the same time the Church, which had been one of the bulwarks of absolutism, and had stood for authority and unity in religion as the monarchy had stood for authority and unity in the State, by reason of its bigotry, its stolid opposition to progress, and its moral laxity, was fast forfeiting all claim to popular esteem : a fact of capital importance, because it goes a long way to explain the scepticism which was so marked a feature of the later eighteenth century, and which was another potent element in the general disintegration of the old order. Hence the universal intellectual ferment of the time. Nothing was any longer regarded as sacred. Everything was questioned, challenged, criticised. The right of the past to dictate to the present was emphatically repudiated. " Dans les salons, dans les cafés, dans les cénacles littéraires, dans les milieux bourgeois comme chez les grands seigneurs, tout était discuté, bafoué, battu en brèche, et le cynicisme des propos rivalisait avec l'audace de la pensée." [1]

It has already been noted that before the end of Louis XIV.'s reign the Court had ceased to exercise an absolute undivided authority over French culture and that the centre of taste had shifted from Versailles to Paris. Among the signs of this change, as the quotation just made will have suggested, was the revival of the *salon,* which once more became powerful. But the spirit of the new *salons* was very different from that of the old. Those of the first half of the century indeed, like that of Mme. de Lambert, still devoted themselves chiefly to the interests of gallantry and fashion ; those of the second half, on the other hand—the *salon* of Mme. Geoffrin, of Mme. Du Deffand, of Mme. Lespinasse—were *centres philosophiques,* which were frequented by the leading thinkers of the day, in which scientific, political, and social questions formed the principal topics of conversation, and which were notoriously " advanced " in their sympathies. But even more important than the influence of the *salons* was that of public opinion, now for the first time the dominating force in French life. As one of Diderot's biographers has pointed out, the evolution of literature in the eighteenth century, and especially from 1750 onward, depended ultimately upon a single " social fact "—" the extraordinary development of commerce and industry," and as a direct consequence of this — a consequence clearly perceived by Voltaire at the time—" the noteworthy progress of the middle classes." [2] The Third Estate, increasing steadily in power and in the consciousness of power, now gave the tone to literature, because

[1] Marquis de Ségur, *Au Couchant de la Monarchie.*
[2] Ducros, *Diderot,* p. 182.

it formed the backbone of that wide reading public to which literature was addressed.

Meanwhile these social and political influences were reinforced by a fresh current which was running strongly in literature itself from its source on our own side of the Channel. For the classicists of the seventeenth century, English literature simply did not exist ; even Boileau, though he had, it is true, read Addison's Latin verses, undertook to discourse on the epic without knowing anything of the greatest of modern epics, *Paradise Lost*, and keenly interested as he was in satire, died in ignorance of Dryden's very name. But in the eighteenth century, English genius and thought everywhere penetrated the genius and thought of France, helping at once to break down the doctrines of classicism and to foster new ideas regarding tolerance, civil and religious liberty, individual rights, the dignity of industry and commerce. The later eighteenth century was indeed an era of pronounced Anglomania ; as a playwright of the time declared :

Les précepteurs du monde à Londres ont pris naissance,
C'est d'eux qu'il faut prendre leçon.[1]

In any consideration of the relations between the two countries during this critical period in the history of European civilisation it must never be forgotten that as Italy had led the way in the great revival of the Renaissance, so England led the way in the eighteenth-century movement of enlightenment and democratic expansion : the starting-point of this being, on the theoretical side, Newton's scientific discoveries and Locke's philosophical and political doctrines ; on the practical, the overthrow of the Stuarts and the foundations of constitutional

[1] Saurin, *L'Anglomane* (1772).

government. But though it originated in England, this movement passed directly to France, and it was France that carried it forward. Hence the significance of the fact that, as we shall see, nearly all the great intellectual leaders in France for a couple of generations before the Revolution had sat at the feet of English masters and were avowedly exponents of their ideas. Equally important was the influence exerted by those more popular writers who represented the middle-class movement in English literature. Defoe, Addison, Richardson, the dramatists Lillo and Moore, strongly appealed to the French *bourgeoisie* by the congenial character and tendency of their thought, especially when, as for example, in the case of Richardson and Lillo, they combined domestic interest and a sound utilitarian morality with a large vein of sentimentalism.

One other important general feature of the literature now to be considered has also to be emphasised—its subordination to directly practical aims. Recognising this, some historians of the period have gone so far as to assert that, though the output of books of all sorts was enormous, literature, in the strict sense of the term, had ceased to exist. This is, of course, a rhetorical exaggeration. But it is certainly true that literature was now on the whole cultivated less for its own sake than as a vehicle of ideas. Taken in the mass the literature of the eighteenth century is, in other words, an applied literature rather than a pure literature, and its interest therefore depends more upon its intellectual content than upon its æsthetic qualities. The great outstanding masterpieces of the period—the works which exhibit its genius at its highest—are not works which belong to the domain of the creative imagination ; they are treatises on political questions, like *L'Esprit des Lois* and *Le Contrat Social* ; on history, like the *Essai sur les Mœurs* ; on education, like *Émile* ; on science, like *L'Histoire Naturelle*. Even poetry and the drama had come to be regarded not as ends in themselves but as means to an end. In particular, in the hands of the dominant "philosophic party," as the leaders of the new movement in thought were collectively called, all types of literature partook of the militant spirit and were employed for propagandist purposes. Critical, sceptical, free-thinking, humanitarian, intensely alive to the abuses of the existing system in Church and State, enthusiastic advocates of progress and enlightenment, sworn foes to obscurantism in every form, the *philosophes* used literature in the main to make war on authority, dogma, and tradition, and to disseminate their political and religious teachings. The work which they produced has great interest from the historical point of view, especially when it is considered in the light of after events, for if its direct effect on the Revolution is sometimes exaggerated, it is clear that it did much both to subvert the old order and to fashion the minds of " the generation of '89." But as literature it necessarily suffered from the over-stress of polemical intention.

41. THE PRECURSORS : FONTENELLE—MONTESQUIEU. —The history of eighteenth-century literature begins with a number of writers who represent the transition from the old to the new, and are commonly described as the precursors of the *philosophes*. We will here confine our attention to two of these—Fontenelle and Montesquieu.

Bernard Le Bouvier de Fontenelle was the son of a sister of Corneille, and was born in Corneille's native town, Rouen, in 1657. He was educated for the law, but, encouraged by his uncle Thomas, turned to literature instead. As a writer for the stage he failed both in tragedy and in comedy, and he achieved only a very moderate success with his *Dialogues des Morts* (1683) and his *Poésies Pastorales* (1688), in connection with which last-named work, as we have seen, he entered the field on the heterodox side in the Querelle des Anciens et des Modernes. He found his true line, however, in his entertaining book of popular science, *Entretiens sur la Pluralité des Mondes* (1686), his *Histoire des Oracles* (1687)—of a decidedly sceptical tendency—and his series of *Éloges des Académiciens* (1708–19), which he prepared in his official capacity as Secretary of the Academy of Sciences, and which analyse and explain with admirable lucidity the contributions made to science by Newton, Leibnitz, Malebranche, and other leading thinkers. Emphatically a man of the new age, he was much attacked and satirised by his older contemporaries, but he lived long enough to witness the spread of many of the ideas in which he had been specially interested, dying a centenarian in 1757. Fontenelle distinctly marks the beginning of a fresh tendency in the literature of his time, for he was, in the phraseology then current, a combination of *savant* and *bel esprit* ; and he is certainly entitled to be regarded as a forerunner of the later eighteenth-century writers for many reasons, and in particular, because of his advocacy of the claims of the moderns in his attack upon the doctrines of classicism, his belief in progress, and his scepticism. The work that he did in popularising science is also significant. " J'ai voulu traiter la philosophie," he declares, in the preface to his *Entretiens*, " d'une manière qui ne fût point philosophique ; j'ai tâché de l'amener à un point où elle ne fût ni trop sèche pour les gens du monde, ni trop badine pour les savants." In thus undertaking to de-specialise science and to make it interesting to the laity, he initiated a movement in which he had many followers, and which before his death had already culminated in the *Encyclopédie*.[1]

Charles Louis de Secondat, Baron de la Brède and de Montesquieu, was born in the Château de la Brède, near Bordeaux, in 1689. He came of a family of distinction in the *noblesse de robe* ; entered the profession of the law almost as a matter of course, became Councillor of the Parliament of Bordeaux in 1714, and in 1716 succeeded his uncle as its President. Meanwhile, however, he had fallen under the influence of Newton, and had turned with great ardour to the pursuit of science. In 1728 he was elected to the Academy, after which he spent three years in travel, investigating on the spot the social conditions and political institutions of various foreign countries. For eighteen months of this time, as it is specially important to note, he resided in England, where he devoted himself in particular to the study of the writings of Locke and the principles of the English constitution. On his return to France he made his home at La Brède, though he paid frequent visits to Paris, finding congenial society in the *salons* of Mme. Du Deffand and Mme. Geoffrin. He died in 1755. Two of Montesquieu's works gave him at once a European reputation, and still assure him a high place among historians and jurists : his *Considérations sur les Causes de la Grandeur des Romains et de leur Décadence* (1734), which is remarkable as an early application of the scientific method to the problems of history ; and his monumental *Esprit des Lois* (1748), an

---

[1] The de-specialisation of knowledge was one very characteristic result of democratic progress in the eighteenth century. Compare Addison's declaration : " It was said of Socrates that he brought philosophy down from heaven to inhabit among men ; and I shall be ambitious to have it said of me that I have brought philosophy out of closets and libraries, schools and colleges, to dwell in clubs and assemblies, at tea-tables and in coffee-houses " (*Spectator*, No. 10).

epoch-making volume which, though necessarily in many ways out of date to-day, laid the foundations of the modern comparative study of governments and legislation. These, however, are technical treatises which do not properly concern us here. His principal contribution to general literature is to be found in his earlier *Lettres Persanes* (1721). The plan of this " most serious of frivolous books " (often imitated since, as, *e.g.*, by Goldsmith in his *Letters from a Citizen of the World*) was not original with him ; he borrowed it from the now forgotten *Amusements Sérieux et Comiques d'un Siamois* (1707) of the playwright Dufresny. He imagines two wealthy and cultivated Persian gentlemen, Rica and Usbek, on their travels through Europe ; they visit Paris ; they see life there under many, to them, most curious aspects ; they exchange their impressions and record them for the benefit of their friends ; while at the same time Usbek is kept informed by his correspondents of intrigues which are going on in his harem at home. By the use of this last device the *Lettres* are made to embody a little Oriental romance of a licentious character which, while it was certainly a concession to the loose taste of the time, helped to carry the writer's ideas into the " têtes bien frisées et poudrées " of his readers. But the entire interest of the book for us lies in the bold satire which his machinery enabled him to direct upon the institutions and society of the day as seen, not by those whose vision had been dulled by familiarity and custom, but through the unprejudiced eyes of two intelligent strangers. Thus the political corruption, the social decadence, the religious insincerity of the last years of the Regency are thrown into high relief. Montesquieu had a keen perception of these things, and whether he writes in a tone of light persiflage of the coquetry of Parisian ladies (26, 52), of the theatres (28), the cafés (36), the mania for gambling (56) ; or introduces character-studies in the manner of La Bruyère (45, 48, 68) ; or, becoming grave, turns his attention to religion (29, 46, 57), government (80), the laws (95, 116, 117, 129), and literature (36, 133, 137) ; or, in the episodical allegory of the Troglodytes (11-14), paints a picture of an ideal republic based on virtue : it is always as the critic and censor of his age. In their direct social and political purpose the *Lettres Persanes* distinctly anticipate the later eighteenth-century literature of reform ; in their combination of solid thought and vivacity of style they quite as distinctly point forward to the great writer who comes next on our list.

42. VOLTAIRE.—François Marie Arouet, who early took the name of Voltaire,[1] was born in Paris in 1694, was educated at the Jesuit Collège Louis-le-Grand, and on finishing his course in the humanities was set by his father, a notary, to the study of law. This, however, proved hopelessly uncongenial to his volatile temperament and was soon abandoned by him. On the other hand, his taste for literature had early asserted itself, and his poetic talents and the wit and charm of his conversation made him popular with the *libertins* of the so-called Société du Temple. In 1717 he had the first adventure of a singularly adventurous life : a satire on the Regent was falsely attributed to him and he was thrown into the Bastille, where he remained nearly a year, occupying himself in his enforced leisure with literary work, and especially with an epic poem which later became *La Henriade*. Soon after his release his tragedy *Œdipe* was performed with brilliant success at the Théâtre Français

---

[1] It is almost, though not quite certain, that this is an anagram of Arouet l. j., that is, Arouet le Jeune : *v* being substituted for *u*, and *i* for *j*.

(Nov. 1718), and at twenty-four he found himself universally acclaimed as the inheritor of the laurels of Corneille and Racine. This play, which marks the real beginning of a literary career which was to extend through sixty years of incessant and varied activity, is also noteworthy because in the famous couplet :

> Nos prêtres ne sont pas ce qu'un vain peuple pense,
> Notre crédulité fait toute leur science—

it opened the crusade which to the very end he was to carry on with unflagging vigour against priestcraft and superstition. For seven years after this he led a strenuous and restless life, fêted by society, busy with his pen, and at the same time industriously engaged in laying the foundations of that splendid fortune which was presently to prove that with all his other talents he possessed those of a clever financier. Then trouble once more overtook him, for as the result of a quarrel with the Chevalier de Rohan he was again lodged in the Bastille (1726). This time his imprisonment lasted only a fortnight, but though he was then liberated, it was on the express condition that he should leave France, and he accordingly crossed to England, where he remained in exile for nearly three years (1726–29). Voltaire's residence in England was in his own opinion the turning-point in his career, and in that of his early biographer, Condorcet, an event of the utmost significance in the intellectual history of Europe. Through the good offices of Bolingbroke, whom he had known in France, he was introduced into some of the best English society, became acquainted with leading men like Peterborough and Chesterfield, and entered into close relations with Pope, Swift, Young, Thomson, and Gay. He learned to read English well and to write and speak it with considerable fluency, and he made himself familiar with a good deal of English literature, including the works of Shakespeare, Milton, and Dryden, besides the writings of the men whom he reckoned among his personal friends. This intimate contact with the English spirit did much to enlarge his outlook and to enrich his mind. But most important of all was the influence exerted upon him by English thought. He studied Bacon, Newton, Locke, and the Deists; he assimilated English ideas about science, religion, philosophy, and government; and what he learned from books, vitalised by his own observation of English political and social conditions, made a profound and lasting impression upon him. It is not too much to say that these English experiences transformed him from a mere wit and dilettante man of letters into a zealous apostle of liberty and enlightenment.

On his return to France he produced in rapid succession a number of tragedies and poems, and in 1731 published his first important prose work, the *Histoire de Charles XII*. The next decisive event of his career, however, was the appearance in 1734 of his *Lettres Philosophiques sur les Anglais*, the direct fruit of his years of exile. The ostensible object of this little book was simply to give some account of English life and thought; its real purpose was to awaken the minds of French readers to a sense of the intellectual and political despotism under which they were themselves suffering. This purpose was well understood, for innocent as the *Lettres* were in appearance they aroused the wrath of the authorities and were condemned by the Parliament of Paris to be publicly burned by the common hangman. Compelled to fly before the storm, Voltaire sought asylum with his friend Mme. du Châtelet at Cirey, in whose château he set up a laboratory and devoted himself to chemistry and physics. After this he found favour for a time at Court, and lived

now in Paris, now at Sceaux, now at Nancy, always busy
with his pen, and producing, among many other things,
the first of his philosophical tales—*Le Monde comme il va*
(1746), *Zadig* (1747), and *Micromégas* (1747). In 1750,
at the invitation of his admirer Frederick II. of Prussia,
he migrated to Berlin, with an official position as king's
chamberlain, a handsome pension, and apartments in
one of the royal palaces. But quarrels soon broke out
between the ill-assorted pair, and, having in the meantime increased the sum of his work by his *Siècle de Louis
XIV.*, Voltaire quitted Prussia (1753), and settled first at
Les Délices, near Geneva (1755–58), where he wrote his
notable poems *Le Désastre de Lisbonne* and *La Loi Naturelle*
(1756) and his *Essai sur les Mœurs* (1756), and then at
Ferney, on the shores of Lake Leman, his home for the
rest of his life. During this closing period the works which
still flowed from his pen—dramas (*e.g.*, *Tancrède*, 1760),
tales (*e.g.*, *Candide*, 1759), literary criticism (*e.g.*, *Commen-
taire sur Corneille*, 1764), history (*e.g.*, *Histoire de la Russie
sous Pierre le Grand*, 1763 ; *Histoire du Parlement de
Paris*, 1769), philosophy (*e.g.*, *Traité sur la Tolérance*, 1763 ;
Dictionnaire Philosophique, 1764)—continued to give
evidence of the immense range of his interests and his
prodigious industry. It was at this time too that he
carried on with greater vigour than ever before his
campaign against despotism, and especially against the
Church—" L'Infâme " as he called it—which was for
him the very incarnation of the spirit of darkness and
oppression. Much of his energy was now indeed devoted,
not to the denunciation of bigotry and superstition in
the abstract, but to the championship of the cause of
the victims of ecclesiastical persecution and political injustice. There were many weaknesses and defects in
Voltaire's character : he was vain, irritable, jealous ; his

moral sense was often at fault ; he was frequently guilty of mean and petty actions and was always too ready on occasion to stoop to the basest arts of prevarication and intrigue. But he was fundamentally noble-minded, generous, and philanthropic, and his sympathies were quickly fired by every instance of concrete wrong. " J'ai fait un peu de bien ; c'est mon meilleur ouvrage," he writes of himself in his *Epître à Horace* ; but when we remember his splendid services to humanity in the case of the Calas family, of Sirven, of La Barre, of Lally-Tollendal, of Montbailli, of the serfs of Mont Jura, we feel that this is a very modest judgment upon his work.

In 1778 the " patriarch of Ferney," long the acknowledged head of French literature, was induced to undertake a journey to Paris, where he had not been seen for more than thirty years. The capital received him with frantic enthusiasm, which culminated in the great scene in the Comédie Française when, after the performance of his last tragedy, *Irène*, his bust was crowned on the stage. Excitement and fatigue proved too much for the frail old man. He was struck down by illness, and after several weeks of alternating delirium and torpor died peacefully on the night of May 30.

Voltaire's writings form a library in themselves ; small and great, they number upwards of 260 separate publications ; they include epic and didactic poems, a large body of miscellaneous verse, tragedies, comedies, histories, biographies, scientific essays, treatises on religion and philosophy, literary criticism, and tales ; while, in addition, he was throughout his life a tireless correspondent with all sorts of people, and more than 10,000 letters, which constitute by no means the least interesting part of it, swell the bulk of his work. Such fertility and variety are amazing. But, on the other hand, it is evident that his versatility of interest was a snare to him ; it led him to scatter his powers ; and the result was that though, as the Academy declared, he tried every kind of literature and failed in none, he rarely did anything that can be regarded as belonging indisputably to the first rank in its class. Obviously no attempt can be made here to deal with his productions in detail. Something will be said later about his poems as poems and his plays as plays (see *post*, pp. 154-55, 162-64). For the moment we will confine our attention to his prose and to the philosophy of which his work as a whole is the vehicle.

Whatever differences may exist regarding the value of Voltaire's matter there can be no dispute as to the supreme excellence of his manner as a prose-writer. He is indeed one of the greatest masters in any language of the purely natural as distinguished from the rhetorical style, and his lucidity, vivacity, ease, and sparkling wit make everything he touches interesting. Of him may be said what has often been said of Macaulay, that he never wrote a dull page or an ambiguous sentence. These qualities are pre-eminent in his brilliant little philosophical tales (*e.g.*, *Zadig*, *Micromégas*, *Candide*) which are perhaps the most thoroughly characteristic of all his writings. They are equally in evidence in his various contributions to history, as, *e.g.*, in his still popular *Histoire de Charles XII.*, which, as Condorcet long ago said, has all the fascination of a romance. But though by sheer charm of treatment Voltaire made history into literature, his substantial claims as an historian must not be overlooked. His *Essai sur les Mœurs*, in particular, is an important landmark in the study of the past. The science of history has developed enormously since his time, and it is easy for us now to detect the faults in this great work—its occasional inaccuracy in detail, the frequent superficiality of its generalisations, the distortion of the author's judgment in many places by prejudice and polemical purpose. But it is still an epoch-making work, because it attempts a philosophy of history in which the conception of natural evolution is substituted for that of supernatural intervention, which had formed the basis of Bossuet's *Discours*, and because it is a record, not merely of wars and dynasties, but also and chiefly of civilisation and intellectual progress. The fact that such historians as Gibbon, Niebuhr, Grote, and Buckle were directly indebted to it will serve to suggest its significance.

Voltaire's interpretation of history leads us directly to his philosophy, but before we consider the substance of this it is necessary that we should say a word about the prevailing tone of his writings. He was, it must be remembered, essentially a wit ; his natural weapons were not denunciation, invective, appeal, but irony, satire, and ridicule ; and these weapons he wielded without the slightest respect for the most deeply cherished feelings of those against whom he turned them. Hence the offence which he gave at the time, and which he still gives to many readers, by his mocking and malicious spirit and by his frequent irreverence in the handling of sacred things. Yet he was, at bottom, in deadly earnest, and was often most in earnest when he seemed to be most flippant. Unless this fact is recognised he can never be properly understood. But though, as Lord Morley has said, he " never played the sentimentalist," [1] and was apt to express his strongest convictions through the medium of his lightest banter, there were occasions on which he was so profoundly moved that he abandoned his usual method, and then the righteous indigna-

[1] *Voltaire*, p. 314.

tion which flames out for a moment in his pages is all the more effective from its contrast with his customary levity.[1]

Having thus cleared the way, we may proceed to a brief epitome of the main principles of his thought. A man of practical and positive temper, he was in philosophy a follower of Bacon and Locke, and his contempt of metaphysics was equalled by his enthusiasm for science. In religion he was bitterly hostile, not to essential Christianity, but to the whole ecclesiastical system of his time, which, with only too good reason, he associated with bigotry, fanaticism, and cruelty ; to Roman Catholicism, which he regarded as a perversion of the teachings of Jesus ; and to dogmatic theology in every form, which was for him the chief enemy of enlightenment and progress. While rejecting all revelation, however, he was a consistent Deist, and held so firmly to his belief in God that in his later years he was sneered at by the rising race of atheists as old-fashioned and reactionary. Yet he did not find in this belief any ready-made explanation of the mysteries of the universe and the anomalies and contradictions of human life. During his earlier manhood he had indeed been an optimist of the school of Leibnitz, Shaftesbury, and Pope. But he was already outgrowing his faith in their flimsy doctrines when it was suddenly shattered by the terrible Lisbon earthquake,[2] and from that time

---

[1] Thus in his persistent and telling attacks upon militarism and the military spirit he is habitually inclined to dwell rather upon the monstrous absurdity of war than upon its wickedness ; or, more correctly speaking, he seeks to reveal its wickedness by exposing its absurdity. But in reproving the clergy for their indifference to this great subject he rises in places to a level of noble eloquence (see, *e.g.*, *Dictionnaire Philosophique*, s.v., *Guerre*).

[2] See his fine poem *Le Désastre de Lisbonne, ou Examen de cet Axiome :
Tout est Bien*, and the corollary of this, the pulverising satire, *Candide ou l'Optimisme*.

onward he relinquished all attempt to solve the ultimate problems of existence and in his further dealings with religion threw his stress entirely upon the practical side. His ethical teachings, as may be anticipated, were utilitarian in the narrowest sense ; " le bien de la société " being for him " la seule mesure du bien et du mal moral." [1] In his social and political views he was, in comparison with many of his contemporaries, distinctly conservative. He was not a utopian, he was not a prophet of any new order ; he was not a revolutionary, the only revolution that he desired being a peaceful change in men's ideas. He had no organised system to proclaim as a cure for all existing ills. Nor had he any quarrel with society and civilisation, the luxuries and refinements of which he good-humouredly eulogised in his poem *Le Mondain*, and later defended against Rousseau. At the same time he never ceased to advocate the constitutional liberty which he had learned to love in England, and was zealous in his insistence on the urgent need of many political reforms. On the whole, however, he had little concern with theories of social regeneration as such. These interested him only incidentally. The movement which he led was primarily intellectual ; it was a movement for the emancipation of the mind of man from the trammels of ignorance and superstition. He fought for reason, freedom of thought, tolerance, and humanity ; and he fought for these great principles with so much courage and success that, however deeply we may at times regret his methods, we must still gratefully acknowledge the value of the work which

---

[1] The thought of duty as the one thing needful in religion is the positive conclusion which emerges out of the philosophic nihilism of *Candide*. " Il faut cultiver notre jardin," is the message with which it concludes ; that is, whatever our hands find to do we should do this with all our might, and not waste our time and energy in futile speculations about things which we can never hope to understand.

he did as one of the progressive forces of eighteenth-century history.

43. DIDEROT AND THE ENCYCLOPÉDISTES.—By his wit and magic of style Voltaire did more than any other man to popularise the ideas of the *philosophes*. A more solid contribution to their propaganda was, however, made by Diderot and the group of writers whom he gathered round him in the *Encyclopédie*.

Denis Diderot was the son of a cutler of Langres, in Champagne, where he was born in 1713 and where he received his early education under the Jesuits. Having angered his father by rejecting all his proposals that he should enter the Church, study law, or qualify as a physician, he found himself thrown on his own resources, and for some ten years (1734–44) lived a life of poverty and hard struggle as tutor and booksellers' hack, in which latter capacity he wrote whatever he was paid to write, including translations, tales designed to meet the lowest taste for garbage, and even sermons. In 1746 his *Pensées Philosophiques* were burned by order of the Parliament of Paris ; in 1749 he compromised himself with the authorities still more gravely by the bold speculations of his *Lettre sur les Aveugles*, for which he was imprisoned in the fortress of Vincennes. For more than twenty years after this (1749–72) he was mainly engaged in the immense and perilous task of the *Encyclopédie*, though he still made time to pour out an enormous number of miscellaneous writings on all sorts of subjects. In later life he fell into serious financial difficulties, from which he was rescued by the Empress Catherine of Russia, who constituted herself his benefactress. After a brief visit to her Court (1773) he returned to Paris, where he lived quietly till his death in 1784.

A man of turbulent, impetuous, prodigal nature,

Diderot squandered his genius as recklessly as he squandered his time, his money, and his health. His mind literally teemed with fresh and original ideas ; the range of his knowledge was so vast that Voltaire called him the " pantophile " ; but while he thought strongly, he could not think coherently, and he lacked entirely the power of concentration. Hence, though he wrote so voluminously, so vigorously, and so suggestively, he left behind him no clear and consistent statement of his philosophy and no finished piece of literary art. Of his general philosophy it is enough to say that he was a thorough-going materialist, though at times his material-ism is hardly distinguishable from pantheism, and that in ethics, while he fully recognised the law of social utility and laid great stress on the · domestic virtues, he championed the rights of the natural man against what he held to be the repressive morality of the Christian schools. In his critical theories he anticipated the romanticists in proclaiming the independence of genius, the rejection of rules and convention, and a return to nature ; and though he did not disparage the classics, he reserved his warmest admiration for such radically un-classical writers as Richardson, Lillo, Moore, and Sterne. To this point we will return later when we come to speak of his plays. Apart from these his most interesting work is to be found in his *Paradoxe sur le Comédien* (1773), which contains a stimulating discussion of the principles of the actor's art ; his curious satire in dialogue, *Le Neveu de Rameau* (1762) ; his novel, *La Religieuse* (1760), a powerful, though painful and rather wearisome study of the conventual life ; and *Jacques le Fataliste et son Maître* (1773), which is often classed as a romance, but is really little more than a series of conversations interspersed with adventures and anecdotes. Mention should also be made of his notes on the exhibitions of the Salon (1761–81), in which he practically inaugurated the literature of æsthetic criticism. In these again the romantic tendency is uppermost. " Et si l'antique n'avait pas existé ? " was the disconcerting question which he was accustomed to propound to painters and sculptors who were for ever prating of the antique.

But the most considerable part of Diderot's work in bulk and in historical importance is that which he did in connection with the *Encyclopédie, ou Dictionnaire Raisonné des Sciences, des Arts et des Métiers*. The immediate model for this great undertaking—in its inception a publisher's speculation—was the English *Encyclopædia* of Ephraim Chambers (1727), but the original plan was modified and expanded by him, and, in a measure at least, under the influence of Bayle's *Dictionnaire Historique et Critique* [1] it became the organ of the philosophic party. As director-in-chief Diderot was primarily responsible for the entire enterprise, and he also provided innumerable articles on history, philosophy, and the applied sciences. But he also secured the co-operation of most of the leading men of the day in all departments of intellectual activity, who wrote on their own special subjects— Montesquieu on taste ; Voltaire on elegance, eloquence, wit, imagination ; Rousseau on music ; Marmontel on literature ; Baron d'Holbach (afterwards famous as the author of the atheistic *Système de la Nature*) on science ; the Abbé Morellet on theology ; Quesnay and Turgot on political economy ; and so on. After Diderot's, however,

---

[1] Pierre Bayle (1647–1706) was the son of a Calvinist preacher of Languedoc. In early life he fled to Geneva to escape persecution as a Protestant, and afterwards held the chair of philosophy and history in the University of Rotterdam until his heterodoxy in turn alarmed the Protestants and he was forced to resign. His *Dictionnaire* (1696) gives him an important place among the precursors of the eighteenth century.

the name most closely connected with the *Encyclopédie* is that of the great mathematician Jean Le Rond D'Alembert (1717–83), who was its joint-editor during its early stages, though he severed his association with it in 1759. His *Discours Préliminaire*, which he wrote as a general preface, though obviously unsatisfactory to us now on both the constructive and the historical side, is still worthy of attention as a noteworthy contribution to the literature of science.

The object of the *Encyclopédie* was twofold : it was intended both as a storehouse of information and as an arsenal of weapons for the use of all who were engaged in doing battle with the forces of ignorance and obstruction. In other words, the aim of the editor and his colleagues was not only to place their readers abreast of the most advanced knowledge of their time, but also, as Diderot himself declared, " de changer la façon commune de penser." Even as an encyclopædia it did good service in the cause of enlightenment. But its principal influence was exerted through the tone and tendency of its thought. On all subjects dealt with it represented the revolt of the modern spirit against authority, tradition, dogmatism, and the dead hand of the past. For this reason it was violently attacked by the conservative party in Church and State ; its articles were mutilated by censorship ; the sale of its successive volumes was more than once prohibited ; its editor was in frequent peril of imprisonment and exile. Only his splendid courage and tenacity of purpose indeed enabled him to carry it forward to its conclusion in the teeth of difficulties and dangers which would certainly have proved overwhelming to any less resolute man.

44. ROUSSEAU.—The *Encyclopédie* was so closely identified with the activities of the philosophic party that

encyclopédiste came to be used currently as a synonym for *philosophe*. We have now to turn to the great opponent of the philosophic spirit, the Swiss " Man of Feeling," Rousseau.

The son of a watchmaker, Jean Jacques Rousseau was born in 1712 in Geneva. He belonged on the paternal side to a French Huguenot family which had sought asylum there about the middle of the sixteenth century, and his mother was the niece of a Swiss Protestant pastor. These facts must be taken into account in any study of his mental and moral evolution, because the Spartan severity of his teaching is in part at least to be explained by reference to his inherited Puritan bias and to the lasting impression made upon him by the austere atmosphere of his native city. But Rousseau's philosophy was one thing, his character quite another, and as the deplorable contradiction between his declamations and his conduct is the most glaring among the many glaring paradoxes in his biography, it is necessary to add that if the ideals which he preached but never put into practice were fostered by the social environment of his childhood, the personal qualities which were to wreck his life—his emotional instability, his inordinate vanity, his morbid self-consciousness, the hyper-activity of his imagination —were meanwhile stimulated by close companionship with his father, a foolish, frivolous, quarrelsome, and absurdly sentimental man. At thirteen he was apprenticed to a notary, who soon discharged him as a blockhead. Then he was set to learn engraving, but after three years of utter wretchedness under a brutal master, he ended his slavery by flight. His aimless wanderings brought him to the village of Confignon, where the parish priest, over a good dinner, converted him to Catholicism and passed him on for further counsel and help to a certain

Mme. de Warens at Annecy, with whom he fell in love on the spot, and who in turn sent him to the Hospital for Catechumens in Turin for proper training in his new faith. In due course he was baptized and cast adrift with the benediction of his spiritual advisers and a gift of twenty francs. He enjoyed himself after his shiftless fashion till the money was exhausted ; spent some months in menial service as a lackey ; and then, becoming restless, made his way back to Mme. de Warens. In the strangely constituted household of this clever but flighty woman he remained for the most part for the next ten years, though the continuity of his life with her was broken by various extraordinary episodes, as teacher of music in Lausanne, secretary to an impostor who gave himself out as an archimandrite of the Greek Church, servant to an officer with whom he paid his first visit to Paris. In 1741, finding himself ousted in Mme. de Warens' affections by an itinerant hairdresser, he made up his mind to seek his fortune in the French metropolis, which he entered with fifteen livres in his pocket, and a comedy *Narcisse* and a new system of musical notation as his passports to fame. But he frittered away his time and his money and accomplished nothing towards the realisation of his ambitions. Then through the influence of two society ladies who had taken him up he was appointed secretary to the French ambassador at Venice. His diplomatic career, however, was at the end of ten months abruptly closed by a violent quarrel with his chief, and he drifted back to Paris, where he settled in a dirty little hotel near the Sorbonne, started to earn his living by copying music, and soon after formed an irregular union with a coarse and illiterate servant girl named Thérèse le Vasseur. Yet though for some years he continued to live in squalid poverty he gradually became intimate with many women of social prominence and with a number of leading men of letters, among them Diderot, at whose invitation he undertook, as we have seen, the articles on music for the *Encyclopédie*.

We now come to the crisis of his life. In 1749 the Academy of Dijon proposed as the subject for a prize essay the question " Si le rétablissement des sciences et des arts a contribué à épurer les mœurs ? " On reading this question in the *Mercure de France*, Rousseau, according to his own statement, was seized with a " sudden inspiration " ; he resolved to compete ; he wrote his essay, which from first to last is a violent diatribe against all culture, in a sort of frenzy ; it was crowned by the Academy ; its publication in 1750 created a furor of excitement ; and at thirty-eight he stepped from his obscurity and on the instant became famous as the audacious and eloquent apostle of a new and piquant gospel—the gospel of " Back to Nature." Four years later he followed this essay up with a *Discours sur l'Origine et les Fondements de l'Inégalité parmi les Hommes*, which further surprised the world by its startlingly radical central thesis that all civilisation is at bottom corruption.

This sensational success gave Rousseau an immense vogue in the Parisian *salons* ; but vain as he was, he was not the man to be tamed by society, and before long he retired in disgust to a cottage called the Hermitage, in the forest of Montmorenci, which had been placed at his disposal by his friend Mme. D'Épinay. There, and a little later at Mont-Louis not far off, he wrote *Julie* (1761), *Le Contrat Social* (1761), and *Émile* (1762). But the political and theological views expressed in the last-named book were unpalatable to the authorities ; it was burned by their order, and an order issued for his arrest. Thereupon he fled from Paris and found shelter for a time at Môtiers in Neufchâtel. Then, driven from this retreat (1764) by the animosity of the inhabitants, which was stirred up against him on religious grounds, he wandered about from place to place, till finally, on the invitation of David Hume, he determined to make his home in England. Long an admirer of England and of many English writers, he came to this country hoping that at length he might reach a haven of rest (1766). But by this time he was a prey to the insidious and subtle form of insanity which is known as the mania of persecution. In his morbid mental state he was suspicious of everything and everybody, and, convinced that the whole world was in league against him, saw only enemies where he had expected to find friends. After months of solitary brooding he returned to France in secret (1767) and for three years led the life of a vagabond. Then, under assurance from the authorities that he would not be molested by them, he settled once more in Paris and to his old task of music-copying. But still his delusions increased ; he believed himself to be dogged by spies as he walked the streets ; he fled in alarm from the very children whom he chanced to meet in his lonely rambles (see his half-crazy dialogues *Rousseau Juge de Jean Jacques*). At length, after eight years of self-torture, he was induced to accept the offer of a cottage on the Marquis de Girandin's estate at Ermenonville, ten miles from Paris. Thither he repaired on May 20, 1778, and there he died suddenly on July 2, less than five weeks after Voltaire.

Though he did not begin his career as an author till he was well on in life, Rousseau's output was very voluminous, and it includes treatises on botany, music, and other special subjects, three comedies (*Narcisse, Les Prisonniers de Guerre*, and *L'Engagement Téméraire*), several operas, a tale (*La Reine Fantasque*), a prose poem (*Le Lévite d'Éphraïm*), controversial essays and pamphlets (*Discours sur les Sciences et les Arts, Discours de l'Inégalité, Lettre à D'Alembert sur les Spectacles*, etc.), and writings of a purely personal character (*Lettres de la Montagne, Rousseau Juge de Jean Jacques, Rêveries d'un Promeneur Solitaire*), besides the four outstanding works with which his name is now chiefly associated—the *Confessions, Julie, Le Contrat Social*, and *Émile*. The *Confessions* occupy a place almost by themselves among the masterpieces of autobiography. It is true that, written as they were in the misery of his later life (1765-70), when his mind was filled with diseased fancies and strange hallucinations, and when he had come to look at every detail of the past and present through a disturbing haze of emotion, they are as a mere record of events entirely untrustworthy. But as a piece of elaborate self-portraiture they are not easily matched in any literature. Rousseau's declared purpose in writing them was to describe himself faithfully and without the slightest reticence—in the words of his motto from Persius, *intus et in cute* ; and if the shameless candour with which he lingers over his sordid intrigues and petty actions is frequently disgusting, his pages none the less provide a painfully interesting study in morbid psychology. *Julie*, better known by its subtitle *La Nouvelle Héloïse*, is a prolix, unwieldy, and incoherent work, which begins with a romance of guilty love and ends tamely enough in a kind of didactic treatise. In form (it is written in letters), in many particulars of its machinery, and in much of its ethical spirit, it is clearly indebted to Richardson's *Clarissa*, which Rousseau pronounced the finest novel in the world, but it is charged with a passion far beyond the little English printer's range of power. As a *roman-à-thèse* it upholds both the sanctity of natural love against worldly convention and the beauty of domestic virtue. A great deal of it is necessarily very wearisome to us to-day, but looking at it historically we can still understand how its overwrought sentiment and its wonderful descriptions of mountains, lakes, and forests seemed nothing short of a revelation of new emotional experiences to the jaded metropolitan readers of its own time. The *Contrat Social* is a work of a very different character ; it is a treatise written in a style of scientific brevity and precision on the fundamental principles of government and civil society. Logical as it is in method, however, this Bible of the revolutionists (as Lecky aptly called it) [1] is entirely utopian in theory, for in it, after his habit, Rousseau ignores historical facts and builds on the sandy basis of abstract speculation. But its bold proclamation of the sovereignty of the people made an immense impression in that era of general political unrest, and so great was afterwards its effect in the hands of the Jacobin leaders that it is no exaggeration to say that, visionary as were Rousseau's doctrines, " his dream became a deed that shook the world." *Émile* is also a treatise, but a treatise thrown roughly into the form of a story. In this epoch-making work the man who had himself been a victim of vicious early influences, had failed as a teacher, and had sent his illegitimate children to the *Enfants Trouvés* because he did not want to be burdened with them, set up as a missionary of pedagogical reform, and produced a programme of " education according to nature," which, with all its extravagances and absurdities, is still recognised as a classic in the literature of its subject. This book is further important because in the long episode of the Vicaire Savoyard it contains the completest exposition of the author's religious faith. Like Voltaire, Rousseau was a deist ; but while the

[1] *History of England in the Eighteenth Century*, v. 345.

" philosophic Deity " of Voltaire was a logical abstraction only, Rousseau's God was a living reality, whose existence was proved, not by the arguments of science, but by the evidence of intuition and by those " raisons du cœur que la raison ne connait pas."

" Tout est bien sortant des mains de l'Auteur des choses, tout dégénère entre les mains de l'homme " : these opening words of *Émile* crystallise Rousseau's philosophy. That philosophy rests on the fundamental antithesis between the natural and the artificial—between " l'homme naturel," or man as benignant nature intended him to be, and " l'homme de l'homme," or the perverted product of a depraved society. What is natural is good ; every departure from the natural is evil ; therefore civilisation itself is a colossal mistake, and the only way of escape lies in a return to nature. The radical unsoundness of such a philosophy is of course apparent. Yet wild, paradoxical, reactionary as it was, full as it was of inconsistencies and contradictions, it still had its roots in certain great truths of which at all times it is well that the world should be reminded and which were specially salutary for Rousseau's own generation. For by preaching a return to nature he at least opened the eyes of his readers to the essential difference between what is factitious and accidental in life and what is intrinsic and permanent, and made them impatient of the parasitic forms and conventions—the simulacra and unveracities as Carlyle afterwards called them—by which elemental realities have been overlaid. The democratic bearings of his teaching must also be emphasised. Tearing away as he did all the fortuitous wrappings of a highly sophisticated civilisation, he laid bare that underlying humanity which is common to lettered and unlettered, noble and peasant, king and clown.

In his repudiation of its cherished ideas about progress and in his attack upon its boasted achievements in science and art Rousseau stood out boldly against the dominant spirit of his age. Furthermore, he sought to break down its hard intellectuality by his appeal to instinct and feeling, to dispel its cynicism by his moral earnestness, to check its effeminacy by his gospel of naturalness and simplicity. At all these points his influence counted enormously ; it swept like a consuming fire through the dry places of the time. In many other ways the potency of his teaching was attested by its amazing practical results. The impulse which he gave to the revolutionary movement in thought, and the sway which he exercised over the minds and the policy of many of the leaders of the Revolution itself, are familiar to every student of history. In literature he is recognised as one of the forerunners of romanticism, which he heralded alike in his passionate love of nature, his extreme individualism, his high‑pitched emotionalism, and his subjectivity. As a stylist, too, he was an innovator and a precursor, for (as I have elsewhere said) he abandoned the formal principles of classical prose-writing and "introduced the long, sweeping rhythm, the extended balanced periods, the colour and the music, afterwards characteristic of the whole romantic school." [1]

45. OTHER PROSE‑WRITERS.—Though the mass of general prose produced in France during the eighteenth century was very great, and often from the point of view

[1] *Rousseau and Naturalism in Life and Thought*, p. 240 note. It should, however, be pointed out that in one important respect Rousseau was distinctly unromantic. Romanticism, as we shall see, was strongly impregnated with mediævalism. He was entirely a man of his time in his admiration of classical antiquity and his ignorance and contempt of the Middle Ages.

of the subjects treated very interesting, only a few other writers need to be mentioned in a short history of literature.   These we will take chronologically.

George Louis Leclerc, Comte de Buffon (1707–88), is chiefly famous for his massive *Histoire Naturelle*, which well exemplifies the eighteenth-century enthusiasm for science and its fondness for reducing all knowledge to system.   The consideration of this work does not fall within our province.   But the *Discours* which he delivered on his admission to the Academy, commonly known as his *Discours sur le Style* (1753), gives him a certain status in literature.   The principal interest of this lies in its emphasis upon the purely individual quality in style— the quality which classicism tended to repress.   Facts and ideas are in themselves impersonal ; " ces choses sont hors de l'homme ; le style est l'homme même."   This often-quoted dictum is certainly illustrated by Buffon himself.   A pompous man, deeply impressed by the grandeur of nature, he strove to make his style consonant with his subject, with the result that it often became inflated and bombastic.

Luc de Clapiers, Marquis de Vauvenargues (1715–47), died too young to leave behind him any adequate memorial of the powers by which he greatly impressed many of his contemporaries, including Voltaire, who had formed a very high opinion of him and was much grieved by his premature death.   But his noble character, his fine stoicism, and his delicate feeling give distinction to his *Introduction à la Connaissance de l'Esprit Humain*, his *Conseils à un Jeune Homme*, and his *Maximes et Réflexions*. As a *pensée*-writer—and as such he is now chiefly remembered—he challenges comparison with La Rochefoucauld.   But his genial and sympathetic spirit and his ardent belief in the essential goodness of human nature bring him into sharp contrast with the great misanthrope whom to some extent he took as his formal model.

Jean Jacques Barthélemy (1716–95) deserves passing mention as the author of *Le Voyage du Jeune Anacharsis en Grèce* (1788), which did much to popularise the rising science of archæology and gave an impulse to the study of Greek. Though we should not now think of using it as an authority, it has a place in that Hellenistic revival which some years before had been inaugurated in France by the Comte de Caylus and in Germany by Winckelmann and Lessing.

The name of Jean François Marmontel (1723–99) has already been mentioned in connection with the *Encyclopédie*. He was a fairly voluminous author who enjoyed a considerable reputation during his lifetime, but he is little read to-day. His *Contes Moraux* (1761) are very dull specimens of the short story ; his *Bélisaire* (1761), which drew down the thunders of the Sorbonne by its advocacy of tolerance, and *Les Incas, ou la Destruction de l'Empire du Pérou* (1767), in which he retorted by exhibiting the evils of fanaticism, are tiresome excursions into that domain of historical-didactic fiction a taste for which had been created by *Télémaque* and to which *Anacharsis* also belongs. His most interesting work is to be found in his *Mémoires* and his *Éléments de Littérature*, which is made up of the articles which he had contributed to the *Encyclopédie*. We shall have to refer to him again as a critic when we come to speak of the eighteenth-century drama.

As a critic, however, he was entirely thrown into the shade by Jean François de La Harpe (1739–1803), whose *Lycée*, a collection of courses of public lectures delivered during many years (published in twelve volumes, 1799–1805), was regarded at the time as the standard authority on the subject. As a comprehensive survey of general literature this work, like Buffon's *Histoire Naturelle* in another field, illustrates the popularising and systematising tendency of the century. It is still a useful manual, and its clearness of style makes it pleasant reading. But it is written so entirely from the classicist point of view that its actual value as a piece of criticism is now little more than historical.

CHAPTER IX

46. POETRY.—Under the blighting influence of Boileau's repressive doctrines and in the unfavourable atmosphere of a rationalistic age, poetry in the France of the eighteenth century almost ceased to exist. The list of the so-called poets is indeed a long one, and collectively they produced much in many forms ; but with little exception their work is uninspired and mechanical, and its value for us to-day is almost naught. A very brief survey of eighteenth-century poetry will therefore suffice.

Though Voltaire's true field was obviously prose he wrote a large amount of verse, and, like his prose, this is very varied in character. His most ambitious effort as a poet is *La Henriade* (1728), an epic in ten cantos, of which the subject is the Wars of Religion, and the hero Henry IV. The choice of such subject and hero was of course dictated by polemical considerations, and the poem is in fact a sustained attack upon superstition and fanaticism and a glorification of tolerance and freedom of thought. In form it is fashioned closely upon the classical epic, especially upon the *Æneid*, the plan of which it follows in many of its structural details.[1] Entirely deficient in imagination, cold in style, and extremely unsatisfactory in its supernatural machinery,[2] it has no claim to a place beside any of the great epics. But it has its redeeming qualities, for the historical narrative in it is clear and interesting, and some of its descriptions—as of the Massacre of Saint Barthélemy (ii.), the Siege of Paris (iv.), the Battle of Ivry (viii.)—are done with much graphic power. Voltaire, however, was more at home in his philosophic poems, as, *e.g.*, *Discours sur l'Homme* and the two really fine poems already mentioned, *Le Désastre de Lisbonne* and *La Loi Naturelle*, and in his *Epîtres*, as, *e.g.*, the early *Aux Mânes de M. de Genouville* (which closes in a strain of unusual tenderness), *Epître à Boileau* (1769), and *Epître à Horace* (1772). His satires (*e.g.*, *Le Mondain*, *Le Pauvre Diable*) have all the piquancy and wit that we should expect from the writer ; but still more characteristic are his " petits vers," or light occasional poems, fugitive things of course, but none the less marked by much ingenuity of fancy, and a never-failing charm of style.

Voltaire's peculiar position in the literature of his century entitles him to consideration in a class by himself. His contemporaries may most conveniently be dealt with in groups defined by the general nature of their work.

[1] Thus Henry tells his tale to Queen Elizabeth as Æneas had told his to Dido, Queen of Carthage, and, like Æneas, he is granted a vision of the future history of his people.

[2] According to classic theory, " supernatural machinery " was an indispensable element in an epic. But while, on the one hand, the use of figures from Christian theology had been proscribed by Boileau (*L'Art Poétique*, iii.), on the other the employment of pagan gods and goddesses would have been absurd in a poem dealing with a modern subject. Voltaire attempts to get out of this difficulty by recourse to allegorical characters—La Discorde, La Politique, Le Fanatisme, La Clémence—who are as lifeless as allegorical characters in general.

In lyric poetry the period produced only one writer of any importance, Jean Baptiste Rousseau (1670–1741), who is not to be confused with his greater namesake, with whom indeed he was in no way connected, but whom he resembled in the unhappiness of his life. The son of a shoemaker in Paris and in youth a disciple of Boileau, this Rousseau had just begun to make a mark for himself in literature when, on charge of writing some defamatory epigrams (the authorship of which is still uncertain), he was banished from France (1712), and the remaining years of his life were spent in exile. The fact that his *Odes* and *Cantates* earned for him the proud title of " le prince des lyristes " is itself sufficient to show the deplorable insensibility of his age to all the higher qualities of poetry, for, though eminently correct in versification, they are frigid, pompous, and artificial. The revival of the true spirit of lyrism which came with the romantic movement proved fatal to Rousseau's claims, and the best that we can now say of him is that more than any of his contemporaries he endeavoured to keep the sacred fire alive.

Didactic verse offered a more congenial field to the writers of the period, but unfortunately, though the moral intention was often excellent, the poetry was generally left out, as in the case of Louis Racine (1692–1763), youngest son of the dramatist, whose Jansenist *La Grâce* (1720) and later and more important *La Religion* (1742) have been warmly commended for their piety, but deserve little other praise. In the closely allied form of satire the principal name is that of Nicolas Joseph Laurent Gilbert (1751–80), whose early death (see his touching *Adieux à la Vie*, which still has a place in the anthologies) cut short a promising career. Gilbert was an uncompromising opponent of the *philosophes*, against whom he wrote two satires, *Le Dix-Huitième Siècle* and *Mon Apologie*. His invectives are often unjust, but the vigour of his verse is beyond question.

Meanwhile the influence of English literature created a taste for descriptive poetry, which for a time enjoyed considerable popularity. *Les Saisons* (1769), by Jean François de Saint-Lambert (1716–1803), who figures prominently in the biographies of Voltaire and Rousseau, is an avowed imitation of Thomson's *Seasons*, but the French writer reproduces and accentuates only the worst characteristics of his Scottish original—his bombast, inflation, and habit of didactic digression—and gives us little or nothing of his real knowledge of nature and feeling for it. This dreary poem was, however, highly approved by the philosophic party in general, whose poetic taste was not their strongest point, and Voltaire went so far as to say of it that it was the only poem of the time which would go down to posterity—a prediction which, as I have elsewhere said, strikingly illustrates George Eliot's dictum that of all forms of mistake prophecy is the most gratuitous. *Les Mois* (1779), by Jean Antoine Roucher (1745–94), and *Les Jardins* (1782), *L'Homme des Champs* (1800), and *Les Trois Règnes de la Nature* (1809), by Jacques Delille (1738–1813), translator of the *Georgics* and later of *Paradise Lost*, are similarly deficient in life, colour, and the true sentiment of the picturesque. Such genuine poetry of nature as the eighteenth century produced is to be sought, not in the prosaic verse of these *descripteurs*, but rather in the poetic prose of *La Nouvelle Héloïse*, the *Rêveries d'un Promeneur Solitaire*, and *Paul et Virginie*.

Far more interesting to us than the ambitious efforts of any of the poets thus far mentioned is the work of some of the writers of lighter verse, two of whom, Gresset and Florian, call for a word of cordial recognition. Jean

Baptiste Louis Gresset (1709–77) tried his hand at serious poetry and at tragedy, but without success. He owes his reputation entirely to one capital comedy, *Le Méchant* (1745), and to a humorous poem, *Vert-Vert* (1734), which was immensely popular at the time and may still be read with pleasure. This lively story of "*un perroquet dévôt*" (under which it is easy to detect a playful but trenchant satire of the monastic life) is indeed written with such a delicate touch and with so much wit and fancy that it remains one of the choicest examples in French literature of the "épopée badine." Like Gresset, Jean Pierre Claris de Florian (1755–94) also lives by virtue of a small part only of his work. He wrote two prose romances of the historical-didactic kind, already referred to, *Numa Pompilius* and *Gonzalve de Cordoue*, *nouvelles*, *pastorelles*, and plays, but to-day he is remembered only for his *Fables* (1792). As a fabulist he possesses this distinction that of La Fontaine's many followers he is the only one whom we should ever think of putting anywhere near that incomparable master. His *Fables* are, however, very different in quality from La Fontaine's: they are less spontaneous than these, less racy, less imbued with the old *esprit gaulois* ; nor do they approach them either in intimate familiarity with the characters and ways of animals or in penetrative insight into human nature. But in their own style they are excellent, for Florian was a skilful story-teller and wrote in easy and agreeable verse. Their moral tone, too, is unimpeachable, though they are often coloured by the melancholy bred in the poet's tender nature by his keen sense of the evils of the troubled times on which he had fallen.

The foregoing sketch will serve to show how much, or rather how little, the eighteenth century contributed to the permanent possessions of French poetry. One writer, however, has still to be considered who stands in a class apart and who, while he belonged entirely to his century, came at its close with the promise of a poetic renaissance after a long period of sterility. André Chénier was born in 1762 at Constantinople, where his father, who was the French consul-general there, had married a Greek woman of great beauty and accomplishments. Taken as a child to France, he was educated at the Collège de Navarre in Paris ; entered the army in 1782, but soon left it, disgusted with military life ; travelled for a time in southern Europe ; and then spent some years in Paris, where, in his mother's *salon*, he became intimate with many artists, poets, and philosophers. From 1787 to 1790 he was secretary to the French embassy in London, but he did not like England or the English people, and his residence here had no influence on his intellectual development. On his return to France he was caught in the political current of the time and became active in journalism. A warm supporter of the Revolution in its early stages he was presently alienated from it by the policy of the Jacobins, whose excesses he denounced. This sealed his fate ; he was thrown into the prison of Saint-Lazare, and six months later (July 25, 1794) perished by the guillotine, one of the last victims of the Reign of Terror, which ended two days later with the fall of Robespierre. Chénier's work, which did not appear in print until a good many years after his death,[1] must be regarded as in the main experimental, but it shows that he was gradually emancipating himself from the cramping conventions of pseudo-classicism and seeking new paths for his genius. His *Élégies* are amorous poems of the artificial kind, in which the influence

[1] During his lifetime he published two poems only, both political, *Dithyrambe sur le Jeu de Paume* and *Hymne aux Suisses de Chateauvieux*

of Tibullus, Propertius, and Ovid is very apparent ; his *Bucoliques* (*e.g.*, *L'Aveugle*, in which Homer sings to some shepherds of Scyros, and *Le Mendiant*, in which a wandering beggar recounts his adventures to his host, who turns out to be his own son) are scholarly productions, rich in details drawn directly from Greek literature, though retouched with real poetic imagination. But while in these collections he depended upon the classics for his inspiration, in *L'Invention* he made a strong plea for a new kind of poetry, modern alike in theme and purpose, though faithful to the principles of the ancients in respect of art :

> Changeons en notre miel leurs plus antiques fleurs ;
> Pour peindre notre idée, empruntons leurs couleurs ;
> Allumons nos flambeaux à leurs feux poétiques,
> Sur des pensers nouveaux faisons des vers antiques.

This declaration, it is true, must be read, not as a formula of what he actually accomplished, but as a programme of what he would have done had his life been spared ; but in *L'Hermès* (which he left a mere fragment) he attempted to realise his ideal of what modern poetry might be by putting the science and philosophy of his time into verse. Hence his work is a rather curious compound of old and new. But perhaps its most important feature is the distinctive quality of its classicism. Half Greek by parentage, Chénier was wholly Greek by temper and sympathy ; he had nourished his genius on Homer and the *Anthology* ; and the blood in his veins, the natural bias of his mind, his direct contact through scholarship with the spirit of antiquity, combined to make his Hellenism a very different thing from the lifeless pseudo-classicism of his contemporaries. For this reason he has sometimes been compared with our own Keats. Except in their instinctive paganism and in the rich voluptuous quality of their imagination the two men had really very little in common, but they resembled one another in this particular, that each of them in his own way revitalised the treatment of classic themes.   On account of the wealth of his imagery, the picturesqueness of his style, the frequent concreteness of his phraseology, and the freedom with which he handled the alexandrine, Chénier has often been described as an ancestor of the romantics. He was, however, rather the forerunner of the Parnassiens—of Leconte de Lisle, for example, and Hérédia—than of such writers as Lamartine, Alfred de Musset, and Victor Hugo.

47. TRAGEDY.—The decline of poetry during the eighteenth century was paralleled by that of tragedy, which meanwhile suffered from a sort of dry rot.   Diderot, of whose attempt to transform the serious drama we shall speak later, put his finger upon the chief cause of this decay when he expressly declared that it was due to the tyranny of pedantic laws and superannuated conventions (*bienséances*).   Tragedy had now indeed become a thing of mere rules and system, in which the old subjects were treated over and over again according to the old methods and the traditional characters, motives, and situations reproduced with monotonous regularity, and in which, as Grimm complained,[1] there was nothing even remotely suggestive of truth or nature.   Hence, though the followers of Corneille and Racine were very numerous, the history of eighteenth-century tragedy is on the whole, as one French writer has put it, little more than " une vaste

[1] Baron Friedrich Melchior Grimm (1723–1807) was a clever and versatile German who spent the greater part of his life in Paris and was an intimate friend of Diderot. His *Correspondance Littéraire, Philosophique et Critique*, in which for some forty years he kept various German princes in touch with the movement in thought in the French metropolis, is of great interest for the student of the history of the time.

nécrologie." [1]   In tragedy proper two writers only redeem the period from the charge of absolute nothingness, and these are Crébillon and Voltaire.

Prosper Jolyot de Crébillon (1674–1762) won his fame early and then sank into oblivion for the rest of his life. The tradition runs that he once defined his own position in the remark : " Corneille a pris la terre, Racine le ciel ; il me reste l'enfer," and though the saying is probably apocryphal it serves to indicate the peculiar quality of his plays.   His aim was to excite terror rather than admiration or pity, and to this end he dealt by preference with violent passions and unnatural crimes (e.g., Idoménée, 1705 ; Atrée et Thyeste, 1707 ; Électre, 1708 ; Rhadamiste et Zénobie—his most notable success—1711).   In style he is unequal, often heavy, sometimes obscure, and his prevailing atmosphere is gloomy and oppressive ; but he reveals in places really great dramatic power.

Crébillon's star, however, soon paled before that of the protean writer who took possession of tragedy as of all other fields, and who alone sustained the great traditions of the seventeenth century till the eighteenth was drawing to its close.   As we have seen, Voltaire's first tragedy, Œdipe, appeared in 1728, his last, Irène, in 1778 ; and in the intervening sixty years no fewer than twelve others (e.g., Brutus, 1730 ; Zaïre, 1732 ; Mahomet, 1742 ; Mérope, 1743 ; Tancrède, 1760) came from his pen.   By his contemporaries he was confidently placed beside Corneille and Racine, and it was even claimed for him that he combined the peculiar excellences of the two.   Modern criticism, on the other hand, lays stress on the fact that he had neither the strength of the one nor the psychological insight of the other, and therefore assigns him to a much lower rank.   Clever his plays unquestionably are, but

[1] Lintilhac, Précis de la Littérature Française, ii. 262.

just as unquestionably they are more than a little factitious, and while their technical skill is often remarkable, their characterisation is generally thin. At the same time no reader of *Zaïre* or *Mérope* will be likely to deny the real tenderness and passion of a few outstanding scenes. That Voltaire used the drama as he used all other forms of literature for the dissemination of his philosophical ideas (*e.g.*, *Mahomet ou le Fanatisme, Les Guèbres ou la Tolérance, Les Lois de Minos*, etc.) is a point to be noted in passing. His place in the evolution of tragedy is a matter of greater importance. In theory he was a stout supporter of the classical tradition of the stage. Yet influenced in part by Shakespeare,[1] he broke with that tradition in several respects, and in particular in broadening the basis and extending the range of tragedy. It had come to be almost a convention within a convention that the subjects of tragedy should be taken from Greek or Roman sources, and that its characters should bear Greek or Latin names. This convention he follows in some of his plays (*e.g.*, *Brutus, La Mort de César, Mérope*), but in others he departs from it ;. in *Tancrède* he takes us to the chivalrous Middle Ages ; in *Alzire* to Peru ; in *Mahomet, Zaïre*, and *L'Orphelin de la Chine*, to various parts of the east ; in *Zulime* to Africa : thus at once exemplifying his own cosmopolitanism and unconsciously preparing the way for what Brunetière calls " la tragédie exotique " of the romantic stage. Even in his purely classical plays, moreover, he anticipates the romantics in his quest for that local colour to which the classical drama before his

---

[1] In his preface to *Zaïre* (a play which clearly owes much to *Othello*) he writes : " C'est au théâtre anglais que je dois la hardiesse que j'ai eue de mettre sur la scène les noms de nos rois et des anciennes familles du royaume. Il me paraît que cette nouveauté pourrait être la source d'un genre de tragédie qui nous est inconnu jusqu'ici et dont nous avons besoin."

time had been utterly indifferent. The fact that in his *Brutus* he insisted that his hero should appear on the scene robed not in eighteenth-century French costume, but as a Roman, is significant in this respect.

48. COMEDY.—The comedy of the first half of the eighteenth century was largely dominated by Molière, as we can see not only in the works of Regnard and Dancourt, which have already been mentioned, but also in such representative plays as *Le Philosophe Marié* (1727) and *Le Glorieux* (1732) by Philippe Destouches (1680–1754), *La Métromanie* (1738) of Alexis Piron (1689–1773), and *Le Méchant* (1747) of Gresset. To the school of Molière also belongs the finest comedy of the period, perhaps of the whole century, and the only one which is really entitled to rank with the greatest work of the master—*Turcaret* (1709), by Le Sage, who if he had never written *Gil Blas* (see *post*, pp. 170-71) would still have a secure place in the history of literature as the author of this brilliant satiric study of the methods and morals of the new race of successful financiers. But in the work of another writer, whom we shall also meet again among the novelists, comedy took an entirely fresh turn. Pierre Carlet de Chamblain de Marivaux (1688–1763), of whose numerous plays, *Le Jeu de l'Amour et du Hazard* (1730), *Les Fausses Confidences* (1737), *Les Sincères* (1739), and *L'Épreuve* (1740) may be mentioned as the most important, was a deliberate innovator, who sought to substitute for the Molièresque comedy of character and social purpose a type of drama which, though still conceived as comedy, should depend for its main interest upon the delicacy of its psychology. His central theme is always love, and the point of his innovation lies in the fact that while his predecessors on the comic stage had treated love simply as an element in their plots, he takes the passion itself

as a subject for analysis. " Dans mes pièces," he writes,
" c'est tantôt un amour ignoré des deux amants, tantôt
un amour qu'ils sentent et veulent se cacher l'un à l'autre,
tantôt un amour timide et qui n'ose se déclarer, tantôt un
amour incertain dont ils se doutent sans en êtres surs, et
qu'ils épient au dedans d'eux-mêmes avant de lui laisser
prendre l'essor." In thus making the psychology of
love the substance of his work, Marivaux undertook to do
in comedy what Racine had done in tragedy : indeed one
of his critics has called him " a Racine in miniature."
The word " marivaudage," which is still used to indicate
excessive subtlety of thought and over-refinement of style,
is enough to suggest his distinctive characteristics.

By the large admixture of sentiment in his plays and
by the expansion which the emotional element underwent in his hands, Marivaux contributed to the development of what is known as the *comédie larmoyante* or
attendrissante, the analogue of the Sentimental Comedy
of our own eighteenth-century stage, and which like this
sought rather to draw the tears of the spectators by the
exhibition of the virtues and sufferings of private life
than to arouse their laughter by ridicule of its follies
and absurdities.   The real founder of this new type was,
however, his contemporary Pierre Claude Nivelle de La
Chaussée (1692–1754), whose highly pathetic dramas (*e.g.*,
Le Préjugé à la Mode, 1735 ; *Mélanide*, 1741) were recognised at the time as an attempt to import the interest of
tragedy into the framework of comedy.   His lead was
followed by a number of minor writers, and curiously
enough even Voltaire, though too good a classicist to
admit any " mélange des genres," yielded a little to the
growing taste for sentimentalism in his *Enfant Prodigue*
(1736) and *Nanine* (1749).   The principal importance of
the *comédie larmoyante*, however, must be sought in its

connection with the *drame*, to which we have next to turn. But it may at once be added that a successful reaction against the long domination of " the goddess of the woful countenance, the Sentimental Muse," similar to that which in the English drama we associate with the names of Goldsmith and Sheridan,[1] was presently initiated by Pierre Augustin Caron de Beaumarchais (1732–99), who, in two sparkling and audacious satirical plays, *Le Barbier de Séville* (1777) and *Le Mariage de Figaro* (1784), revived the hearty laughter which had hardly been heard in any of the higher forms of comedy since the days of Molière and Regnard.

49. THE DRAME OR TRAGÉDIE BOURGEOISE.—Maintaining as they did the complete and permanent separation of the different *genres* of literature, the classicists had drawn a sharp line of demarcation between tragedy and comedy : tragedy according to their theory being essentially aristocratic in the sense that it had to deal with the " sudden turns in the fortunes of illustrious persons " [2] and with characters " raised above the common plane " ; [3] while comedy was confined to the humorous incidents of middle-class or low life. Already, as we have just seen, the *comédie larmoyante* had done something towards the obliteration of this academic distinction. But now the question definitely arose, why should this distinction be maintained ? In other words, why should the doings of the middle classes be always taken on the comic side as matters for amusement only ? Why should not " the misfortunes of private life " [4] also provide subjects of

[1] The quotation just made comes from Sheridan's prologue to *The Rivals*.

[2] D'Aubignac, *Poétique du Théâtre*.

[3] Voltaire, *Remarques sur le Second Discours de Corneille*.

[4] D'Alembert, *Lettre à Rousseau*, in reply to Rousseau's diatribe against the theatre in his *Lettre à d'Alembert sur les Spectacles*.

tragic interest no less than those taken from ancient history or mythology ? Such questions were now seriously discussed by a number of critics, among them Marmontel, who made out a strong case for a " popular tragedy " which should have a recognised status on the boards beside the old " heroic tragedy," and which, while necessarily wanting the " pomp and majesty " of heroic tragedy, would possess the advantage of being nearer to nature and therefore, as the writer argued, more directly influential on the moral side.[1] These new theories, which seemed very radical at the time, were the inevitable result of changing conditions—of the gradual collapse of classicism, the steady progress of the democratic movement in society, the growing sense that the conventional form of tragedy was obsolete or obsolescent, and that something fresh and more vital was needed to take its place. But they were greatly reinforced by English influences. The *London Merchant, or the History of George Barnwell* (1731), by George Lillo, and *The Gamester* (1753), by Edward Moore, both of which were translated, imitated, adapted, eulogised by critics, and received with immense enthusiasm by the public, provided a working-model for those who were convinced that the time was ripe for a new type of play—a *tragédie bourgeoise* (or *drame*, as it was alternatively called), in which all the emotional interest of tragedy should be sought in subjects taken from ordinary domestic life, and which by realism of treatment should bring tragedy back to that simple truth of nature from which it had long been divorced.

The most important of these innovators in weight of influence was Diderot, who put his theories into practice [2]

---

[1] *Poétique Française*, i. 143-50.

[2] For Diderot's dramatic theories, see his essay, *De la Poésie Dramatique : à mon Ami M. Grimm*, and his *Entretiens sur le Fils Naturel*.

in a couple of prose tragedies,[1] domestic in matter and highly didactic in aim—*Le Fils Naturel* (1757) and *Le Père de Famille* (1758). Unfortunately, however, though a very original and stimulating critic, Diderot was a very poor playwright ; his genius was entirely undramatic ; and these two plays of his, with their mawkish sensibility, their endless wastes of verbiage, their everlasting parade of self-conscious virtue, and their stilted style, are hopelessly vapid and dull. A far better example of the *genre sérieux* was provided by Diderot's friend and disciple, Michel Jean Sedaine (1719–97), in his *Philosophe sans le savoir* (1765), a really excellent play, in which a subject, slight in itself, is handled with a capital sense of the stage, and in which there is plenty of clear-cut characterisation and crisp and natural dialogue. After Sedaine, who may justly be regarded as the real precursor of the nineteenth-century *drame*, the new type was industriously cultivated by many writers, of whom Louis Sebastien Mercier (1740–1814), one of the adapters of Lillo's tragedy (*Jenneval, ou le Barnevelt Français*), was the most radical and the most industrious (*e.g., Le Déserteur, L'Indigent, La Brouette de Vinaigre*). Before he scored his great success with his satiric comedies already mentioned, Beaumarchais had also appeared as the author of two *drames sérieux*, written, as he himself explains, on the lines laid down by Diderot —*Eugénie* (1767) and *Les Deux Amis* (1770)—while later he returned to the same type in *Tarare* (1787) and *La Mère Coupable* (1792).

50. THE NOVEL.—As in England, where Lillo's experiment in domestic tragedy closely corresponded in time

---

[1] One aspect of the new realism was the substitution (already made by Lillo and Moore in England) of prose for verse. This specially stirred the indignation of Voltaire, who described the introduction of prose into tragedy as " the abomination of desolation in the temple of the muses."

with Richardson's new lead in *Pamela*, so in France, the combination of forces, which resulted in a transformation of the drama, also brought about a parallel transformation of prose fiction. On the social side the rise of the modern novel, as a type of literature the interest of which is centred in ordinary life and people, was directly connected with the democratic movement. On the literary side it was one aspect of the revolt against the tyranny of the past. In dealing with the development of the novel in eighteenth-century England I have elsewhere written : " As practically a new form of literary art, the novel was a sign that literature was beginning to outgrow the cramping limitations of classicism, and to abandon the doctrine that modern genius was bound to go in the leading strings of tradition. In the epic and the drama it was impossible as yet that men should reject altogether the authority of antiquity. In the novel that authority could be ignored. In general, the novel offered a fresh field in which modern writers were able to work independently." [1] I reproduce these remarks here because they are equally applicable to the development of the novel in eighteenth-century France.

First in order of time of the long line of illustrious French novelists, Alain René Le Sage was born at Sarzeau in Brittany in 1668. As a youth he studied law, and in due course became a member of the Paris bar, but he soon abandoned his profession for literature, and thenceforth till his death in 1747 he was entirely dependent upon his pen. Of his innumerable comedies two only—*Crispin Rival de son Maître* and *Turcaret*—survive ; of his many experiments in fiction again only two—*Le Diable Boiteux* (1707) and *Gil Blas de Santillane* (1715–35). Both the scheme and the title of the former of these Le Sage took directly

[1] *Outline History of English Literature*, pp. 176-77.

from *El Diablo Cojuelo* (1641), of the Spanish writer Luis Velez de Guevara, and his originality was therefore confined to details. The machinery is furnished by the demon Asmodée who carries the student Cléophas with him over the city of Madrid and, lifting the roofs from the houses, enables his companion to see what is going on inside, and what results is not so much a novel as " un petit tableau des mœurs du siècle " (Preface to final edition), or collection of satiric portraits, sketches, and anecdotes, somewhat in the manner of La Bruyère, though set in a fantastic framework. In *Gil Blas* we have another " tableau de mœurs," but on a much larger scale and without the disturbing element of supernaturalism. The hero of this first real masterpiece of French fiction is a young student of Oviedo who, at the opening, sets out to pursue his studies at the University of Salamanca. He is captured by robbers, from whom he presently escapes ; enters the service of a canon ; becomes assistant to a successful physician ; forms a connection with the stage ; after many ups and downs wins the confidence of the prime minister and is appointed his secretary ; gains wealth and power till, by a sudden turn in fortune's wheel, he is overthrown and disgraced ; recovers his position and returns to court as secretary to another influential nobleman ; and ultimately, marrying for the second time, retires to his castle, where he settles down to peace and happiness after the many vicissitudes of his life. As this bare outline of the general movement of its narrative will show, the book belongs to the rambling inorganic type of *picaresque* fiction ; it has no plot, no unity, no logic of events ; its adventures follow one another haphazard ; while, in accordance with the old romantic formula, the main interest is continually interrupted by digressions and intercalated stories in which an unwary reader is likely at times to lose his way.   But if it is, technically considered, little more than a huge bundle of episodes, it is also a kind of " comédie humaine."   The thread of intrigue is nought, but the passage of the hero through all classes of society, from the lowest to the highest, enables the author to present a vast panorama of contemporary life.   Le Sage was a keen observer of all sorts and conditions of men, and his character-studies (some of which, like the famous Dr. Sangrado, have become proverbial), while without any particular psychological depth, are marked by a broad truth to nature.   As a satirist—and he was this from first to last—he dwelt almost exclusively upon the immorality of the world to which he held up his mirror.   Yet his pages are on the whole wonderfully clean, and his temper so genial that his disciple Smollett even complained of his " lightness of touch " in his treatment of evil and folly.   As Sir Walter Scott rightly said of him, " If in his works he has assailed vice rather with ridicule than with reproach, and has at the same time conducted his story through scenes of pleasure and of licence, his Muse has moved with an unpolluted step even when the path was somewhat miry."

The place which Le Sage occupies in the history of French fiction is somewhat analogous to that of Defoe in the history of English fiction : he forms as it were a connecting link between the *picaresque* romance and the true novel of manners.   Another move was made by Marivaux, who at this point may in turn be compared with Richardson.[1]   Marivaux began by parodying Homer

[1] An English translation of *Marianne* appeared in 1736, and it has been suggested that Richardson was to some extent indebted to this in writing *Pamela*.   There appears, however, to be no ground for the supposition.   On the other hand the influence of English literature on Marivaux is shown by *Le Spectateur Français* (1722–23), a kind of sketch-book containing the germs of many subjects afterwards worked up by him in his novels.

(*L'Iliade Travestie*, 1717) and the old romances (*e.g.*, *Pharamond*, *ou Les Folies Romanesques*, 1712), and though these experiments in burlesque have long since been forgotten they are interesting as indicative of the bias of his mind. His two novels, both of which he left incomplete, are *La Vie de Marianne* (1731–41) and *Le Paysan Parvenu* (1735–36) : the former being the auto-biographical memoirs of a certain Comtesse de . . . from her childhood up ; the latter the history of a young peasant, Jacob, who at eighteen quits his native village to seek his fortune in Paris. Like *Gil Blas*, these are entirely inorganic ; as in *Gil Blas*, the adventures, in the one case of the heroine, in the other of the hero, provide the necessary canvas for a series of pictures of life in all sorts of different phases. But Marivaux is more directly realistic than Le Sage. In the first place, instead of disguising his French men and women in Spanish costumes and putting them in a Spanish setting, he portrays them as French men and women moving through French scenes. Secondly, he pays greater attention than Le Sage to the minute details of everyday existence among the " petites gens," who fill a large place in his work ; his description (in *Marianne*) of Mme. Dutour's linen-draper's shop is, to cite only one example, still famous as a piece of *genre* painting, while the episode of Madame's long altercation with the cabman who wants to overcharge her is often reproduced as an admirable specimen of purely realistic art. At one other point Marivaux's originality must be recognised : in his novels as in his plays he gave great prominence to psychological analysis and substituted emotional interest for the interest of satiric humour. With Le Sage we mark the rise of the novel of manners ; with Marivaux that of the novel of sentiment. The novel of passion begins with Prévost. Born in 1697,

Antoine François Prévost d'Exiles commenced life as a soldier, but after many adventures left the army, entered the Benedictine order, and became a priest. For six years he occupied himself with his religious duties and the study of Christian antiquities, but his restless temper got the better of him, and in 1727 he fled from his convent and from France, finding a home first in Holland and then in England. In 1734, under royal permission, he returned to France as a secular priest and almoner to the Prince de Conti. He died suddenly in 1763. Prévost's writings, which fill more than a hundred volumes, include three gigantic works of fiction—*Mémoires et Aventures d'un Homme de Qualité* (8 vols., 1728–32), *Le Philosophe Anglais, ou Histoire de M. Cléveland* (8 vols., 1731–39), and *Le Doyen de Killerine* (6 vols., 1735–40). It should be noted in passing that the dates of these works have a certain importance because they show that though Prévost was afterwards well known as the translator of Richardson, his own novels preceded those of the English writer and were therefore not (as is sometimes loosely asserted) indebted to them.[1] Of his vast output, however, only a very small fragment survives, though this fragment holds a very high place in French fiction—the *Histoire du Chevalier des Grieux et de Manon Lescaut*, which originally formed the seventh volume of the *Mémoires d'un Homme de Qualité*. This deeply pathetic and arresting story can scarcely be said to possess the moral virtue which the author himself claimed for it, but as a study of overmastering passion it deserves the highest praise.

---

[1] At the same time he was much influenced by his residence in England and by English literature. Like Marivaux's *Spectateur Français*, his periodical, *Le Pour et le Contre*, is modelled on the *Spectator* of Addison and Steele. In view of the connection, which we have emphasised, between the Domestic Drama and the novel, the praise which he gives in it to Lillo's *George Barnwell* is significant.

The new fields which had thus been opened up by Marivaux and Prévost naturally proved attractive to many other writers, but the most powerful influence after their time was that exerted by the latter's translations of Richardson's three works. Such influence we have already observed in the one great novel of the second half of the century, *La Nouvelle Héloïse*, and this in turn enormously increased the popularity of fiction among all classes of readers. Only twenty-eight years, it will be remembered, elapsed between the publication of *La Nouvelle Héloïse* and the outbreak of the Revolution, but it is estimated that the novels produced during this short period equalled in number, if they did not exceed, those which had appeared in the preceding sixty years of the century.[1] They fall, roughly, into three main groups —novels of passion, idyllic or pastoral novels, and pedagogic novels—all of which derived more or less directly from Rousseau, but the novel of manners, generally of a licentious character, was also cultivated by a few writers here and there. In all this mass of work, however, there is nothing that need now detain us except the contribution made to it by one of Rousseau's closest disciples, Bernardin de Saint - Pierre (1737–1814). It was after leading an irregular and wandering life for many years in many countries that, on returning from the Île de France (now Mauritius), this self-engrossed egotist made the personal acquaintance of Rousseau, whose full influence his own peculiar character and experiences had prepared him to receive. Under that influence he wrote his *Études de la Nature* (1784), which sets forth a system of natural theology of a very vague and unsubstantial kind, but is now interesting to us only for its descriptions, and the famous story, *Paul et Virginie* (1787), a simple and tender

---

[1] Le Breton, *Le Roman au XVIIIᵉ Siècle*, p. 307.

idyll, the scene of which is laid in the Île de France, and which was designed to illustrate the author's favourite thesis that " notre bonheur consiste à vivre suivant la nature et la vertu." Tastes change, and most mature readers of to-day will probably agree thàt the extreme sentimentalism of this little book seems to them more than a trifle sickly ; but its immense popularity at the time of its appearance is not in the least surprising, for its richly picturesque quality was a fresh thing to its own generation, to whose eyes it also opened up the romance of worlds beyond the sea. Another of Saint-Pierre's writings, *La Chaumière Indienne* (1790),' a mixture of idyll and satire, with a touch of quiet humour not suggested by *Paul et Virginie*, is still sometimes read by admirers of this, but his *Harmonies de la Nature* (1796), a sequel to the *Études*, and other works are practically forgotten.

CHAPTER X

51. THE EARLIER NINETEENTH CENTURY—ROMANTICISM.—It will be convenient for us here to follow the practice of many French historians and to deal with the literature of the nineteenth century in two chronological divisions—the period before 1850, or the Age of Romanticism, and the period after 1850, or the Age of Realism. Owing to the immense wealth and variety of the literature of these two periods we shall be compelled to make our remaining chapters somewhat more comprehensive in character than those which have preceded. While, therefore, our plan will still be to fix attention in the main upon the men of outstanding importance, we shall have to find space for a good many other writers who, whatever their actual status, are of such interest to the modern reader that they merit a certain amount of consideration.

The Revolution, which marks so decisively the beginning of a new era in political history, did not at once inaugurate a new era in the history of literature. The disturbances by which it was accompanied and followed were indeed unfavourable to literary art of any kind, and except in political oratory (which scarcely comes under the head of literature proper) the quarter-century from the fall of the Bastille to the close of the Empire produced comparatively little that will need to concern us in these pages. What is perhaps more remarkable is the fact that while everything else belonging to the old order was ruthlessly thrown into the melting-pot, the writers of the time for the most part continued to adhere with servile fidelity to the principles and practice of the classic school. Thus, though a few attempts were made here and there to revitalise the serious drama,[1] tragedy kept in general to the traditional lines, as in the plays of André Chénier's younger brother, Marie Joseph (*Charles IX*, 1789; *Henri VIII*, 1791; *Jean Calas*, 1791; *Caïus Gracchus*, 1792, etc.); narrative poetry maintained the forms and conventions of the epic (*e.g.*, *Achille à Scyros*, by Luce de Lancival; *L'Atlantide*, by Baour-Lormian); while lyrical verse, as represented by Ponce Denis Écouchard Lebrun (1729–1807), Evariste de Parny (1754–1801), Louis de Fontanes (1757–1821), Charles Louis Julian Lioult de Chênedollé (1769–1833), and Charles Hubert Millevoye (1782–1816), was still strongly marked by eighteenth-century characteristics. It is true indeed that a careful study of some of these poets, and notably of Chênedollé (*Études Poétiques*, 1820) and Millevoye (*e.g.*, *La Chute des Feuilles*, *Le Poète Mourant*), brings to light various pre-monitions of the coming romantic revival, but in the mass we can regard them only as indicating the final exhaustion of classicism.[2]

[1] As, *e.g.*, in *Pinto* (1801), by Népomucène Lemercier (1771–1811), and in the melodramas (*e.g.*, *Victor, ou l'Enfant de la Forêt*, 1798; *Cœlina, ou l'Enfant du Mystère*, 1801) of the " Corneille des Boulevards," Guilbert de Pixérécourt (1773–1844), a sensational writer of immense fertility of invention but absolutely no literary quality.

[2] Reference must, however, be made in passing to the famous outburst of patriotic enthusiasm, *La Marseillaise* (1792), improvised in

But though not operative at the time, the stir of new forces through the whole of society was bound before long to be felt in literature, and the destruction of the old social system was presently followed by that of the art which had been fostered by it. What is known as the Romantic Movement, though like all such movements extremely complex in origin and character, may therefore be broadly interpreted as an offshoot from the revolutionary movement in politics or, more correctly speaking, as another phase of that same great general intellectual upheaval of which the Revolution itself had been the principal manifestation in the sphere of practical activity. This point was seized by Victor Hugo and put by him with his customary emphasis in the preface to his *Hernani* : " Le romantisme, tant de fois mal défini, n'est . . . que le libéralisme en littérature." Hugo often indulged in rhetorical fireworks, and many of his critical pronouncements are too childish for serious consideration, but in this case he certainly hit the mark. In romanticism, standing as it did primarily and fundamentally for the rejection of external authority, ready-made rules and standards, tradition and convention, and for absolute freedom and the right of every one to his own individuality, we have simply the revolutionary spirit of emancipation expressing itself in the new field of literary art.

At bottom, therefore, romanticism was essentially individualistic. In contrast with classicism, the ideal of which, as we have seen, had been uniformity, and which had striven to eliminate the merely accidental and exceptional, it threw its stress entirely upon personality, dis-

---

a moment of intense poetic fervour by a young officer of the engineers, Claude Joseph Rouget de Lisle (1760–1836). One of the world's great martial songs, this stands by itself, outside the limits of any formal classification.

carded uniformity, cultivated the accidental and exceptional, and proclaimed the liberty and spontaneity of
genius. Hence its impatience of the formal restraints of
art, its constant striving after originality, its frequent
extravagances ; hence its subjectivity, its devotion to
the " culte du moi," and that intimately confidential
quality which is one of the salient features of romantic
literature as a whole. On this side romanticism meant
the substitution of sincerity and of the genuine expression of real and fresh emotion for the stereotyped plati-
tudes and conventional rhetoric of the decadent classic
school. Its repudiation of the principles of that school—
in other words, its assertion of the right of genius to be a
law unto itself—was in part the result of this individualism, but in part also of the growing conviction that any
art which depends upon the mechanical imitation of
models must necessarily lapse into sterility, and that a
new age demands a new literature to express its spirit
and satisfy its needs. The significance of romanticism
from this point of view was neatly defined by Stendhal
in his *Racine et Shakespeare* : " Le romantisme est l'art
de présenter aux peuples les œuvres littéraires qui, dans
l'état actuel de leurs habitudes et de leurs croyances, sont
susceptibles de leur donner le plus de plaisir possible. Le
classicisme, au contraire, leur présente la littérature qui
donnait le plus grand plaisir possible à leurs arrière-grands-
pères." This view we shall meet again presently in the
writings of Mme. de Staël. But while in this sense
romanticism implied the renovation of literature by contact with the living forces of the contemporary world, it
none the less nourished itself upon the past, for its abandon-
ment of classical antiquity was accompanied by a return
to the Middle Ages as a fresh source of inspiration and
material. The mediævalism which was (in France as

well as in Germany and England) so conspicuous a characteristic of the whole romantic movement that writers like Heine and Mme. de Staël regarded it as its very essence, was the product of many co-operating causes, particularly of the Catholic revival, which profoundly affected the imaginations of many writers who were not touched by it on the religious side, and of that growing sense of nationality which turned the minds of men back with quickened interest and curiosity to the history and traditions of their own country. But whatever the origin of this renaissance of Gothicism, it is evident that the romantics were naturally carried away by it, because in the literature, art, and legends of the mystical and chivalrous Middle Ages they found precisely the picturesque qualities, the imaginative freedom, the emotional fervour, the combined beauty and strangeness [1] for which they yearned. In the same way, and by immediate reference to the peculiar temper of romanticism, we can account for that passionate feeling for nature (especially for wild nature), that love of exotic landscape, and that thirst for local colour which we also recognise among its important components. The prevailing melancholy, which was another of its distinctive notes, was again directly associated with its highly wrought sensibility and intense emotionalism, but in this case emphasis must be laid upon the powerful influence of social and political conditions. The failure of the glorious humanitarian promises of '89 —the moral exhaustion which followed the abnormal excitement of many eventful years and the long strain of the Napoleonic wars — the sweeping conservative

---

[1] Cp. Walter Pater's doctrine that while " order in beauty " is the " essential classical element," it is " the addition of strangeness to beauty that constitutes the romantic character in art " (*Appreciations : Postscript*).

counter-revolution which was ushered in by the Congress of Vienna and Waterloo and for a time crushed the hopes of democracy : all these things combined to breed in the new generation that spirit of disenchantment, dejection, and aimless unrest which in our own literature we epitomise under the name of Byronism.

Freedom, subjectivity, mediævalism, picturesqueness, and melancholy, varying of course in their degrees, proportions, and forms of expression in different writers in accordance with each one's personal idiosyncrasies, may therefore be regarded as the principal elements of romanticism. It remains to note that while the new movement was to a large extent indigenous, it was at all points greatly stimulated by the influence of the foreign literatures which now took the place of the literatures of Greece and Rome. The men of the seventeenth and eighteenth centuries had found their permanent standards of taste in the masterpieces of classical antiquity. The men of the earlier nineteenth century turned from these to the more congenial literatures of the north, and sought fresh inspiration in Bürger's ballads, Goethe's *Leiden des jungen Werthers*, Schiller's *Die Räuber*, Hoffmann's fantastic tales, the plays of Shakespeare, Young's *Night Thoughts*, the poems of Ossian, and a little later the work of Byron and Scott.

This brief preliminary inquiry into the meaning of romanticism has been undertaken only to prepare the way for the more detailed study of the representative writers of the period now under review. Two of these have first to engage our attention who belong to the time immediately preceding the rise of the romantic movement, and are specially important as its recognised precursors—Mme. de Staël and Chateaubriand.

52. MME. DE STAËL.—Anne Louise Germaine Necker

was born in Paris in 1766, and was the daughter of the famous Swiss banker and financier and of Suzanne Curchod, who in earlier life had been wooed by young Edward Gibbon.   A precocious girl, early accustomed to the stimulating atmosphere of the society which gathered at her father's home, but at the same time an enthusiastic student of Richardson and Rousseau, she grew up intellectually eager and restless, yet dreamy, sentimental, and imaginative.   At twenty she married the Baron de Staël-Holstein, Swedish ambassador in Paris, but the union proved an unhappy one, and a separation took place in 1798.   Meanwhile, ten years before this, she had published *Six Lettres sur le Caractère et les Écrits de J. J. Rousseau*, which show how powerful was the influence that the author of *La Nouvelle Héloïse* continued to exercise over her mind.   After the outbreak of the Revolution she remained in France until the ascendancy of the party of violence forced her to fly (Sept. 1792) to her father's estate at Coppet on the Lake of Geneva, whence she issued an eloquent pamphlet in defence of Marie Antoinette.   She was in Paris in 1795 and again in 1797, having between these two dates published an essay, *De l'Influence des Passions sur le Bonheur des Individus et des Nations* (1796) ; but her opinions brought her into collision with Napoleon, by whom she was exiled.   She travelled in Germany in 1803 and 1807, and in Italy in 1805–6, and after her second marriage in 1811 to a young Swiss officer, Albert de Rocca, visited Austria, Russia, and England, and made a third tour in Italy.   It was not until after the fall of Napoleon that she was allowed to return to Paris, where her *salon* at once became one of the centres of intellectual activity.   She died in 1817, leaving behind her the manuscripts of two works, *Considérations sur les Principaux Événements de la Révolution Française* and *Dix Années d'Exil,* which were published after her death.

Mme. de Staël was a woman of strongly emotional nature, and the fever of her life passed directly into her two novels, the immature *Delphine* (1802) and the far more important *Corinne* (1807). Both these prolix and highly sentimental romances of passion (which belong in type to the numerous progeny of *La Nouvelle Héloïse*) are studies of the " femme supérieure " in conflict with her own temperament and with the social prejudices by which her free development is hampered, but they are studies made from different sides, for while the one portrays the tragic fate of a woman who is bold enough to defy public opinion instead of tamely submitting to it, the heroine of the other—an Italian poetess of the richest artistic endowments, in whom we can easily recognise an idealised portrait of the writer herself—discovers that her genius, though a passport to fame, is a fatal obstacle to happiness. Extremely popular at the time of their appearance, these works have inevitably suffered from radical changes of taste, and to-day we find their method antiquated, their sentiment overstrained, and their style too declamatory. The earlier of the two is now indeed scarcely more than a name, while the later is remembered chiefly for its descriptions of Italy and its many eloquent pages on the masterpieces of sculpture and painting.

More interest attaches to Mme. de Staël's excursions into criticism because, whatever judgment may be formed regarding their permanent value, they secure for her the honour which properly belongs to the pioneer. The significance of the first of her two treatises (1800) may be gathered from its title—*De la Littérature considerée dans ses Rapports avec les Institutions Sociales.* This at once suggests the application to the study of literature of a method entirely new to that subject, though it was substantially the same as that which Montesquieu had long before employed in the study of jurisprudence—the method, namely, of comparative criticism. " Je me suis proposé," the author herself explains, " d'examiner quelle est l'influence de la religion, des mœurs et des lois sur la littérature, et quelle est l'influence de la littérature sur la religion, les mœurs et les lois " ; and, she adds, " il me semble que l'on n'a pas suffisament analysé les causes morales et politiques qui modifient l'esprit de la littéra-ture." Her essay of 600 pages is seriously damaged as a whole by the fallacy of its underlying thesis—that of the necessary and continuous progress of the human race : a thesis which Mme. de Staël took over from the doctrinaires of the encyclopædic school,[1] and which forces her to maintain, on purely *à priori* grounds, the superiority of the literature of each successive generation to that of the generation which had preceded it. Her knowledge was also inadequate to her task, and for this reason she often indulges in superficial views and hasty generalisations. But the substantial importance of her innovation is still incontestable. By connecting literature directly with social life and with the changing spirit of the different races and ages, she for the first time sub-stituted the method of historical interpretation (or, as we should now say, the evolutionary method) for that of the old hard dogmatic criticism, which had judged all literature without reference to its social origins and by fixed and absolute standards.

[1] This thesis, it will be remembered, had already appeared among the arguments of the modernists in the Querelle des Anciens et des Modernes. It was widely current in the later eighteenth century, and will be found developed to its most Utopian conclusions in Condorcet's *Esquisse d'un Tableau Historique des Progrès de l'Esprit Humaine* (1794).

In this work Mme. de Staël showed a marked leaning towards the literatures of England and Germany,[1] and this prepares us for her second treatise, *De l'Allemagne* (1810), which, while in part, it is true, dictated by political considerations and the writer's hatred of Napoleon, was still the product of intellectual and artistic sympathy fostered by her visits to Germany and personal association with some of Germany's leading men. The significance of the book lies primarily in the fact that it did for French readers what a little later Carlyle's essays did for English readers —it opened up to them the new world of German poetry, German romance, and German idealistic philosophy, and thus started a current of influence which·was presently to help in the destruction of classicism. The bearings of this influence were, moreover, clearly appreciated by Mme. de Staël herself. Distinguishing between two great schools of poetry—the southern and pagan (otherwise the classic) and the northern and Christian (which she calls the romantic [2])—she argues that a slavish adherence to the principles of the former can result only in poetic impotence among modern peoples, that a country's literature can be a living literature only when it is really national, and that it can be national only when it is directly fed by that country's own history and religion. Hence her depreciation of classic and her advocacy of romantic art. " La littérature des anciens est chez les

[1] One of the most noteworthy chapters in the book is that on Shakespeare (Part I. chap. xiii.).

[2] This early use of the word romantic, which she seems to have adopted from Schlegel, and the sense in which she employs it, should be carefully noted. " Le nom de romantique a été introduit nouvellement en Allemagne pour désigner la poésie . . . qui est née de la chevalerie et du Christianisme. . . . On prend quelquefois le mot classique comme synonyme de perfection. Je m'en sers ici dans une autre acceptation, en considérant la poésie classique comme celle des anciens et la poésie romantique comme celle qui tient de quelque manière aux traditions chevaleresque " (i. 30).

modernes une littérature transplantée. Ces poésies d'après l'antique, quelque parfaites qu'elles soient, sont rarement populaires, parce qu'elles ne tiennent, dans le temps actuel, à rien de national. La littérature romantique est la seule qui soit susceptible encore d'être perfectionnée, parce qu'ayant ses racines dans notre propre sol, elle est la seule qui puisse croître et se vivifier de nouveau ; elle exprime notre religion; elle rapelle notre histoire " (ii. 11).[1]

The importance of Mme. de Staël's work as a preparation for romanticism is now apparent. We have next to learn how her teachings were reinforced and supplemented by that of her contemporary Chateaubriand.

53. CHATEAUBRIAND. — François René, Vicomte de Chateaubriand, was born at Saint-Malo in 1768, and was therefore two years Mme. de Staël's junior. He sprang from an old Breton family which had gradually fallen into decay, and the influence of his Celtic blood can easily be traced in the distinguishing qualities of his character— his strong religious feeling, his visionary tendency, his sensibility, his melancholy. These qualities were further intensified by his solitary wanderings as a boy over the sand-dunes about Saint-Malo, by his lonely life in the Château de Combourg in the midst of the sombre Breton landscape, and later, as he has himself told us, by his study of Rousseau's *Rêveries*, Bernardin de Saint-Pierre's *Études de la Nature*, Goethe's *Werther*, and the poems of Ossian. Reaching young manhood, he served for a short time in the army, and on a visit to Paris saw something of literary society. But from childhood up he had been

[1] Cp. Ruskin's contention that the classical architecture reintroduced at the Renaissance is with us a form of architecture transplanted from alien conditions, and that Gothic architecture is the only natural and proper expression of the ideals and sentiments of northern and Christian peoples.

haunted by dreams of travel, and as his conservative bias made it impossible for him to sympathise with the Revolution, he resolved to set out on quest of adventure beyond the seas. Accordingly, in the spring of 1791, he sailed for North America, where he spent nearly eight months exploring some of the wilder parts of the continent and learning a good deal of native Indian life (see *Voyage en Amérique*, published in 1826, a picturesque record, though of doubtful accuracy). On his return he married ; joined the army of the emigrants ; was wounded at the siege of Thionville ; and with great difficulty contrived to escape to Brussels, whence he made his way first to Jersey and then to England. He remained in London seven years (1793–1800), living as best he could by teaching and translating, and meanwhile reading widely in English literature, to which he afterwards acknowledged his indebtedness. With the permission of the government he then settled again in France and soon established his reputation with *Atala* (1801) and *Le Génie du Christianisme* (1802). The latter work attracted the attention of Bonaparte, who was just then engaged on his policy of reconciliation with the Papacy, and Chateaubriand was appointed secretary to the embassy in Rome (1803) and minister plenipotentiary in the Valais (1804). But the murder of the Duc d'Enghien alienated him from the First Consul, and resigning his official position he started on an extended tour in Greece, Turkey, Palestine, Tunis, and Spain (1806–7) (see *Itinéraire de Paris à Jérusalem*, 1811). After the Bourbon restoration he became an influential supporter of the legitimist cause, was rewarded for his loyalty with many high honours, and for two years (1822–24) was again in London, not now as a struggling refugee, but as ambassador of France at the Court of St. James. His political career closed with the fall of

Charles X. and the accession of Louis Philippe (1830), on which he retired from public life and busied himself with his immense autobiography, *Mémoires d'outre Tombe*. He died in the year of revolution, 1848, only a few months after the proclamation of the Second Republic.

In turning to those portions of Chateaubriand's work of which it is necessary here to take account, we may conveniently begin with *Le Génie du Christianisme*. This voluminous treatise was written, as the author expressly declared, to destroy the influence of Voltaire and the *Encyclopédie* and to rehabilitate Christianity, and such purpose, he afterwards asserted, was in fact accomplished by it. The effect of the book was certainly remarkable, for it fell into line with the strong neo-Catholic movement of the time and did much to stimulate it. As an apologetic, however, its value is very slight, for Chateaubriand was neither a sound thinker nor a trained controversialist, and his defence of the dogmatic principles of the Catholic faith may therefore be ignored. The really interesting parts of the work are those in which he approaches his subject not from the theological but from the æsthetic side, aims to show that Christianity is the most beautiful of all religions, dwells eloquently on the peculiar charm of Christian architecture, symbolism, and ceremonial, and elaborates the thought that the poet or artist in search of fresh inspiration would do well to seek it not in the long-exhausted fables of heathen mythology but in the Bible, in ecclesiastical history, in the lives of the saints and martyrs of the Church. At this point we also note the importance of his detailed examination of some of the representative Christian epics—Dante's *Divina Commedia*, Tasso's *Gerusalemme Liberata*, Milton's *Paradise Lost*, Voltaire's *La Henriade*—which he cites in support of his general contention that as a source of poetic material Christianity is infinitely superior to paganism.[1] But he was not satisfied with the merely theoretical expression of his views ; he undertook to demonstrate them by a practical illustration ; and this he did in *Les Martyrs* (1809), a prose epic in twenty-four books dealing with the persecutions of the early Church under Diocletian. This ambitious attempt to prove his thesis must, however, be pronounced a failure ; a few of its scenes and episodes are still remembered and praised for their genuine passion and remarkable descriptive power ; [2] but as a whole it is ruined by its borrowed epic machinery, while its supernaturalism impresses us as singularly unconvincing and out of place.

It was part of Chateaubriand's plan in preparing *Le Génie* to develop the " harmonies de la religion Chrétienne avec les scènes de la nature et les passions du cœur humain," and out of this sprang one of his most famous works, a " petite histoire " which, intended originally as a mere interlude in his treatise, was detached from it before it was finished and published independently. As in *Le Génie* he had proclaimed the romantic beauty of Christianity, so now in *Atala* he set himself to write of the romantic beauty of nature and " the man of nature " ; and here, despite his protest that, unlike Rousseau, he had no enthusiasm for the actual savage as such (probably because he had seen real savages, which Rousseau had not), the connection between his own work and that of " the sophist of Geneva " is very clear. The scene of *Atala* is laid in the wilds of North America, and its action

[1] It may be mentioned in passing that he afterwards translated *Paradise Lost* into French prose, and published it (1836) with a preliminary *Essai sur la Littérature Anglaise*.

[2] *E.g.* the episode of the druidess Velléda (liv. ix. x.) and the scene in the amphitheatre (liv. xxiv.).

is very simple. The heroine, who gives her name to the
book, is the daughter of the chief of an Indian tribe ;
Chactas, the chief of another tribe, is taken prisoner by
her father's people and condemned to death at the stake ;
she falls in love with him, saves him, and flies with him
into the wilderness. But she had been brought up in
the Christian faith and consecrated by her dying mother
to God and perpetual maidenhood. To this vow she
remains faithful through all the tremendous stress of
passion and temptation, and finally she commits suicide
in a mood of despair. Such is the bare outline of a story
which took the critics by surprise and the public by storm,
but no mere outline suffices to suggest the peculiar qualities which ensured its instant popularity—the power with
which it portrays the tragic love of two primitive natures,
its long highly-wrought descriptions of deserts, forests,
and prairies, the local colour and exotic atmosphere which
even after *Paul et Virginie* were practically new to French
readers. As Chateaubriand afterwards said, " falling into
the midst of the literature of the Empire—of that classic
school whose very sight, like that of a rejuvenated old
woman, inspired boredom," *Atala* " was a production, as
it were, of an unknown kind." A few years later (1807)
he followed up this sensational success with another
episode detached from *Le Génie—René, ou les Effets de la
Passion*.[1] This new romance—the autobiographical character of which is suggested by the fact that its hero bears
the author's own name—is substantially a psychological
study of his temperament and inner experiences during
the days of his youth in Brittany and of his wanderings
in America, when his mind was in a state of ferment, and

[1] *René* had also a place in an immense rambling kind of prose epic,
Les Natchez, which was written while Chateaubriand was in exile in
London, but not published in its entirety till 1826.

he had not yet found a corrective and a stay in religion. But its interest is general as well as personal, because in portraying himself Chateaubriand was also portraying his generation—a generation which had been bred in the scepticism of the eighteenth century, had passed through the storms of the great revolutionary upheaval, and now stood on the threshold of the new age deeply touched by that *mal du siècle* to which reference has already been made. Towards the end of his life Chateaubriand expressed regret at the malign influence which *René* had exerted over the minds of his younger contemporaries ; had it been possible for him to destroy the book, he declared, he would gladly have done so (*Mémoires d'outre Tombe*, ii. 1). Perhaps he was inclined to take too much credit, or discredit, to himself for the practical effect of what he had done. The spirit of romantic melancholy was, as we have seen, in the air at the time,[1] and Young France was as ready to receive and welcome *René* as a little earlier Young Germany had been to receive and welcome *Werther*, and a little later Young England was to receive and welcome *Childe Harold*. But if he did not create the type of the jaded and disenchanted egotist he certainly helped to popularise and to fix it. As Sainte-Beuve put it : " Le petit livre de *René* garde toujours l'honneur d'avoir, le premier, et du premier coup, trouvé une expression nette et précise à ce qui semblait indéfinissable ; il a même donné cette expression tellement noble, flatteuse et séduisante, qu'il a pu sembler dangereux à son heure."

---

[1] This romantic melancholy was, for example, independently expressed in the *Obermann* (1804) of Étienne Pivert de Sénancour (1770–1846), well known to English readers through Arnold's two poems—*Stanzas in Memory of the Author of Obermann* and *Obermann once more*. In his note to these poems Arnold points out the influence of Rousseau upon Sénancour and " certain affinities " between him and those " more famous and fortunate authors of his own day—Chateaubriand and Mme. de Staël."

We are now in a position to realise the importance of the place which Chateaubriand occupies, beside Mme. de Staël, among the forerunners of romanticism. Gautier summed up his influence by saying : " Il a restauré la cathédrale gothique, rouvert la grande nature et inventé la mélancholie moderne," and though allowance has to be made for some rhetorical over-emphasis in this statement, it serves to indicate the threefold significance of his work. In the first place, he stirred the imagination of his readers to the romantic beauty of mediæval Christianity and Gothic art. Secondly, though he did not reopen nature—for Rousseau and Bernardin de Saint-Pierre had already done this—he greatly extended and deepened the feeling for nature by his brilliant and varied word-pictures of Brittany, North America, and the Far East. Thirdly, while it is obviously inaccurate to speak of him as the " inventor " of modern melancholy, he interpreted the new spirit of dissatisfaction, craving, and general unrest with so much power, and embodied it so successfully in a single permanent type—at once, as it were, synthesis and model—that the literature of romantic melancholy may almost be said to date from him. Chateaubriand was not an amiable man ; the personal qualities which are so aggressively prominent in all his work are by no means engaging ; and much of his sentiment seems to us now factitious and theatrical. For these reasons his interest for us to-day is mainly historical. But his imaginative power is undeniable, and as a writer of richly coloured poetic prose he is still recognised as a master.

54. THE CRITICS—SAINTE-BEUVE.—Aided by the immense development of the periodical press after the Restoration, criticism from the early twenties of the century onward became an important and increasingly

popular branch of literature, and what is particularly noticeable is the fact that in its temper and methods it at once began to reveal the quickening and broadening influences of Mme. de Staël and Chateaubriand. This influence is seen even in academic criticism, as in the *Tableau de la Littérature Française au Moyen Âge* and *Tableau de la Littérature Française au XVIIIᵉ Siècle* of Abel François Villemain (1790–1867) who was successively professor at the Lycée Charlemagne, the École Normale, and the Sorbonne. Villemain followed the lead of Mme. de Staël in treating literature throughout in direct connection with the intellectual and moral movements of society. He was also an exponent of the new cosmopolitanism, laying stress on the complex character of French literature (*Tableau de la Littérature Française au XVIIIᵉ Siècle*, xiv.) and paying great attention to its many borrowings from the literatures of other countries (*ibid.*, v., vi., vii., xxvi., xxvii., etc.). Though clear and interesting his work is wanting in depth and precision, but it was extremely useful at the time and still entitles its author to rank among the pioneers. On the other hand, when the romantic movement was in full swing, conservative criticism still rose in protest against it. Saint-Marc Girardin (1801–73), for example, though mainly occupied with the purely moral aspects of literature, showed himself a stout opponent of the romantics in his *Cours de Littérature Dramatique* ; while an even stronger stand was made against them by Jean Marie Napoléon Désiré Nisard (1806–88) in his *Manifeste contre la Littérature Facile* (1833) and his monumental *Histoire de la Littérature Française* (1844–61). A man of ripe scholarship and vigorous mind, Nisard was hostile not only to romanticism in creative art but also to the eclectic, flexible, historical type of criticism which had grown up with it and which he regarded as radically unsound. He is indeed a belated survivor of the old dogmatic school, the last representative of the spirit of Boileau and La Harpe, untouched and unmodified by the ideas of his own time. His method had therefore nothing in common with that of his contemporaries in general. Ignoring altogether the connection between literature and history, repudiating all considerations of the relations of a given piece of literature to its society and age, taking no account even of biography or the personality of the writers to be discussed, he studies the work before him just as it stands as an example of the *genre* to which it belongs, compares it with other works of the same *genre* and with his own abstract conception of what that *genre* should be, and pronounces judgment upon it in accordance with a code of fixed and absolute rules derived from the great classics of the seventeenth century.

While Nisard was thus making a heroic attempt to re-establish dogmatism and to free literature from " the tyranny of the notion that there is no disputing about tastes," the new tendencies against which he fought found full expression in the writings of the greatest of all French critics, Sainte-Beuve. Born in 1804 at Boulogne-sur-Mer, Charles Augustin Sainte-Beuve was on his mother's side the grandson of an Englishwoman who had married a Boulogne sailor, a fact which, in conformity with his own method, we may hold to explain, in some measure at least, his early and lasting interest in English literature. His father, a commissioner of taxes, died before his birth (see his poem *Souvenir*) and he was brought up in straitened circumstances, but his mother none the less contrived to give him a good education. At her desire he took up the study of medicine, and though he had no taste for this and abandoned it as soon as possible, it undoubtedly helped to develop in him that habit of scientific research which was afterwards a factor in his criticism. Meanwhile one of his old teachers at the Collège Charlemagne, M. Dubois, invited him to join the staff of a newspaper, *Le Globe*, which he had just founded (1824), and in miscellaneous work for this he served his apprenticeship as a writer. In 1827 an article on Hugo's *Odes et Ballades* brought him into personal relations with the poet and his *cénacle* (see *post*, p. 203), and as a recruit to romanticism he published the next year a *Tableau de la Poésie Française au XVIᵉ Siècle*, which was designed at once to direct attention to the long neglected poets of the time before Malherbe, and to legitimise the romantic movement by affiliating it upon the work of Ronsard and his school. This was followed in 1829 by a small volume entitled *Vie, Poésies, et Pensées de Joseph Delorme*, a supposed young medical student " mort d'une phthisie pulmonaire compliquée, à ce qu'on croit, d'une affection de cœur," whom Sainte-Beuve had invented as the expositor of his own morbid fancies, and by two collections of verse issued under his own name, *Les Consolations* (1830) and *Les Pensées d'Août* (1837), in which, under the influence of Cowper and Wordsworth, he attempted, though not very successfully, to write a kind of poetry nearer to the humble realities of everyday life and more familiar in tone and style than that of either the classics or the romantics (see, in *Pensées d'Août, À. M. Villemain* and *Monsieur Jean*, appropriately introduced with a quotation from Crabbe). Between these two dates he had also published his one novel, *Volupté* (1834), a minute and painful analysis of passion and suffering. As all these books suggest, Sainte-Beuve was passing at this time through a period of great intellectual and moral unrest ; but after being carried away for the moment by the fervid neo-Catholicism of Lamennais,[1] he subsided into a quiet scepticism, in which for the remainder of his life he found complete satisfaction and peace of mind. Thus far his chief ambition had been to succeed as a poet. Henceforth criticism was to absorb all his energies. In 1837–38 he gave a course of lectures on Jansenism and the Jansenists, out of which presently grew the first of his works in which his peculiar powers were fully manifested, his *Histoire de Port-Royal*. This great undertaking occupied him at intervals for nearly twenty years, the first two volumes appearing in 1840, the fifth and last in 1860, and it is perhaps worth while to note that it indicates very clearly the change which had gradually come over his mind, for he began it in a spirit of strong sympathy with Jansenist mysticism and ended it as a detached spectator of a movement in which he had ceased to have anything but a critical interest. Another course of lectures ten years later, this time at the University of Liége, resulted in a second work on a large scale, *Chateaubriand et son Groupe Littéraire* (published 1860). In the meantime he had been contributing industriously to the *Revue de Paris* and the *Revue des Deux Mondes*, and had published three collections of essays—*Portraits Littéraires* (3 vols., 1840), *Portraits de Femmes* (1840), and *Portraits Contemporains* (1846). The principal work of his life after 1849 is represented by the " feuilletons littéraires " which he wrote for *Le Constitutionel*, *Le Moniteur*, and *Le Temps*, and which were reprinted in his two series of essays, *Causeries du Lundi* (15 vols., 1851–62) and

[1] Félicité Robert Lamennais (1782–1854), who like Chateaubriand was a native of Saint-Malo, was an apostle of democratic and humanitarian Christianity (see, *e.g.*, *Paroles d'un Croyant*, 1834), and one of the most noteworthy figures in the religious revival of the time. His opinions were condemned by Rome, and the work of his last twenty years was done outside the pale of the Church.

Nouveaux Lundis (13 vols., 1863-72). He died in 1869, and by his own wish was buried without religious rites or ceremonial of any kind.

Though he has sometimes been accused of allowing his judgments regarding contemporaries to be disturbed by personal feeling and even jealousy, and, as Flaubert once told him, of depending too much on his " impression nerveuse," Sainte-Beuve's greatness as a critic has never been seriously questioned. He had indeed in a supreme degree the qualities which are essential to the highest work in criticism : infinite curiosity ; the spirit of eclecticism ; hospitality to all ideas, even to those most foreign to his own modes of thought ; the power at once of identifying himself with his subject and of detaching himself from it ; a passion for truth (the English word " Truth " was the motto engraved on his seal) ; wide, varied, and sound scholarship ; a love of accuracy so great that he was willing to spend hours of laborious research in the verification of a single detail ; extraordinary insight, discrimination and tact ; and so remarkable a skill in portraiture that the best of his analytical studies have all the interest and vitality of creative literature. These qualities combine to give to his writings such permanent value that, whatever else he reads or leaves unread, the student of any period of French literature from the sixteenth century to the nineteenth will turn to these as a matter of course. His method may be briefly defined as in essence biographical and psychological. His aim was always to approach his subject in the spirit of scientific impartiality, without bias or prepossession, to penetrate to its centre, to see it on all its sides, to understand, explain, interpret, and to judge it, as it were, from the inside. As early as 1828, in an article on Corneille, he traced the programme which, with certain modifications, he followed

to the end : " Entrer en son auteur, s'y installer, le pro-
duire sous ses aspects divers ; le faire vivre, se mouvoir et
parler comme il a dû le faire ; le suivre en son intérieur
et dans ses mœurs domestiques aussi avant qu'on le peut ;
le rattacher par tous les côtés à cette terre, à cette existence
réele, à ces habitudes de chaque jour dont les grands
hommes ne dépendent pas moins que nous autres, fond
véritable sur lequel ils ont pied, d'où ils partent pour
s'élever quelque temps et où ils retombent sans cesse " :
such in effect he conceived to be the critic's primary business. But in carrying out his task he was careful at all
times to place his author back in the surroundings of his
own time, and to exhibit their influence upon him ; " l'état
général de la littérature au moment où un auteur y débute,"
being, as he further explains in the same essay, as important to a full comprehension of him as " l'éducation particulière qu'a reçue cet auteur et le génie propre que lui a
départi la nature." Criticism in his hands thus became,
in his own phrase, " l'histoire naturelle des esprits."
But while he had, as he more than once asserted against
those who complained that though he was "un assez bon
juge," he was a judge without a code, his own well-
considered method, it was part of that method to reject
formulas and systems of every kind. That he was fundamentally opposed to the classic dogmatism of Nisard was
of course inevitable : " La nature est pleine de variétés
et de moules divers ; il y a une infinité de formes de
talents. Critique, pourquoi n'avoir qu'un seul patron ? "
(*M. Nisard* in *Causeries du Lundi*, xv.). But on the other
hand he protested against the scientific dogmatism of his
own disciple Taine (see *post*, pp. 264-66), who in his anxiety
to explain everything in terms of natural laws and general
causes neglected " l'initiative humaine," or the purely
personal factor in literature. In the tyranny which any

set system exercises over the mind he saw a fatal obstacle to the clearness of vision and the intellectual freedom and flexibility which he regarded as the foundation principles of the critic's art.

55. OTHER PROSE WRITERS. — There was great activity in religious literature during the first half of the nineteenth century, and in this the reaction against the eighteenth century and the spirit of the *Encyclopédie* is very marked, as we can see in the extreme dogmatism of the *Soirées de Saint-Pétersbourg* (1821) and other works of Joseph de Maistre (1753–1821), and the *Recherches Philosophiques sur les Premiers Objets de nos Connaissances Morales* (1818) of Louis Gabriel Ambroise, Vicomte de Bonald (1753–1840), and no less in the fervid and mystical piety of the free-lance Lamennais. In philosophy, notwithstanding the strong impulse given to the scientific movement by the positivism of Auguste Comte (1798–1857), the same influences were at work, the most popular writers at the moment being Victor Cousin (1792–1867) (*e.g.*, *Du Vrai, du Beau, et du Bien*, 1846, etc.), who was much indebted to the German transcendentalists, and his follower, Théodore Simon Jouffroy (1796–1842) (*e.g.*, *Mélanges Philosophiques*, 1833 ; *Cours d'Esthétique*, 1843). In the same way history responded to the dominant romantic tendencies and became essentially picturesque and dramatic in the hands of Jacques Nicolas Augustin Thierry (1795–1856) (*e.g.*, *Lettres sur l'Histoire de France*, 1820–27 ; *Histoire de la Conquête de l'Angleterre par les Normands*, 1825 ; *Récits des Temps Mérovingiens*, 1840) ; of Jules Michelet (1798–1874), who wrote his voluminous *Histoire de France* (1833–67) with a passionate intensity and in a style and manner which have often been compared with those of Carlyle ; and of Michelet's friend Edgar Quinet (1803–75) (*e.g.*, *Les Révolutions d'Italie*,

1848–52 ;   La Révolution, 1865).[1] While his style is
romantic, however, the distinct didactic purpose in
Quinet's work also connects him with the philosophic
school of historians, the chief of which was François
Pierre Guillaume Guizot (1787–1874), who in his *Histoire
de la Révolution d'Angleterre* (1826–56), *Histoire de la
Civilisation en Europe* (1828), and *Histoire de la Civilisation en France* (1829–32) undertook not merely to narrate
events but also to investigate their causes and relation-
ships.   To this school also belong François Mignet (1796–
1884), whose short *Histoire de la Révolution Française*
(1824) is still a standard authority on the subject, and
Charles Alexis Henri Maurice Clérel de Tocqueville (1805–
1859), the author of two very important critical studies
—*La Démocratie en Amérique* (1835–40) and *L'Ancien
Régime et la Révolution* (1856).   Another historian who
must be mentioned, Louis Adolphe Thiers (1797–1877),
stands somewhat apart from both the romantic and the
philosophical group.   His *Histoire de la Révolution* (1823–
1827) and *Histoire du Consulat et de l'Empire* (1845–62)
are characterised by clearness of narrative and great
wealth of documentary material, but they have none
the less been impugned for their want of depth and their
neglect of the moral and intellectual aspects of history.

[1] Both Michelet and Quinet wrote much outside history.   Michelet's
miscellaneous works include a number of curious, rhapsodical, quasi-
philosophical books—*Le Peuple* (1846), *L'Amour* (1858), *La Femme*
(1859), etc.—and some books of popular science (*e.g.*, *L'Oiseau*, 1856).
Quinet was the author, among many other things, of *Ahasvérus* (1833),
a kind of gigantic allegorical mystery-play on the Wandering Jew ;
Prométhée (1838), an epic in which the Titan becomes a symbol of the
martyrdom and redemption of humanity ;   *Merlin l'Enchanteur* (1869) ;
and *Du Génie des Religions* (1842), which is full of the poetic mysticism
which was one product of the spiritual revival of the time.

CHAPTER XI

56. THE ROMANTIC SCHOOL OF POETRY.—The individualism which we have noted as one of the chief features of the whole romantic movement naturally found the fullest expression in its poetry. Though, as always happens when a certain kind of taste becomes dominant, the smaller men were powerfully influenced by the greater, and (as Carlyle would say) there were many echoes to a few genuine voices, still the theory common to all was that, whatever his quality, the poet should be himself, depend entirely upon the promptings of his own genius, and utter his individual thought in his individual way. Sir Philip Sidney's admonition—" Look in thy heart, and write "— might indeed have been taken as their watchword by the entire school. To the critics who continued to praise the classics as the supreme painters of the human heart, Musset replied with the pertinent question—" Le cœur humain de qui? Le cœur humain de quoi ? " and, he would add, " J'ai mon cœur humain, moi ! " And every other poet of the time was equally convinced of the value of his particular " cœur humain " as the ultimate wellspring of inspiration.

A necessary result of this fundamental individualism

was the extreme variety by which romantic poetry was characterised. Yet those who contributed to it, however diverse their aims and methods, were at one in rejecting the restraints and limitations which had been imposed by classicism, its colourless uniformity, and its technical conventions. In language and style they sought what was fresh, personal, concrete, vivid, and picturesque, loading their work with images and adjectives, and enriching their vocabulary with unusual words derived from many out-of-the-way sources, and especially with archaisms. In versification they were also innovators, emancipating the alexandrine from the rigorous rules of Malherbe and his followers, reviving the stanza-forms of ancient French poetry, and experimenting freely in all sorts of new metrical effects.

The romantic movement in English literature before the time of Wordsworth and Coleridge had represented an unconscious striving after fresh ideals in poetry the nature of which was for the moment only vaguely realised. The romantic movement in French literature, on the other hand, was from its inception a conscious and deliberate movement—a movement with a definite theory behind it and a programme. Unlike the English movement, too, it was highly centralised. Two coteries, or *cénacles*, played a prominent part in its history. The first of these, which was founded in 1823, had its headquarters in the home of the eccentric Jean Emmanuel Charles Nodier (1780–1844)[1] and included among its

---

[1] Charles Nodier is better known to-day for this connection with the early development of romanticism than for his own work. He wrote poems (*Essais d'un Jeune Barde*, 1804), romantic novels (*e.g.*, *Les Proscrits*, 1802; *Jean Sbogar*, 1818, etc.), and some excellent stories in the fantastic vein (*e.g.*, *Trilby*, 1822; *La Fée aux Miettes*, 1832; *La Neuvaine de la Chandeleur*, 1839; *Le Chien de Brisquet*, 1844, etc.).

members the poets Chênedollé, Émile Deschamps (1791–1871) and his brother Antoine (1800–69), Jules Lefèvre (1797–1857), and Jules de Rességuier (1796–1857), and the dramatists, Pierre Alexandre Guiraud (1788–1847), Alexandre Soumet (1788–1845), and Jacques Arsène Polycarpe François Ancelot (1794–1854). It was also frequented for a time by Dubois of *Le Globe*, Sainte-Beuve, Lamartine, and Hugo. But this *cénacle* was still too much tinged with classicism to satisfy the more radical among the younger spirits, and about 1828 another was established about the dominating personality of Hugo, who was from the outset accepted as its chief. Within a couple of years this second brotherhood dispersed, but during its brief existence it included, besides several well-known sculptors and painters of romantic proclivities, most of the poets and dramatists who were specially identified with romanticism in the days of its greatest triumphs, among them Sainte-Beuve, Lamartine, Vigny, Dumas, Musset, and Gautier.

The first distinctive note of the new poetry was struck in 1820, in a little anonymous volume entitled *Méditations Poétiques*, which, as Gautier afterwards said, seemed to the world of the time " comme un souffle de fraîcheur et de rajeunissement." It is with the author of this volume, therefore, that our survey of romantic poetry may properly begin.

57. LAMARTINE.—Alphonse Marie Louis de Prat de Lamartine was born at Macon in 1790. He spent much of his early life at home in the companionship of his five sisters, and during his youth read widely in many literatures, fresh fields of interest being successively opened up to him by the Bible, which he was first taught to love by his pious mother ; by Homer, Vergil, and Horace ; by Tasso and Alfieri ; by Shakespeare, Milton, Dryden,

Pope (whom he set above Boileau), Addison, Richardson, Fielding, Young, and Ossian [1]; by the great French writers of the sixteenth and seventeenth centuries; by Rousseau's *Nouvelle Héloïse*, which threw him into a transport of admiration; and by Bernardin de Saint-Pierre, Chateaubriand, and Mme. de Staël. After a visit to Italy (1811–12), during which he met the little cigarette-maker whom he afterwards idealised in *Graziella*, he returned to his country life of desultory study and dreaming, and though on the first Restoration (1814) he took service in the guard of Louis XVIII. he soon gave up all thought of a military career. Inspired by an unfortunate love-passion he then wrote his *Méditations*, the publication of which brought him immediate fame. This was followed by *Nouvelles Méditations* (1823), *La Mort de Socrate* (1823), *Le Dernier Chant du Pèlerinage d'Harold* (1825), which deals with Byron's death at Missolonghi, *Harmonies Poétiques et Religieuses* (1830), *Jocelyn* (1836), *La Chute d'un Ange* (1838), and *Les Recueillements Poétiques* (1839). Meanwhile he had been for some years secretary to the embassy in Florence and had married an Englishwoman, Marianne Birch. After the fall of Charles X. he made an extended tour in Greece, Syria, and Palestine (see *Voyage en Orient*, 1835). On his return he became active in politics and made his mark as a statesman and orator. With the accession of Louis Napoleon he fell into obscurity and poverty, but his hardships were at length in a measure relieved by a tardy

---

[1] The immense influence of the Ossianic poems in Baour-Lormian's translation is one of the most remarkable facts in the early history of French romanticism. "C'était le moment où Ossian regnait sur l'imagination de la France," writes Lamartine himself of the time of his youth (*Confidences*, liv. vi.); and elsewhere: "Ossian fut l'Homère de mes premières années; je lui dois une partie de la mélancolie de mes pinceaux" (Preface to *Méditations*). Cp. *Jocelyn*, vi.

pension from the imperial government. His last works were in prose, and include his *Confidences*, several novels (*Raphaël*, 1849 ; *Le Tailleur de Pierres de Saint-Point*, 1851 ; *Graziella*, 1852), and two histories, one of the Girondins, the other of the Restoration. He died in 1869.

Lamartine was essentially a lyrical poet, and as a lyrical poet he may be studied to greatest advantage in his earlier verse. His real claim to distinction—and it is a very substantial one—lies in the fact that he freed the lyric from the mythological absurdities and conventional commonplaces of effete classicism and restored to it all the vital elements of personal sincerity and truth to nature. His own conception of his part in the literary revolution of his time is clearly set forth in the preface to his *Méditations* : " Je suis le premier qui ai fait descendre la poésie du Parnasse et qui ai donné à ce qu'on nommait la Muse, au lieu d'une lyre à sept cordes de convention, les fibres même du cœur de l'homme, touchées et émues par les innombrables frissons de l'âme et de la nature." His poetry is thus largely the record of his own passions and sorrows (*e.g.*, *Le Lac*, *L'Isolement*, in *Méditations* ; *Le Crucifix*, in *Nouvelles Méditations*), his own love of nature (*e.g.*, *Le Vallon*, *L'Automne*, in *Méditations ; Milly ou la Terre Natale*, *Hymne de la Nuit*, *Hymne du Matin*, in *Harmonies*), his own deep though vague religious faith (see *Harmonies, passim*). His prevailing tone is that of tender and pensive melancholy, and we may say of him what an American critic once said of Matthew Arnold, that he is at his best in the mood of lament. Hence his real greatness as an elegiac poet. His principal defects, over and above his often excessive sensibility, are his too great facility, his want of restraint, his indifference to the claims of art. " Je demande grâce pour les imper-

fections de style dont les délicats seront souvent blessés,"
he writes in the preface to *Harmonies*, and he apologises on
the ground that " ce que l'on sent fortement s'écrit vite."
Over-rapidity of composition, carelessness, and prolixity
have naturally proved most fatal in respect of his longer,
non-lyrical poems. *La Chute d'un Ange* was, as he himself confessed, " une chute," and neither *La Mort de
Socrate* nor *Le Dernier Chant du Pèlerinage d'Harold* now
survives except by name. *Jocelyn*, however, though far
too long, may still be read with interest. As the story,
told in diary form, of a young priest who, driven by the
Revolution to take refuge among the Alps, rescues a
fugitive whom he supposes to be a boy, but who afterwards
proves to be a woman, and whom he is prevented from
marrying by his vows, it represents a first attempt at a
new kind of narrative poetry suitable, as Lamartine himself
believed, to the taste of an age which had lost its interest
in the old " heroic epics " and craved for something more
human and real. *Jocelyn* is in fact an early specimen in
European literature of the since popular novel in verse.

58. HUGO.—Innovator as he was, there was nothing
of the militant quality in Lamartine's disposition, and
notwithstanding his early connection with the two *cénacles*
he took no part in the battle of romanticism and classicism
which excited the French public in the decade following
the publication of the *Méditations*. We now come to the
great leader of the romantics in this struggle, whose
amazing personal force gave precisely the driving power
which they required, and whose genius was a chief factor
in their success. Though Hugo's career extended far
beyond the limits of our present period, we shall deal with
his poetry in its entirety both as a matter of convenience
and because to the end it belonged essentially to the
romantic movement.

Victor Marie Hugo was born at Besançon in 1802—
the year of Chateaubriand's *Génie du Christianisme*. His
father, an officer in Napoleon's army, whose character we
can infer from the incident recorded in *Après la Bataille*
(*Légende des Siècles*), took his family with him as his duties
called him from place to place, and the future poet spent
a roving childhood in Elba, Corsica, Paris, Naples, and
Madrid. His education was thus very irregular, and even
at the Pension Cordier, to which he was presently sent,
he devoted himself with more ardour to poetry than to his
prescribed studies. An extremely precocious boy, he was
early convinced of his vocation in literature ; at fourteen
he wrote in one of his exercise-books: " Je veux être
Chateaubriand ou rien " ; at fifteen he received honour-
able mention for an essay submitted in competition to the
Academy ; at seventeen he was crowned laureate at the
Jeux Floraux of Toulouse ; at eighteen, in collaboration
with his brothers, Abel and Eugène, he started a journal,
Le Conservateur Littéraire, in support of the conservative
party in politics and poetry. In 1822 he published his
first volume of verse under the title of *Odes et Poésies
Diverses*, and four years later reissued this, with many
additions, as *Odes et Ballades*. So far as the contents of
the first collection are concerned, they give little suggestion of originality either in matter or in form, but in the
new ballads there is an unmistakable tendency towards
freshness of subject, metrical freedom, and picturesqueness (*e.g.*, *La Chasse du Burgrave ; Le Pas d'Armes du Roi
Jean*). Then in 1829 came *Les Orientales*, and in this we
are in the full tide of romanticism. Interest in the East,
as Hugo points out in his preface, was very strong in
France at the time, and of this he takes advantage ; but
in so doing he turns it to propagandist account ; " il lui
semble," he writes of himself, " que jusqu'ici on a beau-

coup trop vu l'époque moderne dans le siècle de Louis XIV et l'antiquité dans Rome et la Grèce : ne verrait-on pas de plus haut et plus loin, en étudiant l'ère moderne dans le moyen âge et l'antiquité dans l'Orient ? " Many of his poems are to a certain extent topical in the sense that they are directly or indirectly connected with the Greek war of independence in which Byron had recently laid down his life ; others are lyrics or ballads of a miscellaneous character ; but whatever the theme, they are all marked by gorgeous colouring, intensity of passion, and astonishing skill in versification. In the range and variety of its metrical effects the little book came indeed as a revelation to its first readers, who were equally surprised by the author's happy revival of some of the measures of the older French poets, as in *Sara la Baigneuse*, and by his inventive daring in such a marvellous *tour de force* as *Les Djinns*. Meanwhile Hugo had thrown himself with characteristic impetuosity into the struggle of the romantics with the classics for possession of the stage (*Cromwell*, 1827 ; *Hernani*, 1830), and was also busy with prose romance (*Bug-Jargal*, published 1826, though written earlier ; *Hans d'Islande*, 1823 ; *Notre-Dame de Paris*, 1831) ; but of his work then and later in the drama and the novel we will deal in other places. Four new volumes of verse followed in the next few years—*Les Feuilles d'Automne* in 1831, *Les Chants du Crépuscule* in 1835, *Les Voix Intérieures* in 1837, and *Les Rayons et les Ombres* in 1840—in all of which, though the range of their subject was very wide, the personal note was strong, and which together represent the full maturity of his genius and technique. Politics now began to divide his attention with literature. At the outset a conservative, he had been a warm supporter of the Bourbons ; then he transferred his allegiance to Louis Philippe, by whom he was made a peer (1845) ; but by this time his liberal tendencies were in the ascendant ; after the revolution of 1848 he sat in the Constituent Assembly ; and he was one of those who, in 1851, vainly attempted to rouse the people of Paris against the *coup d'état* by which Louis Napoleon overthrew the constitution and prepared the way for the Second Empire. In consequence he was banished, and for eighteen years lived in exile, first in Jersey, where he discharged his indignation in the bitter political satires of *Les Châtiments* (1852), and their prose counterpart, *Napoléon le Petit* (1853), and then from 1855 to 1870 in Guernsey, where, reverting to literature, he produced a fine volume of verse, *Les Contemplations* (1856), the first part of *La Légende des Siècles* (1859), *Les Chansons des Rues et des Bois* (1865), a curious volume, nominally criticism, really rhapsody, called *William Shakespeare* (1864), and three romances, *Les Misérables* (1862), *Les Travailleurs de la Mer* (1866), and *L'Homme qui rit* (1869). On the fall of the Empire he returned to France, a convinced radical and republican, and from that time to his death in 1885 he was the idol of the French people, who saw in him the very incarnation of the spirit and aspirations of their new democracy. To these closing years belong in verse, among numerous other volumes, *L'Année Terrible* (1871), *L'Art d'être Grandpère* (1877), and the second and third parts of *La Légende des Siècles* (1877, 1883), and in prose, a last romance, *Quatre-Vingt-Treize*.

There is a general consensus of opinion among the critics, native and foreign, that Hugo is the greatest of French poets and one of the greatest of all the poets of modern times. His defects are indeed many and obvious. He was, it is admitted, a good deal of a poseur ; his thought is superficial ; his sentiment is often forced and theatrical ; he is wanting in self-control and in balance ;

he indulges too frequently in mere rhetorical declamation ; his style is at times vitiated by his love of emphasis and antithesis, and his craving for striking and grandiose effects. These faults are especially conspicuous in the poetry of his later years (*e.g.*, *Le Pape*, 1878 ; *L'Âne*, 1879 ; *Religions et Religion*, 1880 ; *Les Quatre Vents de l'Esprit*, 1881), in which he loses himself entirely in nebulous metaphysics and his diction, overloaded with mannerisms, degenerates into a kind of caricature of itself. But when all deductions have been made and we have cleared away a vast amount of perishable material, there remains a body of work immense at once in bulk and range, and stamped with all the highest qualities of poetic genius : prodigious imagination, intensity of vision, astonishing descriptive power, supreme command of all the resources of language, verbal magic, and, on the purely technical side, a virtuosity which has never been excelled. His extraordinary versatility must also be recognised as an element in his greatness. He is the poet of public events and of domestic joys and sorrows ; of the mighty movements of history and of the humble realities of common life ; of romantic passion and the social enthusiasms of the modern world ; of nature no less than of man ; and his verse adjusts itself with absolute perfection to every mood and theme. Much of his poetry is intimately personal in character. But his conception of the powers and functions of poetry was far larger than that of Lamartine or of the romantics in general. He held that in writing of himself the poet should constitute himself the interpreter of that common humanity to which he belongs (Preface to *Contemplations*) and of the whole complex life of his own time (Preface to *Les Rayons et les Ombres*) ; and, for himself, he declares that universal sympathy and the ability, as it were, to gather up and express what the world about him was thinking and feeling, was the ultimate secret of his own poetic success :

> C'est que l'amour, la tombe, et la gloire, et la vie,
> L'onde qui fuit, par l'onde incessament suivie,
> Tout souffle, tout rayon, ou prospice ou fatal,
> Fait reluire et vibrer mon âme de cristal,
> Mon âme aux mille voix, que le Dieu que j'adore
> Mit au centre de tout comme un echo sonore.[1]

Hence the humanitarianism which is throughout a fundamental characteristic of Hugo's poetry, and which expresses itself now in passionate hatred of injustice, oppression, and cruelty, and now in infinite pity for all feeble and defenceless creatures — the old, the poor, the outcast, children, animals. In the comprehensiveness of his sympathy he even found a place for the toad, the spider, the nettle, which he loved because they were generally despised and hated.[2] From this point of view special interest attaches to *La Légende des Siècles*, on the whole the completest embodiment of his philosophy. Suggested apparently by Michelet's *La Bible de l'Humanité*, this gigantic work was intended as an epic of man, in which " successivement et simultanément sous tous ses aspects, histoire, fable, philosophie, religion, science," all the great movements of the world should be depicted " depuis Ève, mère des hommes, jusqu'à la Révolution, mère des peuples " (Preface). This vast design—the vastest perhaps that has ever fired the imagination of any poet—was not fully carried out in the work itself; [3] there are many serious gaps

---

[1] *Les Feuilles d'Automne*, i.

[2] See, *e.g.*, the beautiful but terrible *Le Crapaud* (*Légende des Siècles*), with its plea for " ce pauvre être ayant pour crime d'être laid " ; and *Les Contemplations*, III. xxvii.

[3] Two other poems were designed to supplement the work, *Dieu* and *La Fin de Satan*. These were published after Hugo's death, the latter having been left unfinished by him.

in it ; much of its matter is very insufficiently handled ; and it suffers from want of uniformity and method. But it none the less contains the poet's reading of history and his interpretation of human life. His central thought is that of progress : " Du reste, ces poèmes, divers par le sujet, mais inspirés par la même pensée, n'ont entre eux d'autre nœud qu'un fil qui s'atténue quelquefois au point de devenir invisible, mais qui ne casse jamais, le grand fil mystérieux du labyrinthe humain, le Progrès." In detail the work is gloomy : " Les tableaux riants sont rares dans ce livre ; cela tient à ce qu'ils ne sont pas fréquents dans l'histoire." But its thesis is profoundly optimistic, for to Hugo, with his firm faith in God, in man, and in the future, all history seemed to resolve itself into " un seul et immense mouvement d'ascension vers la lumière."

59. VIGNY.—We enter a very different intellectual atmosphere when we pass from Hugo to the next poet on our list. Alfred Victor, Comte de Vigny, was born at Loches in 1797. He came of a family of soldiers, and at sixteen entered the army. But his literary taste soon asserted itself ; in 1820 he became attached to the romantics and collaborated with Hugo in the *Conservateur* ; in 1822 he published his first volume of verse ; and in 1826 an enlarged edition of this and an historical romance, *Cinq-Mars*. Fourteen years of military service having filled him with disgust with the dull routine of garrison life, he then definitely exchanged the sword for the pen. For some years he devoted himself to the stage (*Othello*, 1829 ; *La Maréchale d'Ancre*, 1831 ; *Chatterton*, 1835) and to prose romance (*Stello*, 1832 ; *Grandeur et Servitude Militaires*, 1835), but except in the case of *Chatterton* he never achieved the popular success of Lamartine or Hugo. Like these two famous contem-

poraries he was presently drawn into politics, but failing to find the opening he sought he abandoned all thought of a public career and retired, with his invalid wife, an Englishwoman whom he had married in 1828, to the solitude of the Château du Maine-Giraud in Charente. He died of a cancer from which he had long suffered while on a visit to Paris in 1863.

As compared with Lamartine, Hugo, and the romantics generally, Vigny was singularly unproductive, for his collected poems, numbering only thirty-five in all, are comprised in a volume of some three hundred pages. Apart from the posthumous *Les Destinées, Poèmes Philosophiques*, which include much of his finest work (*La Colère de Samson, La Mort du Loup, Le Mont des Oliviers, La Bouteille à la Mer, L'Esprit Pur*), these fall, according to his own scheme, into three divisions : *Livre Mystique* (*e.g., Moïse, Éloa, Le Déluge*) ; *Livre Antique*, in two subdivisions—*Antiquité Biblique* (*La Fille de Jephté*, etc.) and *Antiquité Homérique* (*La Dryade*, etc.) ; and *Livre Moderne* (*Dolorida, Le Cor, La Frégate La Sérieuse*, etc.). But while his matter varies his distinctive qualities are everywhere the same. His conceptions are always noble and his temper heroic ; he is, though a very unequal, a very great artist ; his style is characterised by remarkable dignity and strength ; and if at times we may find him a little cold, we cannot fail to be impressed by the stately and sculpturesque beauty of his verse. Above all, however, he appeals to us by the weight and solidity of his thought. Vigny was essentially an intellectual poet, and though he expressed his ideas not in direct argument but through symbols,[1] a consistent and well-considered philosophy lies at the foundation of

[1] " Le seul mérite qu'on n'ait jamais disputé à ces compositions, c'est d'avoir dévancé en France toutes celles de ce genre, dans lesquelles une pensée philosophique est mise en scène sous une forme épique ou dramatique " (Preface to edition of 1837).

his work. The keynote of that philosophy is pessimism. A proud, unhappy man, who seemed even to those who knew him best "olympian" and austere,[1] but whose apparent insensibility concealed unsuspected depths of passion and sympathy, Vigny was profoundly moved by the doom which so often overwhelms the man of genius in a world which is blind to his greatness and deaf to his message. This is the theme elaborated in *Stello* in the histories of three young unfortunate poets, Gilbert, Chatterton, and André Chénier ; it is the theme of *Chatterton* (a dramatic version of the narrative in *Stello*), which depicts " l'homme spiritualiste étouffé pas une société matérialiste " ; it is again the theme, under slight variations, of *Moïse*, *Éloa*, *La Colère de Samson*, *Le Mont des Oliviers*. But while the aristocratic bias of his mind led him to dwell upon the exceptional tragedies of rare and superior natures, he was equally touched by the infinite misery of the common lot of man, and in brooding over this he could find no relief in the ordinary consolations of the moralists, since to him love was a delusion and a snare (*La Colère de Samson*), Nature, chanted by the romantic poets as the beneficent mother of men, only their living tomb (*La Maison du Berger*), and God Himself " sourd aux cris de ses créatures." Vigny's pessimism was thus a very different thing from the sentimental melancholy which a generation which had nourished itself on *René* often cultivated as a fashionable pose, for it was the product at once of temperament and of reasoned conviction. It is, moreover, the pessimism not of a whimperer but of a stoic, who, failing to wring from an indifferent

---

[1] Sainte-Beuve's description of his moral isolation—

> Et Vigny, plus secret,
> Comme en sa tour d'ivoire, avant midi, rentrait—

has long been famous.

heaven any answer to his prayers, is strong enough
to reply

> par un froid silence
> Au silence éternel de la Divinité,[1]

to meet life with a fortitude sustained by the inspiration
of a high ideal (*L'Esprit Pur*), and to face death like the
wolf driven to bay by the huntsmen :

> Gémir, pleurer, prier, est également lâche.
> Fais énergiquement ta longue et lourde tâche
> Dans la voie où le sort a voulu t'appeler,
> Puis, après, comme moi, souffre et meurs sans parler.[2]

For the rest, Vigny's is not a philosophy of mere passive
resignation ; as the superb *Bouteille à la Mer* is written to
demonstrate, every man may find a measure of heroic
satisfaction in work done without thought of reward for
the benefit of humanity. Vigny, as will be seen, is not a
poet for those who love smooth things. Many readers
will doubtless be repelled by his temper and shocked by
his pessimism. But there are others to whom his work
will yield "steel and bark for the mind."

60. MUSSET.—After the poet of virile thought, the
poet of youthful passion. The son of a wealthy official
in the War Office, Alfred de Musset was born in Paris in
1810. While still in his teens he was admitted to Hugo's
cénacle, and at twenty published a volume of dramatic,
narrative, and lyrical verse, *Contes d'Espagne et d'Italie*,
which, while it scandalised the old-fashioned critics by its
ostentatious Byronism, rather frightened the romantics
themselves by its audacity and its extravagances. As
the sequel proved, however, the young poet was as yet
hardly in earnest. Precociously clever, and fully alive
to his cleverness, he had found amusement in imitating

---

[1] *Le Mont des Oliviers.*   [2] *La Mort du Loup.*

the method and style of his friends ; but in his imitation there was a good deal of wilful exaggeration (*e.g.* in his excessive dislocation of the alexandrine), and in the exaggeration something at least of burlesque ; as in the famous *Ballade à la Lune*, which seemed to the classics the last word in romantic impertinence, but which many critics now regard as a kind of caprice, and even as more than half a parody. At any rate he soon abandoned romanticism as a formal creed and went his own way, convinced—and in this he was true to its inner spirit— that the one thing necessary for a poet was, not to have a theory, but, theory or no theory, to find himself and to be himself. His next volume, *Un Spectacle dans un Fauteuil*, comprising two dramatic pieces—*La Coupe et les Lèvres* and *À Quoi rêvent les Jeunes Filles* — and a poem, *Namouna*, in the manner of Byron's *Don Juan*, appeared in 1832, and this was followed during the next few years by other plays and poems in the *Revue des Deux Mondes*. Meanwhile he had passed through the great crisis of his life, his *liaison* with George Sand. The poet and the novelist met in 1833 ; their friendship quickly ripened into love, and at the end of the year they set out together for a tour in Italy. But misunderstandings soon arose between them, and Musset returned to Paris a disillusioned and embittered man (see his autobiographical novel *Les Confessions d'un Enfant du Siècle*, 1836). His disappoint- ment and the mental agony which followed had a dis- astrous effect upon his excitable nature. They stimulated his genius, it is true, and during the next five years he produced his finest work in verse and prose ; [1] but unfor- tunately he sought an escape from his unhappiness in

---

[1] His prose includes, besides the *Confessions*, a number of admirable stories, published at intervals and collected under the title *Contes et Nouvelles*. His plays will be referred to in the next chapter.

dissipation, and in the end became a victim to drink. With his physical and intellectual powers fatally under-mined he sank deeper and deeper into debauchery, and died of heart disease in 1857.

Despite his impatient rejection of all special dogmas and programmes,[1] Musset, by reason of the strong quality of personal emotion which is the foundation of his work, remained a romantic among the romantics and " le type du romantisme sentimental." [2] " Chacun de nous," he wrote early in life to his brother, " a dans le ventre un certain son qu'il peut rendre, comme un violin ou une clarinette. Tous les raisonnements du monde ne pour-raient faire sortir du gossier d'un merle la chanson du sansonnet " ; and this thought of the poet's dependence upon the inspiration of his own nature reappears fre-quently in his verse, as, *e.g.* :

> Tu te frappais le front en lisant Lamartine.
> Ah ! frappe-toi le cœur ; c'est là qu'est le génie,[3]

and

> On m'a dit l'an passé que j'imitais Byron :
> Vous qui me connaissez, vous savez bien que non.
> Je hais comme la mort l'état de plagiaire ;
> Mon verre n'est pas grand, mais je bois dans mon verre.[4]

It is such absolute sincerity to himself, in all his varying moods of pure sentiment, burning passion, bitter irony, tender regret, joy, and sorrow, that gives a distinctive and peculiar charm to his finest (which is always his most

---

[1] For his attitude towards the literary theories and quarrels of his time, see *Dédicace* to *Un Spectacle dans un Fauteuil* and *Les Secrètes Pensées de Raphael* ; for an amusing satire on the attempts of the romantics to define their own aims, the caustic *Lettres de Dupuis et de Cotonet* (1836).

[2] Strowski, *Tableau de la Littérature Française au XIXᵉ Siècle*, 194-5.

[3] *À mon Ami, Édouard B.*

[4] *Dédicace, Un Spectacle dans un Fauteuil.*

directly personal) poetry — to his *Lettre à Lamartine*,
L'Espoir en Dieu, *Le Souvenir*, and the four wonderful
lyrics, *Les Nuits*, which rank in their kind among the
supreme masterpieces of French poetry. His range is
narrow ; he is often negligent in technique ; and sometimes he may give offence by his frank sensuality (as
in *Rolla*), and by what Lintilhac has aptly called his
"Dandysme à la Brummel." But his place with the
greatest of French lyrical poets is secure. That place
has been well defined by M. Pierre Robert. "C'est
le poète de la jeunesse. Il a chanté le plaisir avec une
pointe de libertinage ; puis, frappé au cœur d'un amour
violent et tragique, il a chanté la passion avec une puis-
sance incomparable. Il est le plus personnel de nos poètes,
le plus sincère, le plus vrai." [1]

61. GAUTIER.—Another poet who, like Musset, was
admitted while still very young to the inner circle of the
romantic brotherhood was Pierre Jules Théophile Gautier.
Born in 1811 at Tarbes in the Hautes-Pyrénées, Gautier,
though he was taken to Paris when a child of three,
retained throughout his life his "fond méridional" and a
craving for warm climates and blue skies. His first
ambition was to become a painter, and to this end he
entered the studio of Rioult. But the influence of his
friend Gérard de Nerval,[2] who had been a fellow-student
of his at the Lycée Charlemagne, turned his attention from
art to literature, and, introduced to the *cénacle*, he became

---

[1] *Les Poètes du XIXᵉ Siècle*, p. 377.

[2] Gérard Labrunie, who assumed the name of de Nerval (1808–55),
was one of the many eccentrics who figure in the history of romanticism.
He led a restless, wandering, dissipated life which ended in insanity
and suicide. His *Aurélie, ou le Rêve et la Vie* (1855) has a curious and
painful interest as a record of his own madness. He wrote poems,
plays, essays, and some really fine fantastic stories collected under the
title of *Contes et Facéties*. His translation of *Faust* was highly praised
by Goethe himself.

an enthusiastic worshipper of Hugo, and one of his most ardent supporters in the great " battle of *Hernani* " (see *post*, pp. 226-7).   His first volume of verse, which appeared in 1832, fell flat, but in 1833 he scored a success (which was perhaps to some extent a " success of scandal ") with *Albertus, ou l'Âme et le Péché*, which he himself described as a " légende théologique," but is in fact a wild tale of sorcery, sensuous in tone and full of the " satanism " which was very much to the taste of a time which revelled in everything connected with the black art.   One feature of this poem—its high pictorial quality—deserves special attention because it remained a characteristic of Gautier's work to the end.   It has often been said of him that though he early gave up the brush for the pen he never ceased to be a painter, and as we can see at once from the famous description of the Flemish landscape with which his story opens, his imaginative conceptions took the form of pictures :

> Sur le bord d'un canal profond dont les eaux vertes
> Dorment, de nénufars et de bateaux couvertes,
> Avec ses toits aigus, ses immenses greniers,
> Ses tours au front d'ardoise où nichent les cigognes,
> Ses cabarets bruyants qui regorgent d'ivrognes,
> Est un vieux bourg flamand tel que les peint Teniers.
> Vous reconnaissez-vous ?   Tenez, voilà le saule
> De ses cheveux blafards inondants son épaule
> Comme une fille au bain, l'église et son clocher,
> L'étang où des canards se pavane l'escadre ;
> Il ne manque vraiment au tableau que le cadre
>   Avec le clou pour l'accrocher.

While this firmly plastic quality—this admirable sense of form, colour, and composition—were conspicuous in it throughout, the poem was conceived and executed in the most extravagant spirit of romanticism.   Yet in the same year, in a collection of stories and sketches entitled *Les*

Jeune France, Gautier, with delightful humour, poured ridicule upon the very excesses in which he had himself indulged, and upon the emotional frenzy, the mediæval-ism, and the puerile affectations of the young men of his generation who had been swept off their feet by the romantic tide (*e.g.*, *Onuphrius, ou les Vexations fantastiques d'un Admirateur d'Hoffmann ; Daniel Jovard, ou la Conversion d'un Classique; Elias Wildmanstadius, ou l'Homme Moyen Âge*). At the same time a volume of critical studies in the by-ways of seventeenth-century literature, *Les Grotesques*, showed his keen interest in such long-neglected writers as Cyrano de Bergerac and Scarron, in whom he recognised the real forerunners of modern romanticism. In 1835 he published a brilliantly written but daringly licentious romance, *Mademoiselle de Maupin*, in which he endeavoured, and most successfully, to shock the " philistines," and in 1838 a second long poem, *La Comédie de la Mort*, still, like *Albertus*, romantic in theme, but far more restrained in style. By this time, however, he had been compelled by necessity, though much against his will, to turn to journalism for support, and from 1836 to nearly the end of his life the greater part of his energy was given to task-work as a critic of literature, the drama, and the *salons*. His leisure he spent in extensive travels in Italy, Spain, Turkey, and Russia, turning his experiences to good account in a number of entertaining and picturesque books. Yet amid the incessant claims of the press he still found time for pure literature. His remaining works include *Émaux et Camées* (1852), which contains his finest verse ; in fiction, *Le Capitaine Fracasse* (1863), a novel of adventure on the lines of *Le Roman Comique*, and generally considered his masterpiece in prose ; *Le Roman de la Momie* (1858) ; many shorter novels and tales (*e.g.*, *Fortunio, Une Nuit de Cléopâtre, Jean et Jeanette, Jetta-*

tura, Avatar, La Belle Jenny, La Peau de Tigre, Spirite) ;
two charming animal books, *Le Paradis des Chats* (he had
a passion for cats) and *Ménagerie Intime,* and a curious
Histoire du Romantisme. He died in 1874.

Gautier was not a thinker ; he had no theories to
expound ; he did not trouble himself about politics, or
social movements, or moral problems of any kind (Preface
to *Émaux et Camées*). His philosophy, such as it was,
was purely epicurean : its beginning and its end was his
love of all beautiful things.

> Il est dans la nature, il est de belles choses,
> Des rossignols oisifs, de paresseuses roses,
> Des poètes rêveurs et des musiciens
> Qui s'inquiètent peu d'être bons citoyens,
> Qui vivent au hasard, et n'ont d'autre maxime,
> Sinon que tout est bien, pourvu qu'on ait la rime,
> Et que les oiseaux bleus, penchant leurs cols pensifs,
> Écoutent le récit de leurs amours naïfs ; [1]

and to this race of happy useless creatures he himself
rejoiced to belong.   He was, in a word, the pure artist, for
whom art was an end in itself, and not a means to an end,
and for whom beauty had no connection with utility.   " À
quoi cela sert-il ? " he asks in the preface to his first poems,
and he replies : " Cela sert à être beau.   N'est-ce pas
assez ?   Comme les fleures, comme les parfums, commes
les oiseaux, comme tout ce que l'homme n'a pu détourner
et dépraver à son usage."   The great virtue of his work
is the perfection of its technique, its pictorial quality,
its fine sensuousness, its feeling for form and colour.
" Tout ma valeur," he once told the Goncourts, " est que
je suis un homme pour qui le monde visible existe," and
it was this constant realisation of the visible world as
providing in itself sufficient matter for poetry which set

---

[1] *À un Jeune Tribun.*   Cp. *L'Art* in *Émaux et Camées.*

him in a class apart from the romantics in general, with their intense subjectivity, their preoccupation with their own emotions, and their tendency to effusive lyrism.

62. OTHER POETS.—Among the minor poets of the earlier nineteenth century by far the most interesting to us to-day is Pierre Jean de Béranger (1780–1857), the greatest song-writer that France has ever produced. The amazing popularity which he enjoyed during his lifetime, and which was in part due to his politics—a combination of ardent democracy and devotion to the memory of Napoleon—has indeed been followed within recent years by a reaction which was perhaps inevitable, and criticism is now inclined to treat him with a rather supercilious contempt. Against this official attitude of depreciation, however, a protest should certainly be made. Béranger was a lyrical poet of real genius and inspiration ; he wrote with equal success on many subjects and in many tones ; and the best of his *chansons* have never been surpassed for wit and pathos, lightness of touch, vivacity, and grace. Another poet who, like Béranger, was a strong opponent of the Bourbon Restoration was Jean François Casimir Delavigne (1793–1843), but though his political poems, *Les Messéniennes* (1815–22), created a great sensation at the time of their publication, they are noteworthy rather for their genuine patriotism than for their intrinsic poetical merits. A little later Henri Auguste Barbier (1805–82) also achieved fame as an unsparing satirist of the manners and morals of his age in *Les Iambes* (1831), a collection of poems vigorous in thought but rather coarse in style. Of his many remaining works only one is now remembered, *Il Pianto* (1833), which was inspired by the writer's love of Italy in the hour of its political degradation and servitude. Both Delavigne and Barbier owed much of their contemporary reputation to the " actuality " of their

subjects. The poems of Julien Auguste-Pélage Brizeux (1806–58), on the other hand, are entirely deficient in any such topical interest. Born at Lorient, and a Breton to his finger-tips, Brizeux was throughout his life inspired by a fervent love of his " terre natale "—" la terre de granit recouverte de chênes "—and of. the local legends on which his childish imagination had been fed, and this love was the chief inspiring motive of his verse—of his tender and graceful elegies in the series entitled *Marie* (1831), of his " épopée rustique," *Les Bretons* (1845), and of his *Histoires Poétiques* (1855), in which he drew upon the rich sources of Celtic romance. Brizeux never had a wide public and to-day he is almost completely forgotten. But he was a true poet, if not a great one, and now that the importance of the Celtic Renaissance in literature is recognised there should be an increasing number of readers for his work.

CHAPTER XII

THE EARLIER NINETEENTH CENTURY (concluded)

THE DRAMA AND THE NOVEL

63. THE ROMANTIC DRAMA.—The theatre was the great battle-ground of classicism and romanticism, and it was on the stage that romanticism secured its popular triumph. In the opening years of the nineteenth century classic tragedy, though still supported by the conservative critics, was obviously moribund. But meanwhile many influences were at work preparing the way for a renaissance of the drama in a form which should combine the literary qualities of classic tragedy with the abundant life and vigour of the sensational melodrama, which was the favourite amusement of the general theatre-going public. Mme. de Staël's *De l'Allemagne* had directed attention to the plays of Lessing, Goethe, and Schiller. Currency was given to Schlegel's severe and often prejudiced strictures upon the French school by Mme. Necker de Saussure's translation (1814) of his *Vorlesungen über dramatischen Kunst und Litteratur*. In particular, there was an increasing interest in Shakespeare, whom the classicists continued to disparage as rude and barbaric, but who for the romantics was " ce Dieu de théâtre en qui semblent réunis, comme dans une trinité . . . Corneille,

Molière, Beaumarchais " (Hugo's Preface to *Cromwell*). This interest was greatly stimulated by the appearance in 1821 of a revised edition of Pierre Le Tourneur's bad prose translation (1776–82), with an important introduction by Guizot, afterwards reprinted separately, by Stendhal's work, *Racine et Shakespeare*, and by the essays of Barante and Villemain ; while in 1827 a profound impression was made upon critics and public alike by a series of performances of Shakespeare by an English company in Paris. At the same time the periodical criticisms of the stage in journals of advanced opinions like *Le Globe* and *La Revue Française* helped to spread a feeling of dissatisfaction with the long-accepted conventions of tragedy and a desire for a fresh and freer type of art. Then in 1827 came Hugo's manifesto in his famous Preface to *Cromwell*, in which, amid much fantastic generalisation and a vast amount of rhodomontade, the writer's conceptions of the new romantic drama were boldly set forth. From this Preface, supplemented by the essays which he prefixed to some of his later plays, a clear view of the cardinal principles of the new school may be obtained. In the first place, Hugo proclaims the necessity of a return to nature, or realism. The drama should cease to present an idealised, that is, an artificially simplified, arranged, incomplete, and therefore falsified image of life. It should hold up the mirror to life itself in all its amplitude, variety, and contradictions. Its primary object should be truth—" la résurrection de la vie intégrale." Hence, as no such division exists in actual life, the old arbitrary distinction between tragedy and comedy must be abandoned : the drama must combine both in a single *genre* and find a place in its comprehensive framework for tears and laughter, beauty and ugliness, the sublime and the grotesque. But this return to nature further involves the substitution of the concrete individual for the abstract type ; for the truth to life which the dramatist is called upon to seek is truth, not to the broad features which are common to humanity at large, but to those infinite varieties of it which are produced by different conditions in different ages and countries. This theory of specific truth (which will be recognised as the application to the drama of the general romantic principle of individualism) in turn leads to what Hugo calls " la caractéristique," otherwise " la couleur locale." This for him is essential : " le drame doît être radicalement imprégné de cette couleur des temps ; elle doît en quelque sorte y être dans l'air, de façon qu'on s'apercoive qu'en y entrant et qu'en en sortant qu'on a changé de siècle et d'atmosphère." From all these considerations the rejection of the unities follows as a matter of course. " Croiser l'unité de temps à l'unité de lieu comme les barreaux d'une cage, et y faire pédantesquement entrer, de par Aristote, tous ces faits, tous ces peuples, toutes ces figures que la Providence déroule à si grandes masses dans la réalité ! C'est mutiler hommes et choses, c'est faire grimacer l'histoire." The new drama must be a free drama in form as well as in spirit, and this freedom must prevail no less in its versification. Hugo accepts the alexandrine as the best medium for the poetic drama, but it must be an alexandrine liberated from all external restraints and flexible enough to meet every demand of dialogue. " Malheur au poète si son vers fait la petite bouche ! "

The Preface to *Cromwell* brought the controversy of romanticism and classicism to a head. Two years later it culminated in the great " battle of *Hernani*," of which Gautier has left us a vivid account in his *Histoire du Romantisme*. On the first night of the play the Comédie

Française was packed with an excited crowd composed of the most fiery partisans of the rival schools. " Il suffisait de jeter les yeux sur ce public pour se convaincre qu'il ne s'agissait pas là d'une représentation ordinaire ; que deux systèmes, deux partis, deux armées, deux civilisations même—ce n'est pas trop dire—étaient en présence." All Young France had gathered there, impatient for the fray, conspicuous among its leaders being Gautier himself in his notorious " gilet rouge " ; " l'orchestre et le balcon étaient pavés de crânes académiques et classiques." From first to last the performance was accompanied by lively demonstrations of approval and protest ; every point was made the pretext for charge and countercharge ; the intervals were noisy with disputes in which the opponents sometimes came to blows; and in the end the curtain fell amid a storm. After this, the battle spread from the theatre to the press and raged for many days, but that historic night really assured the victory of romanticism.

64. DUMAS.—While, however, the date of this performance—February 25, 1830—is taken as marking the opening of a new era in the annals of the French drama, *Hernani* was in fact neither the first example nor the first success of romanticism on the stage. The new type of play in all its essentials, though in prose instead of verse, had already been created just a year before (February 11, 1829) by that amazing and fertile genius, Alexandre Dumas (see *post*, pp. 241-43) in his *Henri III et sa Cour*. " Je ne me déclarerai pas fondateur d'un genre," wrote Dumas himself, with his customary generosity, " parce que effectivement, je n'ai rien fondé," and he names among his forerunners Hugo (with reference to the unacted *Cromwell* and its Preface), Mérimée (see *post*, pp. 252-53), and the now-forgotten playwrights Vitet,[1]

---

[1] *Les Barricades, Les États de Blois, La Mort de Henri III* (1827–29).

Lœve-Veimars,[1] and Cavé and Dittmer ; [2] but notwithstanding his disclaimer, the honour of priority really
belongs to him. Independently or in collaboration Dumas
wrote many other plays of the historical-romantic kind, of
which the most important are *Richard d'Arlington* (1831)
and *La Tour de Nesle* (1832), while in *Antony* (1831) he
achieved an equal triumph in the domestic tragedy of
modern life. The real sources of his dramatic inspiration
must undoubtedly be sought in the popular *mélodrame*,
which he simply vitalised by sheer power of genius. In
the higher literary qualities his plays are patently deficient ; in execution they are often crude ; they depend too
much upon purely theatrical tricks and devices ; their
psychology has neither depth nor solidity ; their style,
judged merely as style, is poor. But whatever their
defects as literature, they have extraordinary merits as
plays. As we can realise even in reading them, Dumas
had the keenest sense of the stage. His technique is
bold and simple ; the interest of his plots begins with
the very beginning and is sustained with unflagging
energy to the end ; his dialogue is vivacious and eminently
dramatic ; his characters act their parts before our eyes.
To find examples of these qualities we need go no farther
than *Henri III* and *Antony*. The former is full of life,
movement, and passion, and while it is easy enough to
sneer at the latter as " glorified melodrama," it is still
a masterpiece of clever construction with a *dénouement*
which is one of the most striking on the modern
stage.

65. HUGO.—But though Dumas possessed all the
powers requisite for popular success, he was not the man
to convince the critics of the poetic possibilities of the new

---

[1] *Scènes Contemporaines* and *Scènes Historiques* (1827–30).
[2] *Les Soirées de Neuilly, Esquisses Dramatiques et Historiques* (1827).

type of play. For this a great poet was needed, and such a great poet appeared in Hugo.

As we have seen, Hugo had scarcely won his laurels as a lyrist when he turned his attention to the drama. His first play, *Cromwell*, a huge, straggling piece, which fills a volume of more than 300 pages, was not intended for the stage, and as it stands is quite unactable, but it led the way to *Marion Delorme* (written in 1829 but, prohibited by the censor, not performed till 1831) and *Hernani*. Then followed *Le Roi s'amuse* (1832) ; three dramas in prose, of inferior quality—*Lucrèce Borgia* (1833), *Marie Tudor* (1833), and *Angelo, Tyran de Padoue* (1835) ; *Ruy Blas* (1838), which repeated the brilliant success of *Hernani* ; and a grandiose and incoherent " mélodrame épique," *Les Burgraves* (1843). After the failure of this last effort Hugo renounced the stage. His remaining work in the drama comprises a collection of fanciful little pieces entitled *Le Théâtre en Liberté*, and published after his death, and a five-act tragedy, *Torquemada* (1882).

Hugo's dramatic theories have been sufficiently explained, and it is only necessary now to say that his own plays are written in accordance with them. Yet when we compare his principles with his practice a number of serious inconsistencies come to light. While he rejects the artificial simplicity and dignity of classic tragedy, his return to nature most emphatically does not result in a return to truth, for life as he depicts it is life seen through the medium of an imagination which magnifies and distorts everything he looks at. Even the local colour to which he attached so much importance, and of which he makes such prodigal use, is scarcely more than superficial ; he obtains some wonderfully picturesque effects from the setting of his actions and his minutely detailed reproduction of the manners of the different times and places in which he lays his scenes; but his interpretation of history is as a rule unsound. Moreover, at two other points not yet referred to he fails conspicuously to fulfil the conditions enunciated in his own programme. The dramatist, he had insisted, should avoid the " tirades " of the classic stage, and be careful always, instead of speaking for his characters, to allow them to speak for themselves. But these excellent precepts are perpetually ignored by him. His plays are full of " tirades," often very eloquent and impressive in themselves (instance the great monologue of Don Carlos in *Hernani*, iv. 2), but still " tirades "; while one of his principal failings as a dramatist is his want of objectivity, that is, his inability to stand outside his plot and his characters. Even in theory he had confused the functions of lyrism and of the drama; " c'est surtout la poésie lyrique qui sied au drame," he had written in the Preface to *Cromwell*; and this fundamentally vicious misconception is illustrated at large in his own work. For his plays are not simply poetic; they are essentially operatic, their dialogues continually overflowing into a lyrism altogether in excess of the demands of the situation in hand and often dramatically out of keeping with it. These are grave defects. But even more important are the violence of his plots and the unreality of his characterisation. His ultra-romantic intrigues are fabricated without reference to the logic of events; in his love of sensation he has recourse to the crudest devices and spectacular accessories of melodrama; he revels in the monstrous, in the physically horrible, in the grotesque, which is his substitute for comedy. And as with incident, so with character: truth to nature is everywhere sacrificed to mere effect. His men and women are in a sense alive;

but they live only with the factitious life of the world
beyond the footlights ; they are not so much individuals
as gigantic embodiments of passion—typical creations of
the romantic imagination, like Didier, Hernani, Don Ruy
Gomès de Silva, Ruy Blas, Don César de Bazan, or
strange, incredible compounds of unresolved contradictions, like Cromwell, Lucrèce Borgia, Triboulet. In view
of all these weaknesses it is impossible to class Hugo
among the really great dramatists of the world. But
we must not therefore overlook the extraordinary qualities
which, if they do not redeem his shortcomings, often
make us blind to them—his tremendous power of imagination, his boundless vigour, his wealth of passion, the skill
with which he works up his situations to the highest pitch
of emotional intensity, and beyond and above all, the
marvellous beauty of much of his poetry. We may find
what fault we will with *Hernani* on the score of its fundamental theatricality ; but the wonderful love-duet in the
fifth act deserves to be placed beside the balcony scene
in *Romeo and Juliet*.

66. VIGNY.—Two other writers who have already been
considered as poets also claim attention among the
dramatists of the earlier nineteenth century—Vigny and
Musset.

The contrast which we have noted between Vigny and
Hugo as poets reappears in their work as dramatists, for
while Hugo's plays are compounded of sensational interest
and passionate lyrism, Vigny's belong to the literature of
psychology and thought. His theory of the drama was
entirely romantic : " La scène française," he wrote in
1829, and therefore before the issue had been decided,
" s'ouvrira-t-elle, oui ou non, à une tragédie moderne,
produisant : dans sa conception un tableau large de la
vie, au lieu d'un tableau resserré de la catastrophe d'une

intrigue ; dans sa composition, des caractères, non des rôles, des scènes paisibles sans drame, mêlées à des scènes comiques et tragiques ; dans son exécution, un style familier, comique, tragique, et parfois épique ? " But while he was thus at one with his romantic contemporaries in his general view of the drama, his own distinctive quality is suggested rather by his further remark that " si l'art est une fable, il doît être une fable philosophique " (Preface to *La Maréchale d'Ancre*). He began with two translations, both in verse, from Shakespeare—*Shylock* (1828), which was never acted, and *Othello* (1829), the success of which undoubtedly contributed to the triumph of the romantic cause.[1] His original dramatic work consists of three plays only—a comedy in one act, *Quitte pour la Peur* (1833), and two tragedies in prose, *La Maréchale d'Ancre* (1831) and *Chatterton* (1835). The former of these is an historical study of the minority of Louis XIII., and is, according to the author's own statement, designed to illustrate a number of ideas, and primarily that of the power of destiny, " contre laquelle nous luttons toujours, mais qui l'emporte sur nous dès que le caractère s'affaiblit ou s'altère, et qui, d'un pas très sûr, nous mène à ses fins mystérieuses, et souvent à l'expiation, par des voies impossibles à prévoir." Conscientiously and carefully wrought, this piece however impresses us more by its intellectuality than by its creative force, and while it may still be read with interest, its failure on the stage can easily be understood. *Chatterton*, on the other hand,

---

[1] Dumas, in his *Mémoires*, describes the excitement of the romantics in anticipation of the first performance of this play : " Cette future représentation *d'Othello* faisait grand bruit. Quoique nous eussions mieux aimé être soutenus par des troupes nationales et par un général français, nous comprenions qu'il fallait accepter les armes qu'on nous apportait contre nos ennemis du moment, de l'instant surtout où ces armes sortaient de l'arsenal de notre grand maître à tous, Shakespeare."

has genuine dramatic power, and power of a kind quite different from that which we find in the plays of Dumas or Hugo. Of its central thesis—the tragedy of genius in a materialistic society—and of the connection of this with Vigny's general philosophy, we have already spoken. The point now to emphasise is that this is presented as a tragedy not of outward incident but of the inner life. "Je crois surtout à l'avenir et au besoin universel de choses sérieuses," Vigny declares in his Preface ; " maintenant que l'amusement des yeux par des surpris enfantins fait sourir tout le monde au milieu même de ses grandes aventures, c'est, ce me semble, le temps du *Drame de la Pensée*." And it is entirely as a " drame de la pensée," or psychological drama, that *Chatterton* must be judged. " L'action matérielle est assez peu de chose. . . . C'est l'histoire d'un homme qui a écrit une lettre le matin et qui attend la réponse jusqu'au soir ; elle arrive, et le tue. Mais l'action morale est tout." In working out his theme Vigny purposely confines himself to the severest simplicity of intrigue, and thus approximates to the type rather of the classic than of the romantic drama. But this, like his adherence to the unity of time, is the result of his deliberate concentration of interest, and has nothing whatever to do with mere academic theory. As the title of the play must necessarily be specially attractive to English readers it may be well to add that Vigny did not attempt to give a literal version of the boy-poet's fate. Kitty Bell, her avaricious and jealous husband " gonflé d'ale, de porter et de roastbeef," the good old quaker, Beckford the Lord Mayor, the young Lord Talbot, are all creatures of the imagination, and Chatterton himself is pure idealisation. " Le Poète était tout pour moi ; Chatterton n'était qu'un nom d'homme, et je viens d'écarter à dessein des faits exacts de sa vie pour ne prendre de sa destinée que ce qui la rend un example à jamais déplorable d'une noble misère."

67. MUSSET.—After the success of his *Contes d'Espagne et d'Italie* Musset turned to the drama, but the failure of his one-act play *La Nuit Vénitienne* (1831) was so decisive that he determined to write no more for the stage, and though he continued to use the dramatic form he did so without reference to the practical conditions of representation. Towards the end of his life, indeed, the histrionic possibilities of his plays were suddenly discovered, and henceforth they had their secure place on the boards. But the fact that they were conceived and executed without thought of the mechanical necessities of actual performance is important because it explains one of their salient features—their entire freedom from everything suggestive of theatrical convention. From this point of view Musset is by far the most romantic of the romantic dramatists. His earliest work, *La Coupe et les Lèvres*, a curious compound of Byron and *Die Räuber* of Schiller, and *À Quoi rêvent les Jeunes Filles*, a graceful but fragile fantasy, were, like *Les Marrons du Feu* in the volume of 1830, merely experimental. But his real power was soon shown in the tragi-comedy *On ne badine pas avec l'Amour* and the fine study of character, *Lorenzaccio* (1834). These and the other dramas which from time to time he published in the *Revue des Deux Mondes* were ultimately collected under the general title of *Comédies et Proverbes* (*e.g.*, *Les Caprices de Marianne, André del Sarte, Il ne faut jurer de rien, Il faut qu'une Porte soit ouverte ou fermée*). Many influences have been detected in Musset's dramatic work ; there is something in it of Shakespeare, something of Byron, something of Racine, something of Molière, Marivaux, and Beaumarchais. But in reading it we are after all most impressed by its originality ; it is, we feel,

his work and his alone—work that no other writer could have done. As we should anticipate, he excels particularly in the treatment of love, which he portrays under many aspects, now with delicate badinage, now with tragic intensity, but always with wonderful subtlety and discrimination. His plays abound in fancy, wit, and poetry, and whether in verse or in prose they are characterised by an unfailing charm of style. As literature they must undoubtedly be regarded as the finest products of the romantic drama of their time.

68. OTHER DRAMATISTS.—While the struggle of the romantics and the classics was at its height, one writer of some distinction—the author of *Les Messéniennes*—endeavoured to keep a middle course between the two extremes. Delavigne's first play, written before the romantic movement on the stage had begun, *Les Vêpres Siciliennes* (1819), was entirely classic in form and style, and the enthusiasm with which it was received seemed for the moment to augur well for a revival of the older type of tragedy. But his *Marino Faliero*, produced between *Henri III* and *Hernani*, showed that he was yielding to some extent to the new influences, and in his later historical dramas, *Louis XI* (1832), which was based on Scott's *Quentin Durward*, and *Les Enfants d'Édouard* (1833), which was derived from Shakespeare, these influences were even more pronounced. Delavigne was, however, a very moderate innovator, and his work represents a kind of compromise between the two schools. But a decade later another playwright, François Ponsard (1814–67), made a bold attempt to initiate a classic reaction. His first tragedy, *Lucrèce*, secured a veritable triumph at the Odéon in the very year (1843) in which the failure of *Les Burgraves* brought Hugo's theatrical career to a close. But this success, which was due in large

measure to the genius of the great actress Rachel, was not repeated either by Ponsard himself or by the few other poets who followed his lead. The more extravagant tendencies of romanticism, it is true, were now checked, and Corneille and Racine were restored to the stage ; but a return to classicism was obviously impossible, and, as we shall see later, the modern drama took another direction. Even Ponsard is remembered to-day, not for his regular tragedies, but for his comedy of manners, *L'Honneur et l'Argent* (1853), and his two historical plays, *Charlotte Corday* (1850) and *Le Lion Amoureux* (1866).

The comedy of the first half of the nineteenth century need not detain us, as apart from the writers who have already been mentioned incidentally, it contains only one name of any importance, that of Augustin Eugène Scribe (1791–1861). For upwards of fifty years Scribe was a prolific and successful caterer for the amusement of the theatre-going public, and in collaboration with numerous other playwrights produced nearly 400 pieces, small and large, of various kinds—comedies (*e.g., Valérie, Le Mariage d'Argent, La Camaraderie, Bataille de Dames*) ; farces and vaudevilles (*e.g., La Demoiselle à Marier, Le Charlatanisme*) ; emotional dramas (*e.g., Adrienne Lecouvreur*) ; historical dramas (*Bertrand et Raton, Le Verre d'Eau*) ; opera-librettos (*e.g., La Juive, Les Huguenots, Le Prophète*). His work has very slight literary value, but he was a consummate theatrical craftsman, and if his methods were mechanical, the perfection of his technique must still be recognised.

69. THE NOVEL.—Apart from the highly poetical romances of Chateaubriand and Mme. de Staël the first quarter of the nineteenth century contributed little of value to prose fiction, though one very notable book stands out as an exception, the short semi-autobiographi-

cal *Adolphe* (1816), by the publicist and statesman Benjamin Constant (1767–1830), which, while in the direct line of *René* and *Obermann*, is remarkable as anticipating the more sober and precise methods of the later analytical school. After 1825, however, the novel underwent enormous expansion, and soon became, as it has since remained, the most wide-cultivated and most popular of all the forms of literature. Though, on account of the variety which was henceforth one of its principal characteristics, exact classification is impossible, the prose fiction of our present period may conveniently be treated in three divisions—the historical romance, the novel of sentiment, and the novel of manners, or realistic novel of modern life.

70. THE HISTORICAL ROMANCE : VIGNY—MÉRIMÉE.— The historical romance was a natural product of the romantic movement which, as we have seen, stimulated an interest in history, especially in national history, a love of local colour, and a sense of the picturesqueness of the past. Many influences would thus have to be taken into account in any consideration of the causes of its rise and popularity, but here we need go no farther than that of Scott, who was as much as Shakespeare the idol of the whole romantic school. The historical romance may indeed be found in germ in *Les Martyrs* of Chateaubriand, but in germ only. Its immediate literary source was the Waverley Novels.

The first important example of the new fiction was Vigny's *Cinq-Mars, ou une Conspiration sous Louis XIII* (1826). This was directly inspired by Scott, yet in one fundamental particular Vigny departed from his master's method. It was Scott's habit to concentrate his interest upon his fictitious characters and to introduce his historical characters only in connection with these. Vigny found fault with this practice : " Je pensais que les romans historiques de W. Scott étaient trop facile à faire, en ce que l'action était placée dans des personnages inventés que l'on fait agir comme l'on veut, tandis qu'il passe de loin en loin à l'horizon une grande figure historique dont la présence accroît l'importance du livre et lui donne une date " (*Journal d'un Poète*, 1847). His own method therefore is the reverse of this ; the characters of his " premier plan " are all historical ; his fictitious figures are figures in the background only. But, on the other hand, he claimed the right to treat his historical personages with the utmost freedom and to subordinate them to his philosophic purpose, his principle being that " le nom propre n'est rien que l'example et la preuve de l'idée." It was upon this principle, it will be remembered, that he afterwards dealt with the story of Chatterton. Like *La Maréchale d'Ancre*, therefore, *Cinq-Mars* is written to expound the author's views about history, with the result that the characters are too much simplified in the interest of these views to be quite true to life. Hence, despite its real dramatic power and the erudition which fills its pages, the work is not entirely satisfactory either as fiction or as history. To find Vigny at his best we must turn rather to the three *nouvelles—Laurette, ou le Cachet Rouge, La Veillée de Vincennes*, and *La Vie et la Mort du Capitaine Renaud, ou La Canne de Jonc*—composing the volume entitled *Servitude et Grandeurs Militaires* (1835) : strong and simple stories, imbued with the fine stoical spirit which we have already noted in his poetry.

Another writer of the first rank who helped to create the historical romance, though his greatest work in fiction was on other lines (see *post*, pp. 252-53), was Mérimée, whose *Chronique du Règne de Charles IX* appeared three years after *Cinq-Mars*. This is specially noteworthy as a scholarly and accurate study of the manners of the age with which it deals. But though historical events are introduced into it, its plot, which is composed of the adventures of a young Calvinist, Bernard de Mergy, at the time of the Massacre of Saint-Barthélemy and the siege of La Rochelle, is entirely fictitious.

71. HUGO.—Hugo's place in the development of the historical romance is similar to that which he occupies in the romantic drama ; in each case he had his forerunners, and in each case he established the new type with one brilliant success. His early essays in prose fiction—the wildly extravagant *Hans d'Islande* (1823), the equally extravagant *Bug-Jargal* (1826), and *Le Dernier Jour d'un Condamné* (1829), which, like the later *Claude Gueux* (1834), was a plea for the abolition of capital punishment—are hardly worthy of serious attention. It was in *Notre-Dame de Paris* (1831) that he exhibited all the wonderful powers, and, along with these, all the characteristic weaknesses, which had gone to the making of *Hernani* only a year before. Like *Hernani, Notre-Dame* is a difficult work to appraise. Its crudely concocted plot moves through scenes of violent sensationalism to a catastrophe of undiluted horror ; its characters—the Bohemian girl Esmeralda, Captain Phœbus de Châteaupers (the typical romantic hero), the priest Claude Frollo (the typical romantic villain), the sympathetic monster Quasimodo the bell-ringer (one of Hugo's many grotesques and a kind of parallel to Triboulet in *Le Roi s'amuse*)—are one and all creatures of the melodramatic stage. Yet notwithstanding its incredible intrigue and its flagrant unreality, it is still a powerful and enthralling romance, and its wealth of local colour (its action passes in the last year of the reign of Louis XI.) makes it intensely picturesque. In particular we must lay stress upon the

prodigious graphic power with which in its pages Hugo has brought the whole world of fifteenth-century Paris once more to life. The two chapters in the third book— *Notre-Dame* and *Paris à Vol d'Oiseau*—may be cited, among many others, as masterpieces of descriptive writing.

Later in life Hugo returned twice to historical romance : in *L'Homme qui Rit* (1869), the scene of which is laid in the England of the Stuarts, but which merely caricatures the life and manners of the time ; and in *Quatre-Vingt-Treize* (1872), a drama of the Revolution, grandiose and terrific, but somewhat simpler in plot and more sober in style. But meanwhile his humanitarian enthusiasm had led him to turn from the past to the present, and as in *Notre-Dame* he had painted a detailed picture of Paris in the age of Louis XI., so in *Les Misérables* (1862) he produced an immense and crowded panorama of modern French civilisation. This work is therefore interesting as a striking example of the transformation of the romance of past history into the romance of the history of contemporary life.[1] It is further important as the fullest expression of Hugo's social theories. Straggling and incoherent in plot, it is not so much a novel as a bundle of loosely connected novels, each of which is overlaid with episodes which at times (as in the case of the long account of the battle of Waterloo) have little or nothing to do with the general theme. But confused and digressive as the action is, three main lines of interest may be followed through it : the story of the convict Jean

---

[1] Another modern romance, *Les Travailleurs de la Mer* (1866), may be dismissed with a mere reference. It is a sort of prose epic of the struggle of man with the forces of nature, fantastic in plot, rhapsodical in style, but with many pages of vivid description of the Jersey coast and the sea. It contains one very famous incident—the battle of Gilliatt with the gigantic octopus.

Valjean, which provides a sort of backbone for the whole ; the story of Fantine, her fall, her misery, her love for her illegitimate child, and her death ; and the love-story of this child, Cosette, and young Marius, which occupies the larger portion of the closing books ; and all these are made the vehicle of Hugo's social gospel—of his optimistic faith in the essential goodness of human nature and the reality of repentance and redemption ; of his charge against the whole system of society, which he accuses of being more than half responsible for the crimes which it punishes with a severity which is as senseless as it is brutal ; of his eloquent pleadings for the spirit of brother-hood, sympathy, and love. As a romance, the work is vigorous, dramatic, and, in spite of its inordinate length and prolixity, engrossing. As a social study, it is un-fortunately damaged by the writer's want of mental balance, by its extravagances and violent sensationalism, and even more by its crude psychology, which is still that of melodrama rather than of real life.

72. DUMAS.—While historians of literature are always willing to give the author of *Henri III* and *Antony* a prominent place among the creators of the romantic drama, they are generally inclined to pass over his prose fiction as unworthy of their attention. But it was in prose fiction that his greatest and most enduring successes were achieved, and as a writer of prose fiction he certainly does not deserve the contempt with which he is commonly treated by the critics. The son of one of Napoleon's generals, and the grandson of a full-blooded Haytian negress, Alexandre Dumas Davy de la Pailleterie was born at Villers-Cotterets (Aisne) in 1802 or 1803. He began life with a magnificent constitution, boundless energy, and an insatiable thirst for adventure, and during a career crowded with varied incident he travelled much,

dabbled in politics, founded magazines, edited newspapers, made fortunes and lost them, and all the time maintained an almost incredible literary activity. Worn out with his incessant labours, he died in 1870 at his son's villa at Puys near Dieppe. Dumas' collected works fill 277 volumes, and include books of travel, plays, and a large number of miscellaneous writings (one of which, *Mes Bêtes*, is a delightful record of his love of animals), besides the prose fiction now in question. His reputation rests in the main upon two cycles of romances—the D'Artagnan trilogy (*Les Trois Mousquetaires*, *Vingt Ans Après*, and *Le Vicomte de Bragelonne*, which Stevenson declared to be the finest romance in the world) and the Valois trilogy (*Marguerite de Valois*, *La Dame de Monsoreau*, and *Les Quarante-Cinq*)—and a few independent romances, like the ever-famous *Comte de Monte-Cristo*; though two other series—the Regency cycle and the Marie Antoinette cycle—must also be taken into account. Though he introduces an abundance of fiction into his narratives, he depends for his chief interest upon historical events and characters, very freely handled, and his work may thus be defined as romanticised history rather than historical romance. In regard to the two charges continually brought against him—that of wholesale plagiarism and that of manufacturing his books with the aid of numerous assistants ("Dumas et Compagnie" early became a familiar gibe)—little needs to be said. He certainly acted upon the Molièresque maxim of taking his own wherever he found it, and was often guilty of barefaced thefts, and it is equally certain that he was scarcely more than the editor or reviser of a good deal of the matter which appeared under his name. But the distinctive qualities of his work—the fecundity of invention, the wit, the vivacity, the racy and dramatic dialogue, the easy swing of the narrative, the high spirits, the contagious zest of adventure—are all his own. His history may be unhistorical, his characterisation superficial, his style careless and faulty. But one merit he has which even the most exigent critic cannot deny him—the gift of story-telling. The wonderful chapters in *Monte - Cristo* describing Edmond Dantès' imprisonment and escape from the Château d'If would alone entitle him to a place with the greatest story-tellers in literature.

73. THE NOVEL OF SENTIMENT : GEORGE SAND.—The novel of sentiment, or idealistic novel, which flourished side by side with the historical romance, was not like this the creation of the romantic movement ; it was rather the continuation of the tradition initiated by *La Nouvelle Héloïse* and carried on in the early nineteenth century by *René, Delphine,* and *Corinne.* Fundamentally personal and subjective, it lent itself freely to all kinds of didactic purposes, and thus easily passed into the *roman à thèse.* Naturally, it proved specially attractive to women-writers, one of whom has a recognised standing among the greater novelists of the time. Armandine Lucile Aurore Dupin, whom we always know under her pen-name of George Sand, was born in 1804 in Paris, but spent much of her girlhood at Nohant in Berri, in which beautiful region, which is one of the loveliest in all France, she imbibed that love of nature which was ever after a passion with her. In 1822 she married the Baron Dudevant, but after nine years of unhappiness separated from him and settled in Paris, with the intention of making her living by her pen. Forming an association with Jules Sandeau (from whom she took her pseudonym) she collaborated with him in a novel, *Rose et Blanche* (1831), which was the first step in her literary career. Her later connection with Alfred de Musset has already been referred

to. After the revolution of 1848 she gave up her Bohemian life and retired to Nohant, where she passed her remaining years, and where she died in 1876. Her numerous novels fall into four well-defined groups, the divisions between which are mainly though not entirely chronological. She began with novels of passion and revolt, in which she gave unrestrained expression to her own turbulent feelings, and into which she put a great deal of her personal experience; *e.g.*, *Indiana* (1832), *Valentine* (1833), *Lélia* (1833), *Jacques* (1834), all of which deal more or less with the tragedy of misplaced love and uncongenial marriage, and are strongly " feminist " in tone. Then under the influence of Lamennais and Pierre Leroux the Saint-Simonian, she turned her fiction to the service of humanitarian and religious ideas, and wrote the socialistic romances *Les Maîtres Mosaïstes* (1838), *Le Compagnon du Tour de France* (1840), *Le Meunier d'Angibault* (1845), and the mystical *Spiridion* (1840). To this group also belong two of her best-known works, *Consuelo* (1842) and its sequel *La Comtesse de Rudolstadt* (1843), which together contain the life-history of a famous singer (*tempo* 1740–86), and are curiously compounded of humanitarian theories and sensationalism. A third division is composed of her *romans champêtres*, or idyllic stories of the peasantry and country life—*La Mare au Diable* (1846), *La Petite Fadette* (1849), *François le Champi* (1850), *Les Maîtres Sonneurs* (1853), etc. Finally, in *Les Beaux Messieurs de Bois-Doré* (1853), *Le Marquis de Villemer* (1860), *Jean de la Roche* (1861), and other novels, she went back to the purely romantic type of her earliest work, though her manner was now much more subdued and her feminism far less aggressive. George Sand was a rapid and fluent writer, and her novels are largely improvisations. Deficient in restraint and in the faculty of self-criticism, she gave free rein to her exuberant genius, with the result that nearly all her books suffer from prolixity. Her strength lies in her passion, in her emotional sincerity, in her wonderful descriptions of nature, and in the flow and charm of her style. These qualities are to be found in all her writings. But on the whole her simplest work is her best. She is now remembered mainly for her tender and wholesome peasant stories, which, though highly idyllic in tone, are marked by great truth of detail, and which thus most fully achieve her own avowed aim as an artist—" idéalisation du sentiment . . . dans un cadre de réalité " (*Histoire de ma Vie*, IVᵉ partie, chap. xv.).

74. THE REALISTIC NOVEL : BALZAC.—The realistic movement in fiction, aiming as it did at the faithful and impersonal representation of life, was fundamentally opposed to romanticism and arose in reaction against it, yet, as we shall see on turning to the great founder and master of the new school, it was in its inception closely connected with the historical 'romance. Honoré de Balzac was born at Tours in 1799. His father was a southerner, his mother a Parisian and *mondaine*, and efforts have been made to explain by reference to his parentage the " double nature " of his genius, or combination of romantic and realistic tendencies in it : " father and mother," it has been wittily said, " continued their household disputes in the brain of their son." He was educated at the Collège de Vendôme in his native city (for reminiscences of his schooldays, including his boyish experiments in poetry and his chilblains, see the early part of *Louis Lambert*), and presently put to the study of law ; but he had made up his mind to be an author, and having obtained his father's consent to a two years' probation, he settled at twenty in a garret in Paris,

resolved to succeed in literature or perish in the attempt. He tried his hand first in a tragedy on Cromwell, but this proving a total failure, he began to write tales of the most extravagant and sensational kind, which were sold for what they would fetch, published anonymously or under various pseudonyms, and never afterwards acknowledged by him. This hack-work continued for seven or eight years.[1] His real career opened with *Les Chouans* (1829), a kind of historical novel written under the inspiration of Scott, and the powerful excursion into supernaturalism, *La Peau de Chagrin* (1831) : books which together mark the transition from his early to his later work. Meanwhile, misled by his inordinate craving for wealth and singularly sanguine temper, he was involving himself in the commercial enterprises and speculations which were to be the curse of his life. His fertile mind teemed with plans for making huge fortunes rapidly, but the practical result was that he was always burdened with debts and harassed with financial difficulties. This fact had a direct bearing upon his literary production and methods. Forced to toil like a slave for publishers to whom he mortgaged his brain and who often paid him outright for a novel before a single page of it had been written, he worked for twenty years at the highest pressure, sitting at his desk sometimes for eighteen or twenty hours at a stretch and keeping his imagination in a sort of fever by enormous potations of coffee. In these circumstances the wonder is, not that he broke down when he did, but that even his " constitution of an ox " stood the strain so long. He died of heart disease in 1850.

In many of the qualities of his work—in the exaggera-

[1] The immediate models of these frenzied productions were the tales of Mrs. Radcliffe, " Monk " Lewis, and R. C. Maturin, for which he had an admiration which clearly shows the romantic bias of his mind.

tion so often conspicuous in his characterisation, in his love of the gigantic and the abnormal,[1] in his over-wrought sentimentalism, in his occasional tendency to mysticism, and in the melodramatic machinery of some of his plots—Balzac shows his intimate connection with the romanticism of his generation. But in theory he conceived the novel as a realistic representation of life, and in so doing placed himself beside the historian. The commonly accepted romantic principle was that a writer of fiction must select his material and arrange it with a view to artistic effect. This principle he rejects. Like the historian the novelist is concerned neither with selec-tion nor with arrangement, neither with beauty nor with morality; he must take life as he finds it and aim only at truth. In this conception he started from Scott. He saw that the author of *Waverley* had endeavoured to reproduce the past with a great wealth of realistic detail, and he maintained that what his romances had done for the past, the modern novel should do for the present : that is, that it should still be historical, only its history should be that not of some bygone period but of con-temporary society. But while his theory began with Scott it was greatly developed and amplified by certain scientific ideas which he took over from the biologists, especially Cuvier and Sainte-Hilaire. In the animal world species exist, and these species have been moulded and fashioned by the influence of their environments. In the social world species of men exist, and these too have

---

[1] He once admitted to George Sand that in his own way he was as much an idealist as she was herself. " J'aime aussi les êtres excep-tionels ; j'en suis un. . . . Mais ces êtres vulgaires m'intéressent plus qu'ils ne vous intéressent. Je les grandis, je les idéalise en sens inverse, dans leur laideur ou leur bêtise. Je donne à leurs difformités des proportions effrayantes ou grotesque " (G. Sand, *Histoire de ma Vie*, IVe partie, chap. xv.).

been made what they are by their environments. According to Balzac, therefore, men must be considered not as mere individuals but as social units—as members of this or that group, class, profession ; they must be placed in their *milieu* and viewed in their relationship with it ; the whole body of society must be studied as a background and setting for each individual life. Hence the enormous amount of attention which he bestowed not only upon the physical, intellectual, and moral attributes of his characters, but also upon their ancestry, antecedents, surroundings, conditions, habits, and the long explanatory essays with which he continually interrupts his narratives. At the outset, he wrote his social studies independently one of another, but he presently conceived the vast ambition of combining them all into a comprehensive whole—a *Comédie Humaine*, as he ultimately called it— which should give in the imaginary society represented in it a complete picture of the real society of the time. "J'ai entrepris l'histoire de toute la Societé," he wrote to a correspondent in 1846. " J'ai exprimé souvent mon plan dans cette seule phrase : une génération est un drame à quatre ou cinq mille personnages saillants. Ce drame c'est mon livre " (cp. his General Preface of 1842). As it stands (and it is scarcely necessary to say that the immense design was never carried out in its entirety), the *Comédie* consists of ninety-six novels, tales, and short stories, which, according to his own rather arbitrary arrangement, fall into a number of subdivisions : *Scènes de la Vie Privée* (*e.g.*, *La Maison du Chat-qui-Pelote, La Messe de l'Athée*) ; *Scènes de la Vie de Province* (*e.g.*, *Eugénie Grandet, Illusions Perdues*) ; *Scènes de la Vie Parisienne* (*e.g.*, *Le Père Goriot, César Birotteau, La Cousine Bette*) ; *Scènes de la Vie Politique* (*e.g.*, *Une Épisode sous la Terreur*); *Scènes de la Vie Militaire* (*Les Chouans*) ; *Scènes de la*

Vie de Campagne (e.g., Le Médecin de Campagne) ; *Études Philosophiques (e.g., La Peau de Chagrin, La Recherche de l'Absolu)* ; and *Études Analytiques (e.g., Petites Misères de la Vie Conjugale)*. Taken as a whole, the *Comédie* is by no means so complete ·or so· logical in composition as it pleased Balzac to suppose ; there are enormous gaps in it, while some of the stories (*e.g., Sur Catherine de Médicis*) are simply forced into the scheme. Yet it none the less presents a wonderfully rich, varied, and living picture of French society during the first half of the nineteenth century.[1] It is interesting to note that Balzac systematic-ally employs the device of continually re-introducing the same characters in different books for the purpose both of binding them together and of giving substantial reality to his imaginary world ; men and women who fill import-ant rôles in one portion of the *Comédie* reappear in minor rôles in other portions, while some of them, like Rastignac, De Marsay, Bixiou, Horace Bianchon and Vautrin, play conspicuous parts in many dramas. Balzac himself said that his work would need a biographical dictionary. Such a dictionary now exists in a volume of over 500 pages.

Two aspects of Balzac's realism deserve special atten-tion. The first of these is his preoccupation with what novelists hitherto had ignored as vulgar detail. Love, generally in its vicious phases, fills indeed an immense place in his books ; but money rather than love is the motive force in the society which he portrays. He is quite as much interested in the business activities of his

[1] Omitting a few works which have no real place in it, the period covered by the *Comédie* is practically coextensive with Balzac's own life. It may be said to begin in *Les Chouans* with the Breton rising of 1799, the year of his birth, and to end in 1846, when, in *La Cousine Bette*, the infamous Baron Hulot (brother of the General Hulot of *Les Chouans*), after the death of his saintly wife, marries his cook.

characters, in their incomes, investments, and speculations, as he is in their intrigues and marriages ; he has, in fact, a perfect mania for figures and statistics, and there are pages in some of his novels—*César Birotteau* is an excellent example—which make us wonder whether we are reading a novel or a financial newspaper. Secondly, his theory of realism led him unfortunately to dwell with monotonous iteration upon the base and ugly side of life. The view which he gives us not only of society but also of human nature itself is profoundly gloomy and even repulsive. There are a few exceptions to be allowed for, but speaking generally the *Comédie Humaine* is a big bundle of tragedies, and tragedies of the most sordid and depressing kind. His stress is laid for the most part upon evil and depravity in all their forms, and though at times he attempts by way of contrast to portray simple goodness and virtue, he rarely succeeds in making them anything but silly and ridiculous. Thus his world is not a healthy world to live in. But it is a world which only the mightiest power of genius could have called into being. With all his defects and limitations he is one of the greatest of novelists. His interpretation of life is falsified by over-emphasis and one-sidedness ; the philosophy which he is so fond of parading at times savours of charlatanism ; he is often heavy and dull ; his style is forced, tortuous, pedantic, and frequently bad. But as a creator of character and as a painter of manners he ranks with the supreme masters of fiction.

75. STENDHAL—MÉRIMÉE.—Balzac shows us the transformation of the historical romance into the novel of manners. In the hands of Stendhal the novel of sentiment develops into the psychological novel. Henri Beyle, generally known by his pen-name of Stendhal, was born at Grenoble in 1783 ; served for a time in the Napoleonic

army ; followed the disastrous Russian campaign of 1812 ; lived now in Paris and now in Italy ; was consul at Trieste from 1830 to 1833, and at Civita Vecchia from 1833 to 1841 ; and died in Paris in 1842. Of a strongly analytical and critical habit of mind, he wrote on art (*Histoire de la Peinture en Italie*, etc.), on music (*Vie de Rossini*, etc.), on psychology (*De l'Amour*), on literature (*Racine et Shakespeare*). His work in fiction comprises three novels, the early and negligible *Armance* (1822), *Le Rouge et le Noir* (1831), and *La Chartreuse de Parme* (1839), and the same analytical and critical quality is uppermost in these. We have seen that he made common cause with the romantics and contributed to their propaganda ; but romanticism for him meant freedom from tradition and formula and the assertion of individuality ; its imaginative excesses, its emotional fervour, its mysticism and sentimentalism were entirely foreign to his positive and cynical temper and his devotion to " de petits faits vrais." Even his manner of writing was as far as possible removed from the lyrical and rhetorical style so much in favour with his contemporaries ; he abhorred " le style contourné," cultivated the plain and exact expression of his ideas, and boasted that while engaged in composition he would read " chaque matin deux ou trois pages du Code Civil afin d'être toujours naturel." In the matter of his novels he reveals the influence of romanticism in the melodramatic machinery of his plots and in his fondness for dealing with exceptional characters (like Julien Sorel in *Le Rouge et le Noir*, and Fabrice del Dongo in *La Chartreuse de Parme*) in exceptional circumstances. But his strength lies in his close and patient attention to minute detail and the rigorous precision of his psychological analysis.

Though Stendhal was little appreciated during his lifetime—he said himself, " j'aurai du succès vers 1880 "—

he had a small group of admirers, prominent among whom was Prosper Mérimée, whose name is now very commonly linked with his own. The son of a well-known painter, Mérimée was born in Paris in 1803 ; after 1830 entered the service of the government ; held various important offices ; under the Empire was closely associated with the Court, and died in 1870, soon after the fall of the dynasty to which he had long been personally attached. Essentially a scholar by temperament and training, he did much sound work in historical research, but his archæological and critical writings need not now detain us, though it may be mentioned, as an illustration of his breadth of interest and cosmopolitanism, that he was the first to " discover " Russian literature and to introduce such masters as Pushkin and Turgenev to the French public. Here we are concerned only with his original contributions to literature. Early in life he fell under the influence of romanticism and began his career with two clever mystifications, *Le Théâtre de Clara Gazul* (1825), a collection of plays which he gave out as translations from a Spanish actress, and published with a portrait of himself disguised in female costume as a frontispiece ; and *Guzla* (1827), which in the same way he offered as a literal version of some Illyrian poems. To this period also belong an historical drama, *La Jacquerie* (1829) and the *Chronique du Règne de Charles IX*, to which reference has already been made. But all this work was little more than experimental. He found his true line later in a series of tales and stories, about twenty in number, all of which are excellent, while some of them (*e.g., Columba, Mateo Falcone, Carmen, la Vénus d'Ille, L'Enlèvement de la Redoute, La Partie de Trictrac*) are masterpieces in their kind. Like Stendhal he was fond of exploring the psychology of strong and unusual characters in strikingly dramatic situations ; like Stendhal he had a keen sense of the value of significant detail—" trouver le trait qu'il faut," he wrote in his essay on Pushkin, " c'est là le problème a résoudre." But while Stendhal had chosen a large canvas he on the other hand sought concision and concentration. More than Stendhal, too, and more than any other writer of the time, he adopted an attitude of complete detachment from his subjects and the impassivity and impartiality of the pure artist. His work is remarkable for the rare combination in it of strength with sobriety and restraint, and his style for its purity and precision.

76. OTHER NOVELISTS.—The output of fiction during the second quarter of the nineteenth century was so enormous that only a few other writers can even be mentioned here, and so varied that any exact classification of these would be impossible. Our simplest plan therefore will be to take them chronologically.

First in sequence of date, and during his long lifetime one of the most popular of all, comes Charles Paul de Kock (1794–1871), whose novels, which number nearly a hundred, and of which the earlier *Gustave le Mauvais Sujet* (1821), *Frère Jacques* (1822), and *La Laitière de Montfermil* (1827) will serve as typical examples, deal almost entirely with the contemporary world of shopkeepers, students, *grisettes*, and the *petite bourgeoisie*. Carelessly written, and coarse though genial in tone, these belong to the old *gaulois* tradition in French literature, and while they have little other claim to attention (except perhaps as amusing pictures of the manners of the time) they have plenty of spicy humour and vivacious dialogue. Xavier Boniface Saintine (1798–1865), a voluminous writer of plays, survives as the author of one book of a very different character, the still familiar *Picciola* (1836), a highly pathetic story of a political prisoner and his flower. Charles de Bernard (1804–55), though now, unaccountably, almost as much neglected by the critics as either of these, was a writer of far greater importance. He was a friend and in a sense a disciple of Balzac, but the influence of the master upon him must not be exaggerated, for his temper was much less pessimistic, his touch much lighter, and he excelled particularly in a field in which Balzac failed, that of social comedy and satire ; as, *e.g.*, in *Gerfaut* (1836), his best work, *Les Ailes d'Icaire* (1839), also a thoroughly good novel, *L'Homme Sérieux* (1847), etc. He has sometimes been compared with Thackeray, who greatly admired his work and took one of his stories as the foundation of his own *Bedford Row Conspiracy*. His exact contemporary, Delphine Gay, Madame de Girardin (1804–55), was also successful as a painter of society (*Lettres Parisiennes*, etc.) and as a story-teller of much delicacy and grace (*e.g.*, *Le Lorgnon, Contes d'une Vieille Fille à ses Neveux, La Canne de M. Balzac*, etc.). Jules Gabriel Janin (1804–74), who gave most of his energies to dramatic criticism, belongs on the contrary to the romantics, though the best known of his fantastic tales, the strange and bizarre *L'Âne Mort et la Femme Guillotinée* (1827), is rather a parody of the "genre frénétique" than a serious contribution to it. Émile Souvestre (1806–54) deserves to be held in kindly remembrance for his stories of his native Brittany (*Les Dernier Bretons*, 1835–37, *Le Foyer Breton*, 1844, etc.), and no less for one very charming little book of quite a different class—*Un Philosophe sous les Toits* (1850). The many novels of the journalist and miscellanist Jean Baptiste Alphonse Karr (1808–90)—the autobiographical *Sous les Tilleuls* (1833), the very clever *Fa Dièze* (1834), *Feu Bressier* (1848), etc.—also stand apart from and well above the average fiction of their generation, for they are original in idea, full of humour, and fresh in style. Léonard Sylvain Jules Sandeau (1811–83), who has already been named in connection with George Sand, was a successful playwright who also wrote novels of a leisurely kind, in which we have an agreeable blend of sentiment and satire, romance and realism, and which are specially excellent for their pictures of old-fashioned country life and society ; as, *e.g.*, *Mademoiselle de la Seiglière* (1848), *Sacs et Parchements* (1851)—the former dramatised under the same title, the latter as *Le Gendre de M. Poirier*—*Le Docteur Herbieu* (1841), *Madeleine* (1848), etc. These still make pleasant reading, but it can hardly be maintained that literature would be much the poorer for their loss. On the contrary, one work by Henry Murger (1822–61) keeps its place as a genuine human document of unique character and interest—his *Scènes de la Vie de Bohème* (1845). Murger was personally familiar with the by-ways of Bohemia, with its struggling young artists and poets, their ambitions, their poverty, their dissipations, and the tragedy and comedy of the *Scènes*— and they are rich alike in pathos and in humour—are directly made out of the materials furnished by his own experiences. Though he returned several times to the same region for his inspiration, as in *Les Buveurs d'Eau* and *Le Pays Latin*, his other books are of a much more commonplace kind. This one production, however, is his sufficient passport to immortality.

It remains to note that the introduction in the late thirties of the " système du roman feuilleton," or practice of running a novel in sections through a newspaper, gave an enormous impetus to the manufacture of fiction intended for popular consumption. With the exception of Dumas, by whom this system was freely employed, the most famous of the feuilletonists was Eugène Sue (1804–

1857), who after experimenting with no great success with a number of Byronic romances and romances of the sea, made a tremendous hit with *Les Mystères de Paris* (1842), a gigantic and lurid melodrama of the underworld of the capital, and *Le Juif Errant* (1844–45), in which the legend of the Wandering Jew is utilised for another thrilling narrative of a very similar kind and on the same vast scale. Very long, very complicated in plot, compounded of entanglements, surprises, and horrors of all descriptions, and entirely innocent of any quality of art, these depend for their interest wholly upon the excitement of their sensationalism. It should, however, be added that they are novels of direct humanitarian purpose, and that they did so much to spread socialistic ideas among the masses that their author has a substantial claim to a place among the literary precursors of the revolution of 1848. Sue's chief rivals were Frederic Soulié (1800–47), with his *Deux Cadavres* (1832), *Mémoires du Diable* (1837–38), etc., and Paul Féval (1817–87), with his *Club des Phoques* (1841), *Les Mystères de Londres* (1844), *Le Fils du Diable* (1847), etc. Innumerable other writers followed the lead of these with more or less success, but we cannot burden our pages with their names, for their work scarcely attains the dignity of literature.

CHAPTER XIII

THE LATER NINETEENTH CENTURY

GENERAL PROSE

77. THE LATER NINETEENTH CENTURY. — By the
middle of the century romanticism had spent its force.
It had done a magnificent work for literature ; it had
liberated genius from the trammels of artificial rules and
conventions ; it had opened up fresh sources of inspiration ; it had revivified poetry, the drama, fiction, and even
criticism. It thus left behind it a rich heritage and in
many directions a permanent influence. But it was as
a movement too violent to be lasting, and an inevitable
reaction against its excesses presently set in which in
turn affected all departments, even poetry, in which it
had naturally been strongest. Thus in general terms
it may be said that as, in the mass, the literature of the
first half of the century had been imaginative and
emotional, so in the mass, that of the second half was
intellectual and critical. As we may put it in a phrase,
a period of dominating romanticism was now succeeded
by a period of dominating realism, though it must not be
forgotten that before the century closed the excesses of
realism itself led to a revival of the idealistic spirit. The
reaction in question might on a broad view be interpreted

simply as an illustration of the familiar principle that as generation follows generation the pendulum of taste often swings from one extreme to another. But it was also in large measure the result of the co-operation of many extra-literary causes ; of political changes after the revolution of 1848 and again after the disaster of 1870 ; of the ever-deepening influence of science and scientific methods ; of the growth of industrialism and commerce. Such movements in thought and in society all contributed to the formation of a positive and utilitarian temper, a temper at once anti-visionary, anti-utopian, and anti-sentimental—in a word, anti-romantic. This was now the prevailing temper in literature, which exhibits the general tendency of the time in its impatience of everything mystical and extravagant and its preoccupation with actuality and concrete fact.[1]

It will be noted that in the rapid survey which follows a very small space is given to general prose. The significance of this brevity of treatment will be readily understood in the light of a single consideration. One very marked tendency in the intellectual as in the industrial evolution of the period in question was the tendency towards ever-increasing subdivision of labour and concomitant specialisation. The result was that while literature as a whole was moulded by the new influences and impregnated with the new ideas, an immense and varied body of purely

---

[1] The fundamental change in the character of French literature during the period now under review, and which the reader may study in detail in M. Georges Pellissier's admirable work, Le Mouvement Littéraire au XIX⁰ Siècle, was of course only a local phase of a general change which came over all European literatures about the same time. It is particularly interesting at this point to compare the whole movement of French literature between 1850 and 1880 with that of our own literature of the mid-Victorian era, for which see my Short History of English Literature in the Nineteenth Century, Part II. chap. i.

professional literature now sprang up—a literature produced by experts and addressed primarily to experts. Such literature, while extremely valuable in itself, does not, however, properly fall within the scope of a book like the present. It belongs rather to the history of the particular subjects concerned or to that of general culture and intellectual development. The case of history itself may be cited as an illustration. The most salient feature of history as written in the later nineteenth century is that in spirit and method it is essentially scientific. But a scientific treatise on history no more comes under the head of general literature than a treatise on biology or economics. The name of Numa Denis Fustel de Coulanges (1830–89), for example, has a high place among those of the founders of the modern historical school, but his *Cité Antique* and *Institutions de l'Ancienne France* are works of science, not of art. Hence rich, varied, and important as is the prose literature of the later nineteenth century on many lines, it provides comparatively little of which we have here to take cognizance. As students of literature we are concerned only with writers whose productions, whatever their subject-matter, have in themselves an independent interest as literature. Such interest certainly attaches to the work of the great historian Renan, who, though he gave most of his life to labours in a highly specialised field, was at the time of his death universally regarded as the first man of letters in France, perhaps in Europe.

78. RENAN.—Ernest Renan was born in 1823 in the little cathedral town of Tréguier (Côtes-du-Nord). His father, the captain of a fishing smack, belonged to an old Breton stock, and though his own character was curiously modified by a strain of Gascon blood, which he derived from his mother's side, and which has been held to explain

his vivacity and his epicureanism, the roots of his essentially poetic nature, as he himself insisted, ran deep down into his native soil. He was thus one of those great writers, like Chateaubriand and Lamennais, who " have small share in that Latin order which is the birthright of a Bossuet, a Racine, or even a Voltaire," and whose " genius is a sort of hippogriff, as Renan used to say of himself, belonging to no known race of mortal herds." [1] A boy of deeply religious nature, he was early destined for the priesthood, and underwent the necessary training in the seminaries of Saint-Nicolas du Chardonet, Issy, and Saint-Sulpice. But the study of Hebrew, which he took up as part of his curriculum, and of German, which he added on his own account, unsettled his mind, and in 1845, having completely lost his faith in Christianity, he quitted Saint-Sulpice and gave up all thought of the Church. He now turned with increased enthusiasm to history and philology, especially to the history and philology of the Semitic races, and soon established his reputation with a volume on *Averroës et l'Averroïsme* (1852), which shows an extraordinary knowledge of the philosophic thought of the Middle Ages, and a *Histoire Générale des Langues Sémitiques* (1854), which is still regarded as marking an epoch in the study of the Semitic tongues. After travels in Italy and the East, undertaken with a view to his future work, he was appointed in 1861 Professor of Hebrew in the Collège de France, and though on the publication of his *Vie de Jésus*, which raised a storm, he was deprived of his chair, he was reinstated in the College as Director by the Republican Government in 1870. For twenty-two years more he led a life of quiet but ceaseless activity, patient, cheerful, and serene under all the weaknesses and pains which advancing age brought

[1] Mme. Darmesteter, *Life of Renan*, pp. 3, 4.

with it, happy in his family and his friendships, happy in the work which with unfailing courage he carried on to the end. He died in 1892.

Apart from those already mentioned, Renan's writings on his own special lines of study include some collections of essays and lectures on religious and ethical questions and a large volume, *L'Avenir de la Science* (written in 1848, but not published till 1890), besides the two closely connected series of works on which his fame as an historian rests, *Les Origines du Christianisme* (*Vie de Jésus*, 1863 ; *Les Apôtres*, 1866 ; *Saint-Paul*, 1869 ; *L'Antéchrist*, 1873 ; *Les Évangiles*, 1877 ; *L'Église Chrétienne*, 1879 ; *Marc-Aurèle*, 1881) and *L'Histoire du Peuple d'Israël* (5 vols., 1888–92). Regarding the scholarship of these twelve massive volumes only the expert is qualified to speak, and we will therefore confine our attention to their general characteristics of spirit, method, and style. Despite his early rupture with Christianity, Renan retained a profound emotional sympathy with the faith he had left behind him. Late in life it gave him a peculiar pleasure to recall not only the surroundings of his childhood at home and in the quaint old-world city of his birth, but also the years he had spent in his preparation for the career he had been forced to abandon and their lasting influence upon his mind. In the beautiful opening paragraph of the Preface to his *Souvenirs d'Enfance et de Jeunesse* he wrote : " Une des légendes les plus répandues en Bretagne est celle d'une prétendue ville d'Is, qui, à une époque inconnue, aurait été engloutie par la mer. On montre, à divers endroits de la côte, l'emplacement de cette cité fabuleuse, et les pêcheurs vous en font d'étranges récits. Les jours de tempête, assurent-ils, on voit, dans le creux des vagues, le sommet des flèches de ses églises ; les jours de calme, on entend monter de l'abîme le son

de ses cloches, modulant l'hymne du jour. Il me semble
souvent que j'ai au fond du cœur une ville d'Is qui sonne
encore des cloches obstinées à convoquer aux offices sacrés
des fidèles qui n'entendent plus. Parfois je m'arrête pour
prêter l'oreille à ces tremblantes vibrations, qui me parais-
sent venir de profondeurs infinies, comme des voix d'un
autre monde." Such a passage as this enables us to
understand why, heterodox as he was (and " pour moi,"
he declares at the end of the same preface, " je ne suis
jamais plus ferme en ma foi libérale que quand je songe
aux miracles de la foi antique "), his attitude towards the
traditional faith was so entirely different from that of the
contemporary rationalistic school.[1] He wrote as one
who had indeed emancipated himself completely from all
theological prepossession and modes of thought but was
still inspired by the deepest religious feeling. And as in
spirit, so in method he was only partly modern. He proclaimed his adherence to the principles of scientific history
by the emphasis which he laid upon the importance of
patient and laborious research, the disinterested examination of every text and document, the need of an alert and
vigilant criticism to control every detail. But he claimed
a right to do precisely what the scientific historian was
most sedulous to avoid—to allow his imagination to play
freely upon the materials provided by research. The
mere collection and colligation of facts was important,
but for him it was only the first step ; " le talent de
l'historien consiste à faire un ensemble vrai avec des
traits que ne sontvrais qu'à demi " (Preface to *La Vie de
Jésus*, 13th edition), and for a reconstruction of the past
one thing besides scholarship is always necessary : " c'est

---

[1] Compare, for example, his own tender and human, if romantic,
Vie de Jésus with Strauss' hard and entirely destructive *Leben Jesu*,
the translation of which was George Eliot's first work in literature.

que les textes ont besoin de l'interprétation du goût, qu'il faut les solliciter doucement " (*Vie de Jésus*, Introduction). In his "gentle solicitation" of his documents he certainly took great liberties with them, trusting too much to his intuition and often letting his fancy lead him too far into the bypaths of speculation. Herein lies the weakness of his work on the scientific side. But however much the historian may be impugned, the artist remains supreme. It is his power to evoke the past and to make it living to the imagination, his extraordinary skill in description and portraiture, and, added to these, the rare and winning beauty of his incomparable style, that in their combination have secured for his historical writings a place among the masterpieces of nineteenth-century prose literature.

Outside such special work Renan is best remembered for his charming and tender *Souvenirs d'Enfance et de Jeunesse* (1883), which are not only delightful as auto-biography but are furthermore invaluable for the light which they throw upon his complex and elusive char-acter. But his *Dialogues Philosophiques* (1876) and *Drames Philosophiques* (1878–86) have also to be taken into account. These two series—the pastime of his leisure hours—have earned for their writer a somewhat equivocal reputation ; he has been accused of exhibiting in them a spirit of flippancy in the treatment of serious things and even of moral laxity. They must however be read as the expression, under a light ironical form, of one of his deepest convictions—the conviction, namely, that as absolute truth is everlastingly beyond our reach, all questions may be regarded from many sides. This explains his choice of the dramatic method as the one most suited for his purpose. " La forme du dialogue est, en l'état actuel de l'esprit humaine, la seule qui, selon moi, puisse convenir à l'exposition des idées philosophiques.

Les vérités de cet ordre ne doivent être ni directement niées, ni directement affirmées ; elles ne sauraient être l'objet de demonstrations. Ce qu'on peut, c'est de les présenter par leurs faces diverses, d'en montrer le fort, le faible, la nécessité, les equivalences. Tous les hauts problèmes de l'humanité sont dans ce cas " (Preface to *Drames Philosophiques*). However disturbing some of the results which Renan attained by its use, this method harmonised admirably with the qualities of his intellect, which was as supple and " ondoyant " as that of Montaigne himself, and as free from every trace of dogmatism. In this respect he presents a striking contrast with the masterful and aggressive writer who comes next on our list.

79. TAINE.—Hippolyte Adolphe Taine was born at Vouziers (Ardennes) in 1828, studied at the Collège de Bourbon and the École Normale Supérieure, and early made his mark with two works in which not only the peculiar vigour of his mind but also the essentials of his critical method were already exhibited — his doctoral thesis (1853) on La Fontaine (later revised and amplified into a volume entitled *La Fontaine et ses Fables*, 1860), and a prize essay on Livy (1854). Debarred by his religious opinions from following a university career, he devoted himself for the next ten years to independent literary work, but his steadily growing reputation as a thinker ultimately broke down the opposition of the conservative party, and in 1864 he was appointed to the chair of æsthetics at the École des Beaux Arts in Paris. Four volumes on *La Philosophie de l'Art* (1865–69) stand to his credit as the direct products of his academic lectures, but in the meantime his interest in psychology continued unabated, and in 1870, in his treatise, *De l'Intelligence*, he made a noteworthy contribution to the constructive

thought of the scientific or materialistic school. After this he turned to history, and was occupied till his death in 1893 with a series of volumes on *Les Origines de la France Contemporaine* (*L'Ancien Régime*, 1875 ; *La Révolution*, 1878–85 ; *Le Régime Moderne,* left incomplete, 1890), which he undertook as an exhaustive inquiry into the causes and results of the Revolution, and which, by the solidity of their erudition, their vast accumulation of details, the breadth and clearness of their design, the range of their generalisations, their analytical and synthetic power, and the energy and incisiveness of their style, take rank among the greatest achievements in modern historical literature.

Varied as Taine's writings are in subject-matter, they are marked by a fundamental unity of purpose and method, for whether he deals with psychology, or with art, or with literature, or with politics and society, his aim is always to reduce his facts to order and system by the help of the same general laws. These laws he took over from biology. Thus the division of his work which is of greatest interest to us here—his literary criticism— represents a bold attempt to apply to the phenomena of literature the evolutionary principles which had gradually been established·in the domain of physical science. His method is fully explained in the introduction to the work in which it is illustrated on the largest scale—his *Histoire de la Littérature Anglaise* (1863). No writer, however great, however independent he may seem to be, is really original. He does not stand outside of or above the conditions of time and place. On the contrary, he and the creations of his genius are the resultants of certain co - operating factors — the race to which he belongs, and whose temperament and disposition he shares ; the complex of physical and social surroundings into which he is born ; and the dominating tendencies in the society and culture of his country and time. Hence the triple formula of " the race, the *milieu*, and the moment," by the use of which Taine " explains " Shakespeare, Bacon, Swift, Byron, Dickens, as he had previously explained La Fontaine and Livy, and as elsewhere in his *Essais de Critique* (1858, etc.) he explains Racine, Stendhal, and Balzac, and in his writings on art, Phidias, Raphael, and Rembrandt. The *Histoire* is a learned, brilliant, and fascinating work which no English student of English literature should leave unread. But it has the defects which we should anticipate. The method adopted is fruitful and stimulating, and is a fine corrective of the lyrical vagaries of romantic criticism. But in his rigorous application of the deterministic theory Taine leaves no room for the incalculable element of individuality or the initiative power of genius, and while properly emphasising the influence of the age upon even the greatest writer he ignores the influence which in turn every great writer exerts upon his age. Moreover, he is too systematic, and is at times guilty of forcing his facts to fit into his generalisations. Thus, though in his attempt to reduce criticism to a " histoire naturelle des esprits " he derived directly from Sainte-Beuve, his work throughout is marked by a rigidity and a dogmatic hardness against which, as we have seen, Sainte-Beuve was himself among the first to protest.[1] But as both philosopher and critic he came precisely at the time when the world was ready for him ; and he summed up the new tendencies in thought and expressed them with so much power that more than any other single writer he contributed to the general movement from romanticism to realism.

80. OTHER CRITICS.—In the enormous development of

[1] See *Causeries du Lundi*, t. xiii.

criticism along many different lines during the second half of the nineteenth century the writer who in weight and influence stands nearest to Taine is Ferdinand Brunetière (1849–1907), a man of sound and massive learning, dictatorial temper, and very pronounced views. The most important feature of his criticism on the theoretical side is his application to literature of the principle of evolution in his doctrine of the " évolution des genres," or gradual transformation of the various types of literature—epic, drama, lyric, and so on—under the changing influences of successive generations (see, *e.g.*, *L'Évolution des Genres dans l'Histoire de la Littérature*, 1890 ; *L'Évolution de la Poésie Lyrique au XIXe Siècle*, 1893 ; *Histoire de la Littérature Française*, 1880–98 ; *L'Évolution de la Critique*, 1890). Guided by this principle, Brunetière is specially strong in analysing movements and tendencies. But he did not, like Taine, merge criticism in history or content himself with a mere scientific " explanation " of authors and their works. He reserved the right of passing judgment, and in so doing he was largely swayed by ethical considerations. He was firmly convinced of the moral responsibilities of literature, and for this reason was an uncompromising opponent of the doctrine of art for art's sake and the theories and practice of the realistic school of fiction (*Le Roman Naturaliste*, 1883). Another critic who was similarly concerned with the ethics of literature is Edmond Henri Adolphe Scherer (1815–89). Clear in thought and independent in opinion, but deficient in flexibility and apt to be too severe where his sympathies were not engaged, Scherer cared far more about the philosophic content of literature than about its form and style, and was on the whole singularly indifferent to all questions of art. Yet he too conceived it as the business of the critic to " account for " his author by placing him back in his environment before proceeding to a judicial estimate of his production. He had a wide and accurate knowledge of English literature, and his studies of English writers in his *Études Critiques sur la Littérature Contemporaine* (1863–95) are of great value. Differing widely in temper and outlook Brunetière and Scherer alike represent the historical tendency in the criticism of their time. On the other hand, in the writings of Émile Faguet (b. 1849) (*e.g.* his series of *Études* on the sixteenth, seventeenth, eighteenth, and nineteenth centuries) we find the eclecticism, the breadth and the disinterested curiosity of Sainte-Beuve, while in those of Jules Lemaître (b. 1853) (*e.g.*, *Les Contemporains*, 1886–96 ; *Impressions de Théâtre*, 1888, etc.) criticism is avowedly treated only as a record of personal taste. For Paul Charles Joseph Bourget (b. 1852), as for Taine, the task of the critic is that of an experimental psychologist ; in his *Essais de Psychologie Contemporaine* (1884–85) he undertakes a minute and systematic inquiry into the mental and moral qualities of the authors chosen for discussion, and who are so chosen because he regards them as in their various ways typical of their age. Finally, to mention only one more representative writer, we have in Émile Hennequin (1858–88) a further development of the scientific method. His *Critique Scientifique* (1889) is an essay in what, with a lapse into barbarism which horrified the purists, he called " esthopsychologie." His procedure, however, is very different from that of Taine, for he rejects Taine's fundamental hypothesis of the fixed relation between an author and his race and *milieu*, and treats individual genius not as a resultant but as an original and creative force. His book is much marred by its scientific terminology, but it is ingenious and suggestive.

CHAPTER XIV

THE LATER NINETEENTH CENTURY (*continued*)

POETRY

81. TRANSITIONAL POETRY.—In following the change which came over French poetry with the exhaustion of romanticism we find, as we should expect, a certain number of writers who represent the transition from old to new. Foremost among these is one who has already been considered, Théophile Gautier, in whose work we have noted the rise of a reaction against the extreme subjectivity of romantic literature, who boasted, as we remember, that for him the "visible world" existed, and who, when he laid it down as a rule "qu'un homme ne doit jamais laisser passer de la sensibilité dans ses œuvres, que la sensibilité est un côté inférieur en art et en littérature," clearly formulated that doctrine of impersonality in poetry which was to be one of the central principles of the Parnassian School. With him we have now to associate two of his friends and disciples, Banville and Baudelaire.

Théodore Faullain de Banville (1823–91) resembles Gautier in his devotion to "le réalisme pittoresque," and in the immense importance which he attached to form (see his *Petit Traité de la Versification Française*, 1872). His work as a whole (*e.g., Les Cariatides*, 1842 ; *Les*

Stalactites, 1846 ; *Les Exilés*, 1867) is marked by a wonderful technical perfection, and his mastery of the most intricate and difficult stanzaic forms, like the *ballade*, the *rondeau*, and the *rondeau double* of the mediæval poets, earned for him the nickname of " le roi des rimes." It is, however, in general the work of a consummate virtuoso, and it suffers from want of substance and from its poverty of both thought and passion. It is, in a word, a poetry of beautiful form but without soul. He is at his best in his lighter moods, and notwithstanding his theoretical impersonality, the real charm of his verse as of his prose (*e.g.*, *Mes Souvenirs*, 1852 ; *Esquisses Parisiennes*, 1859) lies in its essentially personal qualities—in his gaiety, his wit, his cheery pagan temper. This is especially true of the " clowneries," or humorous fantasies, of his *Odes Funambulesques* (1857, 1867), and of his *Ballades Joyeuses* (1873).

Charles Pierre Baudelaire (1821–67) published only one volume of verse, *Les Fleurs du Mal* (1857), which was dedicated to Gautier, and which gained temporary notoriety through the criminal prosecution of its author on the ground that it contained offences against morals. His other writings include a collection of *Petits Poèmes en Prose*, a book on Wagner (1861), some critical essays on art and literature, and a volume, partly original, partly made up of matter derived from De Quincey and Edgar Allan Poe, entitled *Les Paradis Artificiels : Opium et Haschich* (1861). He also made an admirable translation of Poe's *Tales*, his enthusiasm for the American writer being a clear indication of the bias of his own genius. A man of morbid and brooding temperament, haunted by melancholy fancies which, like funeral hearses, passed unceasingly through his mind (*Spleen*), loathing the simple and the natural, and living habitually in the region of strange sensations and abnormal ideas, Baudelaire everywhere shows a perverse love of dwelling upon monstrous and repulsive subjects, and despite his rich imagination and the solemn music of his verse (*e.g.*, *L'Albatros*, *Don Juan aux Enfers*, *Le Balcon*, *Madrigal Triste*, *Spleen*, *L'Horloge*), the atmosphere of his poetry is profoundly unwholesome. That atmosphere cannot perhaps be better suggested than by a quotation from the poem, *Ave atque Vale*, inscribed to his memory by his great English admirer, Swinburne :

> Thou sawest, in thine old singing season, brother,
> Secrets and sorrows unbeheld of us ;
> Fierce loves, and lovely leaf-buds poisonous,
> Bare to thy subtler eye, but for none other
> Blowing by night in some unbreathed-in clime ;
> The hidden harvest of luxurious time,
> Sin without shape, and pleasure without speech ;
> And where strange dreams in a tumultuous sleep
> Make the shut eyes of stricken spirits weep ;
> And with each face thou sawest the shadow on each,
> Seeing as men sow they reap.

In his adherence to the doctrine of art for art's sake, and in his preoccupation with sensuous beauty, Baudelaire was a follower of Gautier.   On the other hand, in his fondness for seeking out the latent affinities which exist between dissimilar things—" les parfums, les couleurs et les sons se répondent " (*Correspondances*)—he anticipates at one point the later Symbolistes.

82. THE PARNASSIENS. — From these transitional poets we pass to the so-called Parnassian School, who represent the dominant tendency in French poetry between 1860 and 1880. The title Parnassian is in no sense descriptive ; it arose accidentally out of a publisher's anthology, *Le Parnasse Contemporain* (1866), and was to begin with used only as a collective name for the contributors to this enterprise ; but it presently came to be

transferred to the group of young poets (chiefly composed of these contributors) who gathered about Leconte de Lisle in his *salon*, and were more or less in sympathy with him in his æsthetic ideas regarding the impersonality of all great art, the elimination of the disturbing element of individual feeling in the treatment of external things, and the supreme importance of form. The members of this new *cénacle*, however, differed widely among themselves in quality and aim, and "Parnassian" must therefore be regarded as a term of very general connotation. In fact, strictly speaking, there are only two among the many poets to whom it was applied who fully embody the principles of the school—Leconte de Lisle himself and Hérédia.

Charles Marie René Leconte de Lisle (1818–94), though of French parentage, was a native of the Île de Bourbon, a fact which helps to explain the exotic character of much of his work. After travelling in the East, he settled in Paris in 1845, and for a time was active in politics, but on the establishment of the Second Empire he withdrew from public affairs, and henceforth devoted himself entirely to literature. His principal collections of original verse are *Poèmes Antiques* (1852), *Poèmes Barbares* (1862), and *Poèmes Tragiques* (1884). In these his subjects are largely mythological or legendary, and are taken mainly from Greek antiquity (*e.g.*, *Helène*, *Niobe*, *L'Enfance d'Héraklès*) [1] or from the East (*e.g.*, *Bhagavat*, *Surya*, *La Vision de Brahma*, *L'Apothéose de Mouca-al-Kebyr*, *Qaïn*); though he makes occasional excursions into other times

[1] It is significant of Leconte de Lisle's Hellenism that both in his original poems and in his translations of Theocritus, the *Iliad* and the *Odyssey*, he breaks with the long-accepted tradition of Latin classicism, and not only uses Greek proper names instead of their Latin equivalents, but also spells these approximately in the Greek way. Thus he substitutes Zeus for Jupiter, Héraklès for Hercule, Alkestis for Alceste, *Les Moires* (Μοῖρα) for *Les Parques*, and so on.

and regions (*e.g.*, *Le Cœur de Hialmar*, *Les Elfes*), and often confines himself to the painting of exotic landscapes (*e.g.*, *La Bernica*, *La Fontaine aux Lianes*) or to the description of wild animals (*e.g.*, *Le Rêve du Jaguar*, *Les Éléphants*, *La Panthère Noire*, etc.). His work is thus substantially a series of *tableaux historiques* interspersed with scenes from nature, and both in its range of matter and in the power with which it presents the spirit of the ages dealt with in concentrated imaginative form it may be compared with *La Légende des Siècles*. Unlike Hugo, however, Leconte de Lisle was inspired with no didactic aim, and indeed expressly asserted his complete detachment from all personal and social considerations. " Bien que l'art puisse donner, dans une certaine mesure, un caractère de généralité à tout ce qu'il touche," he wrote in the preface to the first edition of his *Poèmes Antiques*, " il y a dans l'aveu publique des angoisses du cœur une vanité et une profanation gratuites. D'autre part, quelque vivantes que soient les passions politiques de ce temps, elles appartient au monde de l'action ; le travail spéculatif leur est étranger. Ceci explique l'impersonnalité et la neutralité de ces études." [1] Yet in spite of his firm conviction that art should have nothing to do with the private sentiments and opinions of the artist, he does not succeed in his attempt to escape completely out of himself, and his poetry, while only rarely directly expressive of his ideas, is throughout a luminous record of the impressions which life makes upon him. Like Vigny he is a pessimist, whose imagination is burdened with a persistent sense of the sufferings of the world and the tragedy of man :

---

[1] This preface was omitted in later editions, but it should be consulted as a clear exposition of the writer's principles. The student of English literature will do well to compare Matthew Arnold's views as set forth in the preface to his poems of 1853.

Sombre douleur de l'homme, ô voix triste et profonde,
Plus forte que les bruits innombrables du monde ;
Cris de l'âme, sanglot du cœur supplicié,
Qui t'entend, sans frémir d'amour et de pitié ? [1]

But in his pessimism he differs from Vigny at two important points ; he does not find a stronghold in stoicism, but
turns rather to Buddhism with its doctrine of Nirvana,
or the extinction of the individual consciousness (*e.g.*,
Si l'Aurore, Dies Irae) ; and he seeks spiritual solace and
refreshment in nature (*e.g., Nox, Midi*). His poetry is
laboriously fashioned and finished, and has great beauty
of form ; his versification is pure and regular ; his austere
style, as Gautier put it, has something of a " neigeuse et
séreine froideur."

Leconte de Lisle's closest disciple, Jose Maria de
Heredia, or in the commonly adopted French form of
the name, Hérédia (1842–1905), was born in Santiago de
Cuba and was a descendant of one of the old Spanish
conquistadores, though he had some French blood in him
on his mother's side. Educated in France, where he
finally made his home, he early became attached to
Leconte de Lisle, whose ideas about form and the impersonality of art he accepted to the full, though he did
not share his pessimism. His work consists almost
exclusively of sonnets, written during many years, published separately or in small groups from time to time in
the reviews, and ultimately collected, 118 in number,
under the title of *Les Trophées*, in 1893, when the movement out of which they had sprung was already a thing
of the past. They resemble Leconte de Lisle's poems in
presenting us with a succession of pictures and portraits,
taken mainly from the past or from remote countries,[2]

---

[1] *Bhagavat*, in *Poèmes Antiques*.
[2] It should be noted that the selection of subjects distant in time

and they were arranged by the author himself in sections according to the subject-matter : Greece (*e.g., Hercule et les Centaures*), Rome and the Barbarians (*e.g., Antoine et Cléopâtre, La Trébbia, Aux Montagnes Divines*), the Middle Ages and the Renaissance (*e.g., Vitrail, Le Vieux Orfèvre, Émail, Les Conquérants*), the Orient and the Tropics (*e.g., La Vision de Khêm, Les Samurais*), with a concluding section entitled Nature and Dreams (*e.g.* the sequence, *La Mer de Bretagne*). Hérédia was a consummate literary craftsman, who deliberately adopted the sonnet as " le plus beau des poèmes à forme fixe," the very brevity and difficulty of which seemed to him to demand " une conscience dans l'exécution et une concentration dans la pensée qui ne peuvent qu'exciter et pousser à la perfection l'artiste digne de ce beau nom " ; and in the flawless precision of his workmanship he deserves a place among the greatest sonnet-writers of the world. His radical defect is perhaps the result as much of his theories as of his genius—a want of breadth and humanity. Even more than his master he was an exponent of the principle of artistic detachment and indifference, and his complete objectivity is the more striking, because in all times and countries the sonnet has generally been adopted as a medium of personal expression.

In the work of another of Leconte de Lisle's personal adherents, René François Armand Sully - Prudhomme (1839–1907), we have a body of poetry which, though starting from the Parnassian doctrine, has little in common with its extremer implications. His first book of verse, *Stances et Poèmes* (1865), was warmly praised by Sainte-Beuve, and this was followed by a number of other

---

and place was a natural corollary of the theory that the poet should get as far away from himself as possible. Cp. Matthew Arnold's preface, just referred to.

volumes of which *Les Épreuves* (1866), *Les Solitudes* (1869), *Les Vaines Tendresses* (1872), *La Justice* (1878), and *Le Bonheur* (1888) are the most important. He also wrote several suggestive works on æsthetics and philosophy, and in 1901 was awarded the Nobel Prize for literature. Sully - Prudhomme's. earlier poetry was Parnassian in its plastic quality and in its attention to form, but he never sought, or at least he never attained, the indifference which for the moment was the reigning ideal in art. On the contrary, even his first writings contained many revelations of his tender and sympathetic nature and of his preoccupation with the inner world of thought and feeling, and this subjective side of his genius found freer and fuller expression in his later work. Ultimately his interest in science and metaphysical problems led him on to philosophical speculation, and convinced that it was within the capacity of poetry to embrace and interpret " outre tous les sentiments, presque toutes les idées," he wrote *La Justice* and *Le Bonheur*. Though marked by high purpose and great nobility of thought, these experiments in didacticism cannot, however, be regarded as successes; they have many memorable passages, but judged as wholes they prove very clearly that the writer lacked the intellectual and imaginative power necessary to surmount the difficulties of his ambitious task. He will be remembered rather for some of his shorter poems—as, *e.g.*, *La Vase Brisée*, *Jeunes Filles* (*Stances et Poèmes*), *Première Solitude* (*Les Solitudes*), *Homo Sum*, *Un Songe* (*Les Épreuves*), *Aux Amis Inconnus*, *La Coupe*, *L'Étoile au Cœur* (*Les Vaines Tendresses*)—which are characterised by great subtlety, delicacy, and grace.

Another writer who is commonly included in the same group, but whose association with it was hardly more than personal, is François Édouard Joachim Coppée (1842–

1908), a very attractive poet, whose work deserves to be better known to English readers than it is. Coppée began as a Parnassian in *Le Reliquaire* (1866), but he soon detached himself from the school, finding his true line as a realistic poet of modern life—of the city streets and faubourgs, the working - classes, the sorrows and heroism of the poor—in *La Grève des Forgerons* (1869), *Les Humbles* (1872), *Promenades et Intérieures* (1872), *Contes en Vers* (1881, 1887), etc. This rejection of the aristocratic ideal of art was, it may be mentioned in passing, strongly disapproved by Leconte de Lisle himself, who saw in it only a sacrifice on the altar of popularity. Coppée's literary ancestry has been sought by critics who are determined to find a pedigree for everybody, in Victor Hugo (*e.g.*, *Les Pauvres Gens*) and in Sainte-Beuve, and through the latter it may be traced back to Cowper, Crabbe, and Wordsworth. But such an inquiry into origins is, I think, ingenious rather than convincing, and it seems safer to connect the realistic movement in poetry directly with the spread of social interests and the parallel realistic movement in the drama and the novel.[1] Coppée is not always successful in overcoming the difficulties which confront the poet who seeks his material in the commonplaces of actual life ; he lapses occasionally into the baldly prosaic, and on the other hand his sentiment is sometimes strained into sentimentalism. But at its best his work has strength and true pathos.

Among minor writers of the Parnassian group we may just mention Armande Silvestre (1837–1901), who achieved some distinction as a poet with *Les Renaissances* (1869), *La Chanson des Heures* (1878), and *La Chanson des*

[1] Another writer of some note, Eugène Manuel (1823–1901), may also be mentioned as an independent representative of the same tendency in verse. See his *Pages Intimes* (1866) and *Poèmes Populaires* (1871).

Étoiles (1885), though his contemporary popularity rested upon his Rabelaisian tales in prose ; Léon Dierx (b. 1838), a compatriot of Leconte de Lisle (*e.g.*, *Poèmes et Poésies*, 1864; *Les Lèvres Closes*, 1867); Henri Cazalis (1840–1909), a physician, who published a beautiful poem of oriental mysticism, *L'Illusion* (1878), under the pseudonym of Jean Lahor; and Catulle Mendès (1841–1909), whose verse (*e.g.*, *Philomèle*, 1863 ; *Hespérus*, 1872), while excellent in technique, is deeply tainted with the sensuality which mars his numerous unwholesome novels. These, however, are scarcely important enough to call for more than casual reference, and the many other members of the school must be passed over in silence.

83. THE SYMBOLISTES.—During the seventies of the century the domination of Parnassianism, which was largely neo-classic in tendency, was definitely challenged, and about 1880 it was finally broken, by a revival under a changed form of the spirit of romanticism. The poets who rose in reaction against the clear-cut precision and the technical restraints of Leconte de Lisle and his school first called themselves Décadents, but afterwards adopted the name of Symbolistes. The title was not well chosen, but it served to indicate one special feature of their new conception of art—its mystical or transcendental quality. Their principle was to proceed not by exact statement but by subtle suggestion ; to substitute impression for mere description, and instead of addressing the intellect, to evoke moods and feelings by the magic of words and the rhythm of verse. Hence their deliberate cultivation of the vague and obscure, their love of elusive fancies, fleeting sensations and half-realised ideas, their attempt to penetrate beneath the surface òf conscious experience into that twilight region which in turn seemed to them to lead out into the infinite. Hence their further develop-

ment of Baudelaire's doctrine of latent analogies and correspondences. Hence, too, their repudiation of the Parnassian theory in accordance with which poetry had been correlated with painting in favour of a diametrically opposed theory which associated it with music as intellectually the least substantial and emotionally the most suggestive of all the arts.

The leader and theorist of this new school was Stéphane Mallarmé (1842-98). Yet Mallarmé's influence, immense as it was, was mainly a matter of personal ascendancy ; he was the guide and inspirer of the many young men who, Tuesday by Tuesday, sought his companionship in his rooms in the Rue de Rome ; [1] but he was himself a very unprolific writer, and what is most important in his work, including his admirable translations of some of the poems of Poe, will be found in two slender volumes, *Poèmes Complètes* (1887) and *Vers et Prose* (1893). No one who reads *L'Après-Midi d'un Faune*, *Les Fenêtres*, *L'Azur*, and *Hérodiade* can doubt for a moment that he was a true poet if not a great one. But on the whole his paradoxical attempt " after an impossible liberation of the soul of literature from . . . the mere literature of words " [2] ended, as might have been expected, in unintelligibility. As Faguet has said, we read him as we should listen to a piece of music, " sans le moindre intention de comprendre ce qu'il veut dire et en goûtant seulement la suggestion des mots et des sonorités." [3]

It is as a theorist only that Mallarmé deserves the place of priority in the history of the Symbolist movement. The one really important original representative of that movement is Paul Verlaine (1844-96), whose biography

[1] For an account of his *salon* see Arthur Symons' *The Symbolist Movement in Literature*, pp. 155 ff.

[2] Symons, *op. cit.* p. 126.

[3] *Petite Histoire de la Littérature Française*, p. 298.

is a pitiful record of vagabondage, dissipation, repentance, remorse, relapse, poverty, beggary, and disease, but who had in him the soul of a poet and was endowed with a marvellous gift of song. Verlaine's earlier work, the *Poèmes Saturniens* (1866), *Les Fêtes Galantes* (1869), and *La Bonne Chanson* (1870), show in various ways the influence of Banville, Baudelaire, and Leconte de Lisle. His distinctively personal note was first heard in *Romances sans Paroles* (1874), and then again, after a long period of silence, during which he had undergone a term of imprisonment and had been converted to Catholicism, in *Sagesse* (1881), a collection of lyrics steeped in the spirit of mystical piety. His later volumes include *Jadis et Naguère* (1884), *Amour* (1888), *Parallèlement* (1889), and *Bonheur* (1891). A creature of instinct and impulse, weak, undisciplined and capricious, and wholly lacking in self-restraint and intellectual balance, Verlaine was essentially the poet of fugitive moods and passing impressions. His conception of poetry will be found in the verses entitled *Art Poétique* (in *Romances sans Paroles*), and in these, as the following extract will show, he embodies some of the leading ideas of the whole Symbolist school :

> De la musique avant toute chose.
> Et pour cela préfère l'impair
> Plus vague et plus soluble dans l'air,
> Sans rien en lui qui pèse ou qui pose.
>
> Il faut aussi que tu n'ailles point
> Choisir les mots sans quelque méprise ;
> Rien de plus cher que la chanson grise
> Ou l'Indécis au Précis se joint. . . .
>
> Car nous voulons la Nuance encor,
> Pas de couleur, rien que la Nuance !
> Oh ! la nuance seule fiance
> Le rêve au rêve et la flûte au cor !

These stanzas may be taken as a key to his own poetry, which, generally vague, frequently obscure, and sometimes apparently without any definite meaning—even his landscape painting, as Mr. Symons has said, " is always an evocation in which outline is lost in atmosphere "— is often exquisitely beautiful in its verbal magic and haunting melody. In his metrical freedom (a freedom which we are told by one who knew him well, he learned in part from his study of English models) [1] he broke away more completely than any writer hitherto had done from the rhetorical and prosodial traditions of French verse, and at this point his influence was very strong on the younger generation of poets.[2]

84. OTHER POETS.—Though few poets of the closing decades of the nineteenth century detach themselves conspicuously from the mass, the period was one of great activity, and in the more important writers, as in their minor contemporaries, we find, not a single central movement, but a bewildering diversity of tendencies and aims. There were those who, calling themselves " Vivants," returned to the earlier traditions of Romanticism, like Jean Richepin (b. 1849), a man of strong personality and robust and unconventional style (*e.g.*, *La Chanson des Gueux*, 1876 ; *Les Blasphèmes*, 1884). There were those who showed the influence of Parnassianism in their leanings towards the antique and the plastic quality of their art, like Henri de Régnier (b. 1864) (*e.g.*, *Poèmes*,

[1] Symons, *op. cit.* p. 84.
[2] The prosodial revolution which he may be said to have inaugurated was carried on by a small group of writers—among them Marie Krysinska, Gustave Kahn, René Ghil, Viélé-Griffin, and Francis Jammes—who adopted in part or entirely the so-called *vers libre*—verse irregular in metrical construction and sometimes unrimed. This innovation in French poetry can, however, for the present at least, be regarded only as an experiment, and we must not be tempted into any discussion of it here.

1887, 1892, 1896 ; *Les Jeux Rustiques et Divins*, 1897 ; *Les Médailles d'Argile*, 1900). There were those in whom, as in Albert Samain (1859–1900), the Parnassian influence was blended with that of Symbolism (*e.g.*, *Au Jardin de l'Infante*, 1893 ; *Aux Flancs du Vase*, 1898). There were those who, like Jean Moréas (1856–1910), a naturalised Greek, were alternately Parnassian, romantic, and symbolist (*e.g.*, *Les Cantilènes*, 1886 ; *Le Pèlerin Passioné*, 1891 ; *Poésies*, 1898) ; those who like Francis Jammes (b. 1868) may be connected with the religious element in Verlaine (*e.g.*, *Géorgiques Chrétiennes*, 1911–12), and those who, like Maurice Bouchor (b. 1855), were specially marked by their mystical idealism (*e.g.*, *Les Symboles*, 1888–95). But we cannot now undertake any further inquiry into the various developments of recent French poetry. A mere catalogue of names would have little interest, and the subject is too large for detailed treatment in these pages.

CHAPTER XV

THE LATER NINETEENTH CENTURY (*concluded*)

THE DRAMA AND THE NOVEL

85. THE COMÉDIE DE MŒURS.—The failure of *Les Burgraves*, which as we have seen brought Hugo's connection with the theatre to a close, also marked the end of romantic tragedy. At the same time, and notwithstanding his momentary success, Ponsard's attempt to initiate a classic revival proved completely abortive. The rising realistic tendency in literature was in fact fatal to both the romantic and the classic type of play, and under the combined influence of Scribe on the stage and of Balzac in the novel, the older forms of tragedy gave way to a drama of serious purpose based on the facts and problems of modern life. Though generally called the *Comédie de Mœurs*—a very appropriate title, since it was the analogue and in part the product of the *roman de mœurs*—this new type may also be regarded as a transformation of the eighteenth-century *drame*.

The two great masters of the *comédie de mœurs* are the younger Dumas and Émile Augier.

Alexandre Dumas *fils* (1824–95) was the natural but legitimised son of the famous romancer, and it is a curious fact that though the strongest affection existed between the two, the younger man's rigid moral idealism was in large measure a reaction against the elder's bohemianism and disorderly habits of life. In 1848 he made a great hit with a novel of passion, *La Dame aux Camélias*, and after this produced other novels (*e.g.*, *L'Affaire Clémenceau*, 1866). But the immense success of the dramatised version of *La Dame* (1852) attracted him to the stage, and it was for the stage that his best work was done. Of his sixteen plays *Le Demi-Monde* (1855), *La Question d'Argent* (1857), *L'Ami des Femmes* (1864), *Les Idées de Madame Aubray* (1867), and *Une Visite de Noces* (1871) are generally considered the most important. Dumas inherited from his father a real dramatic instinct, a strong sense of the stage and a keen feeling for theatrical situations and effects, and, along with these, a pronounced romantic bias often noticeable in the character of his plots and his fondness for the violent and the abnormal. But he was by conviction and purpose a realist and a didactic realist, who conceived the stage as the most fitting place for the discussion of moral problems and believed that it could be used as a powerful agent in social reform. Both his matter and his manner were often, as he admitted, calculated to upset " les idées reçues, des conventions établies, les préjugés et le qu'on dira-t-on, dans lesquelles la société vit tant bien que mal " (Preface to *Le Fils Naturel*), and his plays in fact seldom failed to arouse a storm of controversy ; but he never deviated from the course which he had marked out for himself in advance. As a moralist he worked in two different directions, for while on the one hand he pleaded the cause of the victims of social prejudice and legal injustice, and especially that of the women against whom the unchristian bigotry of the world bars the way to redemption, on the other he sought to arrest the decomposition of modern society by proclaiming the sanctity of marriage and the family. As a dramatist he insisted upon the substitution of the logic of passion for the arbitrary procedure of the romantic stage : " 2 et 2 font 4, et 4 et 4 font 8. Le théâtre est aussi impitoyable que l'arithmétique " (Preface to *Les Idées de Madame Aubray*). The chief defect of his plays as plays is the occasional subordination of dramatic interest to thesis, and their consequent tendency to run into talk, discussion, and declamation : one of their most significant structural features being the frequent introduction of a character (technically known as *raisonneur*) whose function is that of chorus to the action and who is really the representative of the author and the mouthpiece of his ideas (*e.g.* Olivier de Jalin in *Le Demi-Monde*). But their genuine acting quality is amply attested by their practical success on the boards, while their intellectuality, their dialectical subtlety, their mordant wit, and their brilliant and incisive style make them always remarkable as literature. As the principal founder of the modern problem-play Dumas has an important place in the history of the European drama.

More broadly, a large share in the evolution of that drama must also be assigned to his contemporary Guillaume Victor Émile Augier (1820–89). Under the influence of Ponsard and Delavigne, Augier began with a number of plays in verse—*La Ciguë* (1844), which is Greek in theme, *Un Homme de Bien* (1845), a comedy of the older classical type, *L'Aventurière* (1848), the scene of which is laid in the Italy of the Renaissance, etc. From these experiments he passed on to *Gabrielle* (1849), which, though still in verse, was modern in subject and realistic in manner, and which, as the younger Dumas declared, was " la première révolte contre le théâtre de Scribe " ; meaning thereby, the first revolt, not against the technique of Scribe, which indeed both he and Augier largely adopted, but against his mechanical methods in the handling of passion and character. Then following the lead of Dumas, Augier turned to the prose comedy of manners, and in 1854 produced in *Le Gendre de M. Poirier* [1] one of the classics of the modern stage. This, however, was only the opening of a career of unbroken and well-earned success, the principal landmarks of which are perhaps *Les Effrontés* (1861), *Maître Guérin* (1864), and *Les Fourchambault* (1878). In a general estimate of Augier's work there is little need for qualifications. His plays, one and all, are admirable in structure and composition, thoroughly dramatic in interest, robust and natural in style, and full of sound, generous, healthy sentiment and sane and practical morality. In particular, stress must be laid upon the vitality of his characterisation ; his personages are not mere puppets ; they are figures of flesh and blood, and some of them, like M. Poirier, Maître Guérin, and Giboyer, have definitely taken their places as types beside the great creations of the older drama. Voltairian in his opinions and thoroughly anti-romantic in temper, Augier was a capital representative of what was best in the middle classes of his time and a consistent interpreter of many of their ideas regard ing love, marriage, and the family. Yet he was an outspoken critic of their weaknesses and failings, and continually satirised their sordid notions of worldly success and their besetting sins of narrowness and hypocrisy.

86. THE LIGHTER DRAMA.—Side by side with the more serious comedy of manners the various lighter forms of drama flourished greatly, especially under the Second Empire. Among the innumerable caterers for public

---

[1] This, as we have already noted, was based on Sandeau's novel, *Sacs et Parchements*, and was written with Sandeau's co-operation.

amusement none was more successful than Victorien Sardou (1831-1908), whom we include under the present head because, whatever the nature· of his work, it was designed expressly for the footlights and to meet the demands of popular taste. Sardou was a man of extraordinary versatility of talent, and in his long and prolific career produced plays in all sorts of styles : vaudevilles (*e.g., Divorçons*) ; comedies of manners (*e.g., Nos Intimes, La Famille Benoîton*) ; comedies of intrigue (*e.g., Les Pattes de Mouche*) ; political comedies (*e.g., Rabagas*) ; historical dramas (*e.g., Madame Sans-Gêne, La Haine, Patrie, Thermidor*). Many of his later melodramas (*e.g., La Tosca*) were written for Sarah Bernhardt, and he also provided two plays for Sir Henry Irving—*Robespierre* and *Dante*. Sardou was the successor of Scribe, and what has been said about Scribe may with equal justice be applied to him. He was an adroit and dextrous craftsman and a master of all the resources of the stage, but despite his surprisingly clever technique he cannot be described as a great dramatist, because his work as a whole is devoid of depth and sincerity. Far less copious, but possessed of a much higher literary quality, Édouard Pailleron (1834-99) deserves to be remembered as the author of one delightful piece of "marivaudage," *L'Étincelle* (1879), and one very brilliant satirical comedy, *Le Monde où l'on s'ennui* (1881). Of the many other successful playwrights of the time we must not pause here to take account, but an exception must be made in favour of one of them—the inimitable Eugène Marin Labiche (1815-88)—who was for many years the most popular dramatist in France, and whose popularity rested on really firm foundations. Labiche worked in the lighter forms of comedy only, but his humour was so abundant, his wit so spontaneous and keen, his dialogue so racy and sparkling, he had such a wonderful fertility in the invention of comic incidents and situations and such a happy knack of hitting off characters, that in his own special way he is fully entitled to a place among the masters. There is moreover at times a deeper meaning to his mirth than might at first sight be supposed. Plays like *La Cagnotte* and *Un Chapeau de Paille d'Italie* may be little more than tissues of irresistible buffooneries, but in *Le Voyage de M. Perichon*, for example, and *La Poudre aux Yeux*, there is more genuine human nature and more psychology than in many far more pretentious pieces.

87. THE DRAME NATURALISTE AND THE ROMANTIC REVIVAL.—The evolution of the realistic novel of manners into the *roman naturaliste* of Zola and his school was followed by a parallel movement in the drama. Zola himself and a few other theorists under his immediate influence made the first attempts in the *drame naturaliste*, but without much success, and the new type is principally associated with the name of Henri Becque (1837–99), who illustrated its formula in some half-dozen plays of which *Michel Pauper* (1870), *Les Corbeaux* (1882), and *La Parisienne* (1885) will serve as examples. Becque's avowed purpose was to liberate the drama entirely from all lingering theatrical and literary conventions, and to make it the absolutely faithful reflection of life as it is. He wrote, accordingly, without the slightest concern about technique in the usual acceptation of the term ; reduced his plots to the smallest possible proportions, providing only just enough thread of intrigue to hold the successive scenes together ; handled these scenes without regard to progression, climax, or mere stage effect ; and in the fashioning of his dialogue aimed at all times to avoid those very qualities of wit and fancy which the ordinary dramatist was most sedulous to cultivate for the display

of his own cleverness. Though it was part of his programme to present his "tranches de vie" not only without commentary but also without any disturbing touch
of doctrinal purpose, he showed the bias of his school in
his preoccupation with the sordid and ugly, and the
general tone of his work is profoundly pessimistic and
even brutal. With his vigorous propaganda in favour of
naturalism we must also connect the foundation in 1887
by an enterprising actor, André Antoine, of the Théâtre
Libre, which was opened to give hospitality to those
native playwrights of talent whose ideas about art were
too advanced for the general public, and which also served
to introduce to a select circle of enthusiasts the works of
some of the leaders of the new drama abroad, like Tolstoi,
Ibsen, and Hauptmann. In its more aggressive features
the whole movement was scarcely more than a passing
fashion. But it certainly helped to broaden and deepen
the art of the stage and to break down the Sardouesque
tradition of the "well-made play," and its influence is
clearly marked in the later French drama, as, for example,
in the writings of Georges Ancey (*L'École des Veufs*, 1891,
L'Avenir, 1899, etc.) ; Jules Lemaître (*Le Député Leveau*,
1891, *Mariage Blanc*, 1891, etc.) ; Eugène Brieux (*Blan-
chette*, 1892, *L'Évasion*, 1896, etc.) ; and Paul Hervieu
(*Les Ténailles*, 1895, *La Loi de l'Homme*, 1897, etc.).

Meanwhile the poetic drama, though apparently dead,
was only dormant, and after the disasters of 1870 it began
to evince fresh signs of life, the excesses of naturalism
presently causing a distinct reaction in its favour. In
1875 a friend and disciple of Hugo, Henri de Bornier
(1825–1901), made a strong appeal to romantic sentiment
with *La Fille de Roland*, and he was followed by Coppée
(*Les Jacobites*, 1881, *Severo Torelli*, 1883, *Pour la
Couronne*, 1895, etc.) ; by Richepin (*Nana Sahib*, 1883,

Par la Glaive, 1892, *Le Chemineau*, 1897, etc.), and by
other writers. But it was reserved for Edmond Rostand
(b. 1864) to prove triumphantly with *Les Romanesques*
(1894), *Cyrano de Bergerac* (1897)—the most brilliant
theatrical success of recent times—and *L'Aiglon* (1900),
that public and critics alike were ready and eager to
welcome an author who was at once a dramatist and a
poet, and who was able to captivate their imaginations
with dashing romance and enchant their ears with
musical verse.

88. THE ROMAN RÉALISTE.—The influences which we
have traced in the development of the drama in the later
nineteenth century also, and even more powerfully, affected
prose fiction : the novel of sentiment and the historical
romance lost their vogue, and for some thirty years the pre-
dominant type was the realistic novel of contemporary life.
In the decade following Balzac's death an active campaign
in favour of realism was conducted by a number of young
writers who fought under his banner, foremost among
whom was Jules Fleury-Husson, always known by his
pen-name of Champfleury (1821–89), whose novels (*e.g.*,
Les Bourgeois de Molinchart, 1855), though now almost
forgotten, embodied and helped to popularise the leading
ideas of the school. But the triumph of that school
dates from the publication in 1857 of *Madame Bovary*, by
Gustave Flaubert (1821–80), in which Sainte-Beuve at
once detected the rise of a new force in literature and
which critics as far apart as Zola and Brunetière afterwards agreed in regarding as a landmark in the history
of the modern novel. Flaubert has been described as a
romanticist born out of his proper time, and there was
indeed a great deal of romanticism in his intellectual composition ; he confessed himself to a natural taste for the
extraordinary and the fantastic ; and in *Hérodias* and

La Légende de Saint-Julien l'Hospitalier (in *Trois Contes*), in *La Tentation de Saint-Antoine* (1874), as well as in his second masterpiece, *Salammbô* (1862), he sought an imaginative escape out of that "vie ordinaire" which he held "en exécration." But he subjected his temperament to the severest artistic discipline, and in particular opposed the emotional and sentimental tendencies of romanticism with his central doctrine of the absolute impersonality and indifference of art : " l'artiste doit s'arranger de façon à faire croire à la postérité qu'il n'a pas vécu." Such was his ideal of the "impersonnalité surhumaine" which he admired in Shakespeare. Life for him was in fact only so much subject-matter for art ; its possible ethical significance did not in the least interest him ; his one concern was with the fidelity of his treatment and the perfection of his technique. It was in the spirit of complete detachment and with the most laborious care that in *Madame Bovary* he traced step by step the gradual declension of his heroine from weakness to vice and from vice to suicide, painting his characters in the minutest detail against a background, painted with equal minuteness, and provided by the manners of the provincial *bourgeoisie* to which they belonged ; and though in *Salammbô* he forsook the present to undertake an elaborate reconstruction of Carthaginian civilisation after the first Punic War, his method was still the same, for he prepared himself for this massive work by exhaustive studies and by a journey to Tunis in quest of local colour. Entirely absorbed in his art, Flaubert had a passion for form and style which he carried indeed to the point of mania ; he would spend days in the revision of a page and hours over a single phrase. In *Madame Bovary* he produced what is undoubtedly one of the greatest of realistic novels. But in his other work on the same line he paid the penalty of his " documentary " method, for both *L'Éducation Sentimentale* (1870) and the unfinished *Bouvard et Pécuchet* are as dull as the life which they depict.

This method was carried even further by two brothers, Edmond (1822–96) and Jules (1830–70) de Goncourt, who for ten years wrote in collaboration, though after the younger's death the elder continued to produce novels on his own account. The Goncourts boasted specially of the documentary value of their work : " un des caractères particuliers de nos romans ce sera d'être les romans les plus historiques de ce temps-ci, les romans qui fourniront le plus de faits et de vérités vraies à l'histoire morale de ce siècle " (*Journal*, i. 362).[1] Their novels (*e.g., Charles Demailly,* 1860 ; *Sœur Philomène,* 1861 ; *Renée Mauperin,* 1864 ; *Germinie Lacerteur,* 1865, etc.) are very unequal, generally very tedious, and always very gloomy and morbid ; their interest is pathological rather than psychological ; they are frequently marred by a brutal frankness of description and a grossness of phrase which made even Flaubert declare that henceforth he might be considered as respectable, and they are written in a feverish, contorted style which adds still further to our distress in reading them.

89. THE ROMAN NATURALISTE.—Though it is difficult to draw any clear line of demarcation between realism and naturalism, we will follow the usual practice of French critics and adopt the latter term to designate the particular development of realism which we find in the writings of Zola and his disciples. It was the aim of Émile Zola (1840–1900) to make the novel absolutely scientific by

[1] The novels of the Goncourts are little read now except by professed students of literature, but the *Journal* in which for many years they recorded the events of their lives retains its interest as a mine of information regarding the literary and artistic world and people of their time.

carrying over into it the most modern ideas about determinism, environment, heredity, and physiological psychology which had been expounded by biologists like Claude Bernard and evolutionary philosophers like Taine. In the Preface to the second edition of his early *Thérèse Raquin* (1867) he wrote: " J'ai simplement fait sur deux corps vivants le travail analytique que les chirurgiens font sur les cadavres." In these audacious words he already suggested that conception of the "experimental" novel which he afterwards formulated in full : " Le romancier est fait d'un observateur et d'un expérimenteur. L'observateur, chez lui, donne les faits tels qu'il les a observés, pose le point de départ, établit le terrain solide sur lequel vont marcher les personnages et se développer les phénomènes. Puis l'expérimenteur paraît et institue l'expérience, je veux dire fait mouvoir les personnages dans une histoire particulière pour y montrer que la succession des faits y sera telle que l'exige le déterminisme des phénomènes mis à l'étude " (*Le Roman Expérimental*). Such was Zola's doctrine. Its demonstration is to be found in the twenty inter-related volumes—a new *comédie humaine*, but far more systematic and logical than Balzac's— collectively entitled *Les Rougon-Macquart : Histoire Naturelle et Sociale d'une Famille sous le Second Empire* (1861–93). The design of this colossal work is to follow the fortunes of the various members of a single family through all the different environments in which they respectively play their parts, and in so doing to present a complete picture of the many-sided civilisation of the period. The plan was a great one, and we cannot but admire the consistency with which it was carried out. Unfortunately, however, Zola has chosen a family of degenerates, and his chronicles are a huge mass of corruption, which is often shocking in its intolerable foulness and is vitiated as a social study by its everlasting pre-occupation with " la bête humaine." [1] Moreover, for all his parade of theories, Zola was anything but an impartial observer and "expérimenteur," and in his violence and excesses, and in the imaginative power with which he perpetually intensifies and distorts his subjects, he really belongs to the romantics, though his romanticism, in Brunetière's happy phrase, takes the perverted form of "romantisme à rebours." His scientific pretensions are now exploded and a large part of his work is dead. But three portions of it at least survive—*L'Assommoir*, the most tremendous exposure of the evils of drink in any litera-ture,[2] *Germinal*, which deals with miners and strikes, and has justly been called an "épopée sociologique," and *La Débâcle*, a powerful study of the disasters of 1870. After completing his immense task Zola wrote a second sequence of novels : *Trois Villes—Lourdes, Rome, Paris* (1894–98), and embarked upon a third, *Les Quatres Évangiles*. The latter, left unfinished at his death, was intended to embody his gospel of social reconstruction, and reveals the pessimist of the *Rougon-Macquart* series in the new rôle of apostle of humanity and preacher of faith and hope.

Of the many other writers who are also roughly classed as naturalists the most important are Fabre, Maupassant, Huysmans, and Daudet. The novels of Ferdinand Fabre (1827–98), which, with little grace of style, are marked by great simplicity and truthfulness, are interesting as showing the specialising tendency which has since been increasingly apparent in French fiction, for they deal almost entirely with his native region of the Cévennes

---

[1] For a general summary of the history of this remarkable family, and for their genealogical tree, see the closing volume of the series, *Le Docteur Pascal*.

[2] Dramatised for the English stage, under the title of *Drink*, by Charles Reade.

(*e.g.*, *Le Chevrier*, 1868 ; *Mon Oncle Célestin*, 1881), or with clerical life and manners (*e.g.*, *L'Abbé Tigrane*, 1873). Guy de Maupassant (1850–93) was Flaubert's disciple, and learned his first lessons in the art of literature directly from him. He wrote a number of novels (*Une Vie*, 1883 ; *Pierre et Jean*, 1888 ; *Notre Cœur*, 1890, etc.), but it is as one of the greatest masters of the *nouvelle* and short story that he holds his distinctive place in the history of modern fiction. He was, on the whole, the completest exponent of the doctrines of naturalism, for his one and only aim was to depict life as he saw it (Preface to *Pierre et Jean*), and he never allowed his vision to be disturbed by any ulterior consideration, scientific, philosophical, or ethical. He exhibits at times a genuine quality of humour, though it is humour of a rather grim kind ; but in common with most of his school, he dwells almost exclusively upon the base and evil aspects of life, and the tone of his tales is in general gloomy and depressing. Joris Karl Huysmans (1848–1907) was one of the group of young writers who gathered about Zola in the early years of his propagandism, and formed what was for the moment known as "l'École de Médan." His first novels (*Marthe*, 1878 ; *Les Sœurs Vatard*, 1880, etc.) were heavy, unclean, bitterly pessimistic books, which exemplified the creed of naturalism at its worst. Then he became absorbed in the study of demonology and magic (*À Rebours*, 1884 ; *Là-Bas*, 1890), which however proved to be only the first stage in a long and curious intellectual pilgrimage, which ended at last in mystical piety (see *En Route*, 1895 ; *La Cathédrale*, 1898). Alphonse Daudet (1840–97), while commonly included among the naturalists, really occupies a position far apart from them, for though his watchword was "d'après nature," and his method "documentary," there is nothing in his writings to suggest the aloofness and indifference of the scientific school. On the contrary, the personal note in them is very strong, and much of their peculiar charm is due to his exquisite sensibility, his tenderness, and his emotionalism. These qualities are present in all his work : in *Le Petit Chose* (1868), which is largely autobiographical ; in *Fromont Jeune et Risler Ainé* (1874), perhaps his greatest book and a novel of enormous depth and power ; in *Jack* (1876), a painfully pathetic record of a child's martyrdom ; in *Le Nabab* (1877), *Les Rois en Exil* (1879), and *L'Immortel* (1880), all elaborate pictures of Parisian manners ; in *Numa Roumestan* (1881) and *L'Évangeliste* (1883), the one a study of the southern temperament, the other of morbid piety ; in *Sapho* (1884), which is the tragedy of a young man's infatuation for an artist's model ; and all these show the same wonderful skill in creating character and atmosphere, the same subtlety of insight and fineness of touch, the same vividness of description, the same grasp of life. Daudet, in my own judgment, stands well to the fore among the greatest of European novelists, and he is at the same time one of those writers whom we not only admire, but for whom, as for Dickens, with whom he has often been compared, and by whom he was evidently influenced, we feel a warm personal affection. It is only exigencies of space which compel us here to dismiss him with so brief a reference, for he really deserves a much fuller consideration. It must, however, be added, in order to make our rapid view of him even approximately complete, that two of his books, not yet named, *Tartarin de Tarascon* (1872) and *Tartarin sur les Alpes* (1885), which give the comedy, as *Numa Roumestan* gives the tragedy of the " méridional," are masterpieces of humorous extravaganza, and that the stories collected in *Contes du Lundi* (1873) are unexcelled for delicacy and grace.

90. OTHER NOVELISTS.—Even during the period of its greatest ascendancy the power of realism was often challenged, not only by writers like George Sand, whose work to the last was but little modified by its influence, but also by various younger novelists who still carried on the traditions of romantic idealism. The year after the publication of *Madame Bovary* Octave Feuillet (1821–1890) scored an immense success with his extremely sentimental *Roman d'un Jeune Homme Pauvre*, and this he afterwards followed up with other novels (*e.g.*, *M. de Camors*, 1867 ; *Julie de Trécœur*, 1872) which, though more robust in character, belong to the same general class of society fiction, and are marked by the same aristocratic tone and the same respectable but worldly morality. The *Dominique* (1863) of the celebrated landscape painter Eugène Fromentin (1820–76) also deserves mention as a remarkable piece of psychological analysis in the manner of the earlier generation. Feuillet and Fromentin will serve as examples of the novelists who were entirely independent of the realistic movement. After these we come to a number of writers of varying degrees of merit, who may be described as eclectics, because while they adopted more or less fully the methods of the realists, they did so without reference to any of the special theories of the school ; like André Theuriet (1833–1907), the author of many charming novels of the country and provincial life (*Le Fils Maugars*, 1879 ; *Sauvageonne*, 1880 ; *Le Mariage de Gérard*, 1889, etc.), which though soundly realistic in quality are deeply imbued with sentiment, and in their poetic descriptions of nature often remind us of the idyllic stories of George Sand. Such work as Theuriet's clearly suggests the new and healthy tendency in fiction to break away from the trammels of dogma and system and to develop freely along lines as multifarious as the

personalities of the writers. This tendency became increasingly apparent after 1880, with the result that though the novels produced since that date may still be arranged in groups—autobiographical novels, sociological novels, sentimental novels, novels of provincial manners, historical novels, humorous novels, and so on—the outstanding fact is that " de nos jours les genres les plus divers voisinent sans mésentente." [1] To illustrate this variety it is only necessary to refer to the three most important figures in the literature of the closing years of the century—Paul Bourget, Pierre Loti (Marie Julien Viaud), and Anatole France (Jacques Anatole Thibaut). Of these three Bourget (b. 1852) is most closely associated with the realists, but in fiction as in criticism his chief interest has always been in moral psychology, and his mature novels (*Le Disciple*, 1889; *Cosmopolis*, 1892; *L'Étape*, 1902, etc.) are mainly concerned with the problems of the inner life. Pierre Loti (b. 1850) is less a novelist than a poet and a painter, who has drawn for his materials and settings upon his own experiences as a naval officer in many parts of the world (*e.g.*, *Le Mariage de Loti*, 1880; *Le Roman d'un Spahi*, 1881; *Le Pêcheur d'Islande*, 1886; *Madame Chrysanthème*, 1887), and is specially remarkable for the brilliancy of his word-pictures. But though his strength lies in description he is sharply distinguished from the realists by the essentially personal quality of all his writing ; his art is in fact pure impressionism, and as his transcripts from nature are steeped in the melancholy of his temperament, so his style, technically open to criticism but extraordinarily vigorous and vivid, is absolutely his own. Equally personal in another way is the fascinating work of Anatole France (b. 1844), for whom fiction is in the main a medium of ideas. That work is indeed so varied

[1] *Histoire Illustrée de la Littérature Française* (pub. H. Didier), p. 626.

in character, and so deeply impressed by the changes which the writer's mind has undergone in the course of his long career, that no adequate account of it can be given in a few sentences.   Speaking generally, however, we may say that even when it approximates most closely to the type of the regular novel, as in the delightful *Crime de Sylvestre Bonnard* (1881), *Thaïs* (1890), *Le Lys Rouge* (1894), and that powerful picture of revolutionary Paris, *Les Dieux ont Soif* (1912), it is still everywhere impregnated with his individuality and his philosophy, while in many of his books, as in *Le Livre de mon Ami* (1885), *La Rôtisserie de la Reine Pédauque* (1893), the four volumes making up the *Histoire Contemporaine* (*L'Orme du Mail*, *Le Mannequin d'Osier*, *L'Anneau d'Améthyste*, and *M. Bergeret à Paris*, 1897–1901), and the Swift-like satire *L'Île des Pinguoins* (1909), the form of fiction is employed only as a convenient vehicle of his opinions on men and things.   As a philosopher, Anatole France belongs to the school of Montaigne and Renan ; a man of versatile and acute intellect, he employs his varied and curious learning, his dialectical skill and his irony to ridicule the pretensions of theology, metaphysics, and science in their quest for absolute truth, and to expound a thoroughly subjective conception of life.   But pungent as is his wit, there is nothing hard about his nature ; on the contrary, his universal scepticism is accompanied by cheerful tolerance, and his satire softened by frequent touches of tenderness and sympathy.

It would be out of keeping with the plan of this book to enter into any further consideration of recent French fiction, and I will therefore content myself with saying that it gives every sign of continued vitality and growth. We have only to turn to the sound and admirable work of some of the most prominent of contemporary writers —to *De toute son Âme* (1897), *La Terre qui Meurt* (1899), and the striking story of lost Alsace, *Les Oberlé* (1901), of René Bazin (b. 1853), for example, or to *L'Enfant à la Balustrade* (1904) of René Boylesve (b. 1867), or to *Le Pays Natal* (1900) and *Les Roquevillard* (1906) of Henry Bordeaux (b. 1870)—to feel assured that at least in this one fertile and ever-widening field the French literature of the immediate future will be fully worthy of the great traditions of the past.

INDEX

(1) FRENCH AUTHORS

(2) ENGLISH AUTHORS QUOTED OR REFERRED TO